Rethinking Judicial Power in Papua New Guinea

Bal Kama

Rethinking Judicial Power in Papua New Guinea

A Mandate for Activism in a Transformative Constitution

Springer

Bal Kama
Faculty of Business
Government and Law
University of Canberra
Canberra, ACT, Australia

ISBN 978-981-97-2948-7 ISBN 978-981-97-2946-3 (eBook)
https://doi.org/10.1007/978-981-97-2946-3

This Springer imprint is published by the registered company Springer Nature Singapore Pte Ltd.
The registered company address is: 152 Beach Road, #21-01/04 Gateway East, Singapore 189721, Singapore

Foreword

It is with great pleasure that I write this foreword for Dr. Bal Kama's seminal book on the nature of judicial power in Papua New Guinea (PNG). The book is significant for being the first book on the country's judiciary as we near the country's 50th Independence Anniversary.

Kama provides a comprehensive analysis of the nature of judicial power in PNG as embedded in the Constitution, offering invaluable insights into the judiciary's role and its relationship with the other arms of government. Beginning with the revolutionary processes the Constitutional Planning Committee undertook in the drafting of our autochthonous Constitution, Kama highlights the significance of the Constitution's departure from colonial models and its embrace of unique structures appropriate to the circumstances of the country, including a judiciary imbued with liberal powers.

The major contention of the book for there to be a rethink of the character of the PNG judiciary should invoke much interest. Through its analysis of the various powers of the judiciary, Kama argues for a departure from narrow legalistic approaches towards an expansive understanding of judicial power. Those arguments underscore the vital role of PNG judges as guardians of our democracy.

Kama's analysis on the separation of powers doctrine offers another intriguing perspective, advocating for a departure from the traditional tripartite model where the judiciary is expected to have a restricted role to a modified model that recognises the independent constitutional institutions as a fourth arm of government and a judiciary with a constitutionally mandated 'activist' function. While the analysis reaffirms the pivotal role of our constitutional institutions to work alongside the judiciary, it also challenges us to reconsider how we have interpreted our 'home-grown' constitutional designs.

The book grounded these discussions with the constitutional impasse cases of the *Rooney Case* of 1979 and the *East Sepik Province Case* of 2011 to serve as stark reminders of the costs of competing expectations often placed upon our judiciary and the need to ensure there is a proper understanding of the role of the judiciary as intended within the country's constitutional contexts.

The book offers a stimulating intellectual inquiry that invites us to rethink our established systems and assumptions of judicial power in PNG. I commend Dr. Kama for his scholarly endeavour and trust that his work will inspire and enlighten the public as well as colleague judges, legal practitioners, policymakers, and scholars in their engagements with our judiciary.

Port Moresby, Papua New Guinea

The Honourable Sir Gibuma Gibbs Salika, GCL, KBE, CSM, OBE
Chief Justice Papua New Guinea

Acknowledgments

I am indebted to the esteemed past and present judges of Papua New Guinea, whose commitment to and struggle with enlivening and enriching the liberal character of the judiciary has served as a source of inspiration. Their insightful writings and judicial pronouncements sparked my interest in undertaking an in-depth exploration of the character of judicial power in Papua New Guinea and the transformative potential of the country's 'home-grown' Constitution.

To lawyers and scholars both in PNG and abroad with whom I have discussed this subject, our interactions have been a firm motivation. I hope that this book serves not only as a valuable resource for comprehending the judiciary's unique and indispensable role in the ongoing development of Papua New Guinea but also fosters a deeper appreciation of what it means to have a 'home-grown' Constitution.

I am immensely honoured and thankful to Chief Justice Sir Gibuma Gibbs Salika for the Foreword, lending his esteemed perspective to this endeavour.

To my wife Sonja, whose unwavering support sustained me through the labour of this book, I owe a debt of gratitude. To Bob and Anne in Aotearoa, I am thankful for their generous hospitality which allowed for this book to be completed while visiting their home.

Lastly, I am appreciative of the reviewers and the Springer publishing team whose collaboration enabled this publication. While I acknowledge their invaluable assistance, any errors or omissions in these pages are solely my responsibility.

Dr. Bal Kama, LLB (Hons), BA,
GDLP, Ph.D.

Table of Statutes

Papua New Guinea (Including Pre-independence)

Central Court Ordinance 1925 (Territory of Papua) (Cth)
Constitution of the Independent State of Papua New Guinea 1975 (PNG)
Constitutional Documents (Manner of Proof) Act 1976 (PNG)
Customs Recognition Act 1963 (PNG)
Judicial Conduct (Amendment) Act 2012 (PNG)
Judicial Conduct Act 2012 (PNG)
Judiciary Ordinance 1912–1940 (Cth)
Judiciary Ordinance 1921–1938 (Territory of New Guinea) (Cth)
Justice Ordinance 1920 (Cth)
Local Courts Ordinance 1963 (PNG)
Native Administrative Ordinance 1921 (Cth)
Native Administrative Regulation 1924 (Cth)
Native Local Government Councils Ordinance 1954 (Cth)
Native Regulation Ordinance 1908 (Cth)
Native Regulations Ordinance 1908–1939 (Cth)
Native Village Councils Ordinance 1949 (Cth)
New Guinea Act 1920 (Cth)
Organic Law on the Duties and Responsibilities of Leadership (PNG)
Organic Law on the Guarantee of the Rights and Independence of Constitutional Office-holders (PNG)
Organic Law on the Terms and Conditions of Employment of Judges (PNG)
Papua and New Guinea Act 1963 (Cth)
Papua and New Guinea Act 1966 (Cth)
Papua and New Guinea Act 1968 (Cth)
Papua and New Guinea Provisional Administration Act 1945 (Cth)
Papua New Guinea Act 1949–1954 (Cth)
Papua New Guinea Act 1975 (Cth)
Papua New Guinea Act 1949 (Cth)

Prime Minister and National Executive Council (Amendment No 2) Act 2011 (PNG)
Prime Minister and National Executive Council Act 2002 (PNG)
Supreme Court (Amendment) Act 2012 (PNG)
Supreme Court Ordinance 1949 (Cth)
Supreme Court Ordinance 1949–1959 (Cth)
Territory of Papua Act 1905 (Cth)
Underlying Law Act 2000 (PNG)
Village Court Ordinance 1973 (PNG)
Village Court Regulation 1974 (PNG)
Village Courts Act 1989 (PNG)
White Women's Protection Ordinance 1926–1934 (Cth)

Others

Administrative Decision Judicial Review 1977 (Cth)
British Solomon Islands (Constitution) Order 1960 (UK)
British Solomon Islands Order 1974 (UK)
Canadian Bill of Rights 1960 (Canada)
Commonwealth of Australia Constitution Act 1900 (UK)
Constitution Alteration (Retirement of Judges) Act 1977 (Cth)
Constitution of Massachusetts 1780 (Mass) (US)
Constitution of the Republic of Brazil 1988 (Brazil)
Fiji (Constitution) Order 1966 (UK)
Gilbert Islands Order 1975 (UK)
Judicial Review Act 1991 (Qld)
Statute of Westminster 1931 (UK)
The Constitution of India 1950 (India)
The Constitution of Kenya 2010
The Constitution of the Republic of Namibia 1990 (Namibia)
Tuvalu Independence Order 1978 (UK)

Table of Cases

Papua New Guinea (Including Colonial Cases)

Haiveta v Wingti (No. 3) [1994] PNGLR 197
Hau Koava [1959] PGSC 19
In re Anderson Agiru; Enforcement pursuant to Constitution Section 57 [2002] PNGLR 587
In re Anderson Agiru; Review Pursuant to Section 155*(2) and 155(4) of the Constitution* [2002] PNGLR 27
In re Application for Enforcement of Human Rights under Section 57 *of the Constitution, by Jacob Eddie* [2014] PGNC 133
In re Conditions of Detention at Kimbe Police Lock-up [2006] PGNC 183
In re Constitutional (Amendment) Law 2008, *Reference by the Ombudsman Commission of Papua New Guinea* [2013] PGSC 67
In re Enforcement of Basic Rights under the Constitution of Papua New Guinea, Section 57 [2014] PGNC 18
In re Lack of Correctional Service (CS) Facilities in Enga Province [2010] PGNC 251
In Re Lack of Water Supply to Mount Hagen National Court [2011] PGNC 319
In re Powers, Functions, Duties and Responsibilities of the Commissioner of Police [2014] PGSC 19
In re Re-Election of the Governor General [2010] SC1085
In re Section 57 *of the Constitution of Papua New Guinea, Enforcement of Basic and Human Rights* [2006] PGNC 201
In the Matter of an Application under Section 57 *of the Constitution*
In the matter of enforcement of Basic Rights under the Constitution re conditions of detention at Bialla Police Lock-up (2006) N3022
In the Matter of Enforcement of Basic Rights under the Constitution Section 57 [2006] PGNC 29
In the Matter of Section 18*(1) of the Constitution and in the Matter of Bill Skate MP* [2001] PGSC 6
In the Matter of Section 18*(1) of the Constitution and In the Matter of Application by Anderson Agiru* [2001] PGSC 7
In the Matter of the Organic Law on the Nomination of Governor-General [2004] PGSC 3
Independent State of Papua New Guinea v Transferees [2015] PGSC 45
Jaminyen-Urinjimbi v The Queen [1967] PGHCA 4
Kensi v The State [1983] PNGLR 350
Kipalan v National Parliament [2004] PGSC 42
Kobol v Powi [2018] PGNC 1
Kobol v Powi [2018] PGSC 51
Kobol v Powi [2018] PGSC 68
Komane Wasege v Mathias Karani (1998) N1696
Kristeff v Regina [1967] PGHCA 2
Kwale-Tauwan v Iwas [1960] PGSC 4
Lack of Correctional Service (CS) Facilities in Enga Province, In re [2010] PGNC 251
Loa v Safe [1963] PGSC 42

Lowa v Damena [1977] PGSC 11
Magiten v Beggie (No. 2) [2005] PNGLR 647
Malagigi v Geelan [1953] PGSC 11
Marape v Paraka [2014] PGNC 118
Mase v State [1980] PGNC 82
Matter of Jim Kas, Governor of Madang Province [2001] PGSC 15
Medaing v Ramu Nico Management (MCC) Ltd [2011] PGNC 95
Moiga v Devete [2010] PGNC 240
Morauta v Pala [2016] PGSC 46
Namah v O'Neill [2015] PGSC 77
Namah v Pato [2014] PGSC 1
Namah v Poole [2016] PGSC 34
National Court Circuit, Southern Highlands Province, Re [1989] PGNC 70
Nilkare v Ombudsman Commission [1995] PGNC 29
Ombudsman Commission of PNG v Denis Donohoe [1985] PGLawRp 348
Ombudsman Commission of PNG v Ellis, Constituting the Poreporena Freeway Commission of Inquiry [1992] PNGLR 437
Ombudsman Commission v National Parliament [2003] PGSC 19
O'Neil v Ombudsman Commission of Papua New Guinea [2015] PGNC 1
O'Neill v Eliakim [2017] PGSC 53
Peter v South Pacific Brewery [1976] PNGLR 537
Petrus v Telikom PNG Ltd [2008] PGNC 85
PNG Power Ltd v Augerea [2013] PGSC 53
Premdas v The State [1979] PGSC 20
Public Service Commission v The Independent State of Papua New Guinea [1994] PNGLR 603
Queen v Amuna [1954] PGSC 13
Queen v Creighton [1952] PGSC 1
Queen v Evans [1954] PGSC 1
Queen v Mumford [1953] PGSC 7
Queen v Ofu-Koloi [1956] PGSC 29
Queen v Pamboa-Takai [1962] PGSC 29
Re Bouraga [1982] PNGLR 178
Re Calling of the Parliament [1999] PGSC 55
Re Constitution S23(2), Constitution S225 [1990] PNGLR 82
Re Constitutional (Amendment) Law 2008, Reference by the Ombudsman Commission of Papua New Guinea [2013] PGSC 67
Re Enforcement of Basic Rights under Section 57 *of the Independent State of Papua New Guinea* [2017] PGNC 266
Re Enforcement of Basic Rights under Section 57, *Constitution of the Independent State of Papua New Guinea* [2014] PGNC 222
Re Judicial Act 2012; Special Reference by Morobe Provincial Executive [2012] PGSC 12
Re Motor Traffic Act [1982] PNGLR 122
Re National Court circuit to Bali and Vitu Island [2011] PGNC 266

Re Ombudsman Commission Investigations of the Public Solicitor [1978] PGSC 7
Re Petition of MT Somare [1981] PNGLR 265
Re Reference to Constitution Section 19*(1) by East Sepik Provincial Executive* [2011] PGSC 41
Re Rights of Person Arrested or Detained [1977] PGSC 15
Re s 19 of the Criminal Code [1982] PNGLR 150
Re The King [1950] PGSC 3
Re Tribunal established under the Organic Law on the Duties and Responsibilities of Leadership S27 and Leo Robert Morgan [1978] PNGLR 460
Re Section 57 *of the Constitution of Papua New Guinea, Enforcement of Basic and Human Rights* [2006] PGNC 201
Re Section 57 *of the Constitution of Papua New Guinea, Enforcement of Basic and Human Rights* [2006] PGNC 201
Ref By Simbu Provincial Executive [1987] PGSC 17
Reference by the Executive Council of the Enga Provincial Government [1990] PNGLR 53
Reference by the Ombudsman Commission of Papua New Guinea [2010] PGSC 10
Reference by the Public Prosecutor pursuant to s27(2)(E) of the Organic Law on Duties and Responsibilities of Leadership—in the matter of Hon Sir Moi Avei (2007) N4633
Reference by the Ombudsman Commission; Re Section 19 *of the Constitution* [2010] PGSC 43
Review Pursuant to Constitution Section 155*(2)(b): Application by Herman Joseph Leahy* [2006] PGSC 21
Somare v Geno [2008] PGNC 188
Somare v Manek [2011] PGSC 17
Somare v State [2007] PGNC 34
Somare, Re [1981] PGSC 23
Southern Highlands Provincial Government v Somare, Chairman of the National Executive Council [2007] PGSC 2, [13], [149] (Kapi CJ & Sakora J)
Southern Highlands Provincial Government v Somare, Chairman of the National Executive Council [2007] PGSC 2
Special reference by Allan Marat; Special reference by the National Parliament [2012] PGSC 20
Special Reference By Fly River Provincial Executive Council, Re Organic Law on Integrity of Political Parties and Candidates [2010] PGSC 3
Special Reference by Morobe Provincial Executive [2012] PGSC 12
Special Reference by Morobe Provincial Government [2002] PGSC 9
Special Reference by Morobe Provincial Government [2002] PGSC 9
Special Reference by the Attorney General pursuant to Constitution, Section 19 [2016] PGSC 52
Special Reference by the Morobe Provincial Executive [2005] PGSC 32
State v Winston [2003] PGNC 146
Supreme Court Reference by the Western Highlands Provincial Executive [1995] PGSC 6

Overseas

Plaintiff M68/2015 v Minister for Immigration and Border Protection (2016) HCA 1
R v Henry [2005] 3 SCR 609
R v Kirby; Ex parte Boilermakers' Society of Australia (1956) 94 CLR 254
R v Wilkes [1917] 1 KB 176
Rates Action Group v City of Cape Town (2004) 12 BCLR 1328
State of Tasmania v Commonwealth of Australia and State of Victoria (1904) 1 CLR 329
Theophananous v Herald and Weekly Time Ltd (1994) 182 CLR 104
Victor Chandler International v Customs and Excise Commission and Others [2000] 2 All ER 315
Victoria v Commonwealth (1975) 134 CLR
Victorian Stevedoring and General Contracting Company v Dignan (1931) 46 CLR 73
Waterside Workers' Federation of Australia v J W Alexander Ltd (1918) 25 CLR 434
Webb & Hay v R (1994) 181 CLR 41
Wilson v Minister for Aboriginal and Torres Strait Islander Affairs (1996) 189 CLR 1

Contents

Chapter 1
Introduction

The judicial system in Papua New Guinea was conceived to serve a distinctive role within its society, one surpassing the traditional bounds observed in other post-colonial contexts. Designed to have a liberal, socially engaging and interventionist function, the Papua New Guinea judiciary embodied an undertaking in indigenous constitutional ingenuity that marked the nation's constitutional framework as truly 'home-grown'. Unlike many of their peers in the region, the expectation for judges in Papua New Guinea was to be 'leaders' with a broader role of shaping society. However, this unique character of the judiciary is often challenged and remains obscured, overshadowed by the domineering influence of legal positivism, which constrains judges to a narrower role.

The tension between the judiciary's envisioned liberal role and prevailing legal culture, including transplanted assumptions of judicial power, becomes apparent often in politically charged cases where divergent expectations collide among the populace, political elites, lawyers, and judges. Notable instances, like the *Rooney Case* in 1979 and the *East Sepik Province Case* in 2011, underscored these conflicts, leading to constitutional crises in which the integrity of both the parliament and the judiciary were questioned. In the *Rooney Case*, the intervention of Prime Minister Sir Michael Somare in relation to a Supreme Court judgment caused mass resignation of judges[1] and the *East Sepik Province Case* saw Parliament, through the government of Peter O'Neill, respond to a Supreme Court decision that resulted in Papua New Guinea having two prime ministers for seven months and hostility from the executive government.[2]

These cases accentuate the need to understand the proper role of the judiciary within Papua New Guinea's constitutional framework, especially in a nation

[1] *The Public Prosecutor v Nahau Rooney* (No.2) (1979) PGSC 23 (11 September 1979); David Weisbrot, 'Papua New Guinea: Judges and Politicians' (Part 1) (1979) 4 *Legal Service Bulletin* 240.

[2] *In re Reference to Constitution Section 19(1) by East Sepik Provincial Executive* [2011] PGSC 41 (12 December 2011); Rowan Callick, 'Papua New Guinea in crisis with two PMs, two police chiefs', *The Australian* (online), 14 December 2011.

B. Kama, *Rethinking Judicial Power in Papua New Guinea*,
https://doi.org/10.1007/978-981-97-2946-3_1

marked by high litigation rates and profound socio-cultural and political complexities. These and other cases have not only exposed fundamental misunderstandings about the role of the judiciary under the 'home-grown' Constitution, but also the potential for consequential impacts resulting from the misunderstandings.

To better understand the distinctive role of the judiciary within the arms of government, the book contends for a reimagining of the doctrine of separation of powers in Papua New Guinea. It argues for a departure from the traditional conceptions in which judicial power is restricted to one in which the judiciary is part of a larger constitutional architecture intended to intervene in and engineer societal development and constitutional accountability. A critical part of the reimagining of the doctrine of separation of powers is recognising that the Constitution envisaged four arms of government with the inclusion of the independent constitutional institutions. The book contends that the 'home-grown' constitutional undertaking reconfigured the doctrine of separation of powers, establishing a quadripartite model as opposed to the traditional tripartite model. It argues that reimagining the framework of government in Papua New Guinea through that lenses would enable a better appreciation of the broader interventionist and liberal role of the judiciary.

While the book acknowledges that there are potential challenges for the judiciary in pursuing its broader role, it argues that there is compelling and overriding significance for the judiciary to remain committed to it. It cautions the judiciary on challenges from within the legal system, including influences of judicial methodologies and philosophies developed elsewhere, that are ill-suited to the constitutional intents and context of Papua New Guinea. In conclusion, the book asserts that Papua New Guinea's judiciary embodies a historic indigenous vision of constitution-making and is, uniquely equipped for its context to navigate the nation's complex socio-political landscape. It calls for a steadfast commitment to the 'home-grown' constitutional ethos, ensuring that the judiciary remains a beacon of liberal and societal interventionism in Papua New Guinea.

1 Chapter Overview

The discussions in this book are developed over eight substantive chapters. Chapter 2 discusses the historical background of the Papua New Guinea Constitution, highlighting the revolutionary and exhaustive constitution-making process undertaken by the Constitutional Planning Committee. It explores the 'home-grown' nature of the Constitution, emphasising the intention of the constitutional drafters to reflect the 'will and spirit' of the People and their concerted departure from the colonial models of constitutionalism.

It demonstrates how the resulting Constitution contains some peculiar structures including a judiciary intended to have liberal and interventionist powers.

Chapter 3 examines the development of the court system in Papua New Guinea under colonial rule, focusing on its characteristics and how they are distinguished from the post-Independence judiciary. Examining the German, Britain and later

Australian colonial administrations, the chapter highlights how the colonial judicial systems often prioritised colonial objectives over the justice needs of Papua New Guineans. It highlights decisions of the Territory of Papua and New Guinea Supreme Court and the domineering influence of strict legalism at the High Court of Australia at that time as incongruent to the circumstances of Papua New Guinea. It argues that those conditions provided the impetuses to designing a judiciary that departs from the colonial models and is responsive to the context of the Papua New Guinea society.

Chapter 4 establishes the character of the Papua New Guinea Constitution as transformative, as opposed to its usual characterisation as programmatic or aspirational. It argues that the liberal and interventionist role of the judiciary is a legitimate feature of the Constitution's transformative character. It compares the Papua New Guinea Constitution to other transformative constitutions globally, such as those of India, South Africa and Kenya, to demonstrate that the character of the Papua New Guinea is not isolated from established constitutional frameworks. In arguing the reframing of the character of the Papua New Guinea Constitution, the chapter introduces, for the first time, the doctrine of transformative constitutionalism as a framework for analysing Pacific constitutions.

Chapter 5 identifies twelve textual indicators within the Constitution that demonstrates the liberal and interventionist character of the Papua New Guinea judiciary is firmly entrenched. It contends that these textual indicators provide the mandate for the judges to engage in the social and political realms beyond traditional legalistic approaches.

Chapter 6 analyses the tensions between the executive and the judiciary through two key case studies: the Rooney Case in 1979 and the East Sepik Province Case in 2011. These instances highlight challenges to the liberal role of the judiciary from the political branches and among judges. The resulting tension led to instances of constitutional crises. The chapter explores how misunderstandings of the role of the judiciary stem from outdated doctrinal arguments and discusses the need to rethink the doctrinal basis.

Chapter 7 draws from the doctrinal misunderstandings to propose a modified model of the doctrine of separation of powers to better appreciate the liberal character of the judiciary. It suggests a quadripartite model instead of the traditional tripartite model. This model is described as the 'home-grown' model of separation of powers. It argues that this modified model reflects the unique constitutional landscape of Papua New Guinea. This landscape includes a liberal and interventionist judiciary as well as the fourth arm of government identified by the independent constitutional institutions that do not fall under any of the conventional three arms of government.

Chapter 8 explores how the judiciary's liberal powers have been applied to address social and political issues, transforming judges from their traditional 'guardians of the Constitution' role to being guardians of the Papua New Guinea democracy. It contends that accepting this transformative function not only allows for a better understanding of the character of the Papua New Guinea judiciary, but importantly, that the courts and judges have a legitimate function as agents of social and political development in the country.

Chapter 9 examines the internal and external challenges facing the judiciary in maintaining its liberal and interventionist role, extending beyond tensions with other branches of government. It identifies the domestic legal culture, lawyer training methods in Papua New Guinea, and the utilization of foreign judges as some of the key contributors to these challenges. However, it emphasises the importance of upholding the judiciary's liberal and interventionist role amidst the decline and paralysis of deliberative and accountability institutions. Additionally, it notes the lack of constitutional culture and the legitimate expectation of the people for the judiciary to respond to these conditions beyond the narrow confines of black-letter law.

Chapter 10 concludes that the distinctive constitutional designs in the Papua New Guinea Constitution, resulting from a historic and unparalleled constitution-making process aimed at creating a truly 'home-grown' Constitution, must be given their fullest place and materialise meaningfully in contemporary Papua New Guinean society. It reflects on the ingenious outcome, particularly the establishment of a liberal judiciary with unique social and political interventionist functions and emphasises that the role of the judiciary be reconsidered from traditional conceptions. It urges Papua New Guinean judges not to abdicate their liberal and interventionist powers despite the challenges they face and cautions against supplanting these powers with conceptions drawn elsewhere that may undermine the country's 'home-grown' constitutional contexts and intents.

Chapter 2
The Evolution of the Papua New Guinea 'Home-Grown' Constitution

Abstract This chapter delves into the history of the Papua New Guinea Constitution, showcasing the nation's transition from colonial rule to a historic and comprehensive constitution-making process during the 1960s and 1970s. Led by the Constitutional Planning Committee (CPC), the drafters aimed to harness 'the will and spirit of the people' through extensive consultations. The resulting Constitution emerged as an autochthonous document, tailored to address the deficiencies of colonial governance structures, the complex societal diversities, and the anticipated challenges of the post-independence era. Departing from traditional colonial models, the CPC charted a distinct path for Papua New Guinea through their crafting of unique constitutional designs. A notable institution with novel features is the judiciary. Vested with liberal and interventionist powers, the CPC intended for the judiciary to be distinguished from conventional frameworks. This chapter offers a deeper exploration of the transformative journey towards autonomy and self-governance encapsulated within Papua New Guinea's constitutional evolution.

Keywords Decolonial constitution · Homegrown constitution · Constitution-making · Papua New Guinea constitution

1 Introduction

The Papua New Guinea Constitution was crafted to rectify the legacies of over 90 years of colonial rule and to honor the aspirations of its diverse populace for a governance system aligned with its distinct circumstances. Unlike many other nations decolonising through violent struggle, Papua New Guinea achieved independence peacefully. However, the journey towards self-government was not devoid of challenges, particularly in the formulation of an independent constitution tasked with unifying a nation comprising over 830 languages and approximately 5000–7000 tribal groups. The quest for an autochthonous constitution can be traced back to the late 1960s, gaining momentum into the early 1970s, when a cadre of mostly

B. Kama, *Rethinking Judicial Power in Papua New Guinea*,
https://doi.org/10.1007/978-981-97-2946-3_2

semi-educated yet deeply patriotic indigenous leaders comprising the Constitutional Planning Committee (CPC) embarked on an exhaustive consultative process. Australian jurist John Goldring aptly characterized the consultation endeavor for the independence Constitution as 'unparalleled in comparative constitutional law history'.[1]

The drafters rejected the notion of outsourcing the constitution-drafting process, adamantly advocating for a 'home-grown' or autochthonous approach. Later affirmed by the Papua New Guinea Supreme Court as a sincere effort to 'tap the will and the spirit of the people',[2] the exhaustive consultations sought to ensure that the multifaceted desires of the populace were comprehensively understood and, to the greatest extent feasible, enshrined within the Constitution. Thus, the constitution emerged as a unifying force in a society marked by profound heterogeneity and fragmentation.

The progressive ethos of the Papua New Guinea judiciary finds its roots in the nation's pursuit of a bespoke constitutional framework tailored to its unique imperatives. It included rectifying the deficiencies of colonial governance, notably the lack of governmental accountability prevalent during the colonial era, and a judicial system unresponsive to local exigencies. This chapter examines the historic genesis of the 'home-grown' Constitution, illustrating within the broader context of the book that the establishment of a liberal judiciary in Papua New Guinea constituted a legitimate exercise of sovereignty aimed at redressing the injustices of colonial systems and responding to the contemporary challenges confronting the nation.

2 Impetuses for a 'Home-Grown' Constitution

Numerous factors shaped the method of consultation chosen for crafting the Constitution. While some were explicitly outlined by the drafters, others can be gleaned from the history and context of Papua New Guinean societies. Understanding these factors is paramount before delving into the constitution-making processes, as they illuminate the essence and validity of the proposals within the Constitution. These influencing factors can broadly be categorized as stemming from either the precolonial or colonial period, depending on when they existed in the context of Papua New Guinea.

2.1 Pre-colonial Influences

A central aspect of the exhaustive consultation process underpinning the Constitution is the consensus-based model of governance that prevailed among the societies of

[1] John Goldring, *The Constitution of Papua New Guinea* (Lawbook Co, 1978) 15.

[2] *Ref by Simbu Provincial Executive* [1987] PNGLR 151 (Barnett J) (unnumbered judgment).

Papua New Guinea prior to the imposition of centralised, elitist government structures by the colonial powers.[3]

This governance model prioritises consultation and consensus, and can result in an acceptably lengthy process of decision-making.

The significance of 'consultation' within Papua New Guinean societies is reinforced by Section 255 of the Constitution, mandating that consultations be 'meaningful,' allowing for 'genuine interchange and consideration of views.' According to the drafters of the Constitution (CPC), the process of consultation and consensus requires the people 'to be actively and meaningfully involved in [decisions regarding] their own development'[4] while the PNG National Court has further defined 'meaningful consultation' as requiring 'more in-depth' and elaborate consultations with the people.[5]

This traditional model of governance facilitates access to and direct participation in local affairs, contributing to stable, governed and settled communities rather than nomadic ones. The CPC emphasized in its report for an independent Constitution that '[w]hen Europeans settled in Papua New Guinea, they did not find a political vacuum.'[6]

Instead, they found well-organized, self-sufficient communities with governing systems, with the CPC highlighting that 'the price of the impact of Western colonisation has been the sapping of the initiative of our people.' During his tenure as Minister for Territories between 1951 and 1963, Paul Hasluck, referred to this consensus model of governance among the natives as 'government by jabber'[7], a system based on negotiation, participation, and deliberation without centralized authority.

Ascension to leadership under the traditional model of governance was generally by common consensus as 'bigmen' or 'women of influence' based on an individual's merit rather than hereditary chiefly structures typical of Polynesian societies.[8] Chief Justice Barwick of the High Court of Australia observed, when presiding over a land dispute case between colonists and native Papuans, that 'there were really no chiefs amongst the Port Moresby Papuans' and that ascription of leadership was by 'common consent' among the people.[9]

The absence of hierarchical power structures meant decision-making in traditional Papua New Guinean societies was consensus-driven, embodying collectivist

---

[3] Constitutional Planning Committee *Final Report* 1974 (CPC Report) Chapter 2 [212]–[215] (see online copy http://www.paclii.org/pg/CPCReport/main.htm).

[4] CPC Report 1974, Chapter 1 [16–19], Chapter 2 [106–112].

[5] *Maniwa v Malijiwi* [2014] PGNC 25, [22, 23]. According to the Court, that involves 'go[ing] to the villages…talk[ing] to the landowners, in their families clans and tribes, in the languages they could understand'.

[6] CPC Report 1974, Chapter 2 [97].

[7] Paul Hasluck, *A time for Rebuilding: Australian administration in Papua and New Guinea, 1951–1963* (Melbourne University Press, 1976) 165–166.

[8] Keir Martin, *The Death of the Big Men and the Rise of the Big Shots: Custom and Conflict in East New Britain* (Berghahn Press, 2013) 173; Paula Brown, 'From anarchy to satrapy' (1963) 65 (1) *American Anthropologist* 1, 5.

[9] *Papua & New Guinea v Daera Guba* (1973) 130 CLR 353, [44] (Barwick CJ).

values. Even if some chiefly system is claimed to have existed, decisions, as Papua New Guinea psychologist Leo Marai puts it, were mainly 'through the art of consensus [in] the spirit of collectivism'.[10]

These values were echoed in the CPC Report, which emphasised that 'our people are firmly against elitism which is both unjust and undemocratic' and that 'our ways emphasize egalitarianism' and 'those practices of participation, of consultation and consensus'.[11]

The Supreme Court of Papua New Guinea has expanded on these societal values of consensus and egalitarianism to declare that the people of Papua New Guinea were not meant to be 'mere spectators' in deliberations of government.[12] As the governance model widely practised in traditional Papua New Guinean societies was consensus-based, authority and governance were negotiated rather than imposed, reflecting a fairly democratic society. Bernard Narokobi, the legal adviser for the CPC, attested that 'we are by nature democratic'.[13]

The democratically infused consensus model of governance in Papua New Guinean societies created an innate accountability mechanism for political power, demanding that it be diffused and decentralised. It is receptive to and aligns with the creation of constitutional structures that distribute power and encourage accountability, including a judiciary with liberal and interventionist role equipped for ready oversight over society and other arms of government. This consultative and consensus-based model of governance, integral to Papua New Guinean societies, provided the foundation for an exhaustive consultation process underpinning the Constitution's drafting. It resulted in a 'home-grown' Constitution tailored to Papua New Guinea's own needs and circumstances.

2.2 *Colonial Influences*

Colonial administrations

Britain and Germany formally colonised the territories of Papua and New Guinea respectively in 1884. Germany's annexation of mainland New Guinea was driven by its imperial ambitions, while Britain, under pressure from the Australian colonies, reluctantly annexed the southern part of New Guinea, wary of Germany's proximity as a neighboring power.[14] Britain subsequently offered control over British

[10] Leo Marai, 'The Psychology of Consensus in Melanesia' (2007) 1 (2) *Journal of Pacific Rim Psychology* 54, 55.

[11] CPC Report 1974, Chapter 2 [50], [212–215].

[12] *Reference by the Ombudsman Commission of Papua New Guinea* [2010] PGSC 10, [68].

[13] Bernard Narokobi, 'Experiences in constitutional development in post-independence Papua New Guinea' in Rick Gray, David Lea and Sally Roberts (eds), *Constitutional changes in the 1990s: Proceedings of the 1990 Constitutional Conference, Darwin* (1994) 39.

[14] Hank Nelson, Stewart Firth and James Griffin, *Papua New Guinea: A political history* (Pearson. Education, 1979) 40.

New Guinea (Papua) to Australia in 1902. This transfer was not formalized until 1905 through the passing of the *Territory of Papua Act* 1905 (Cth).

Towards the end of 1914 as German war efforts intensified in Europe, Australian armed forces seized a dwindling German outpost in New Guinea and effectively took military control of the colony.[15] Article 22 of the *Treaty of Versailles 1919* between Germany and Allied Forces allowed for former German colonies to be placed under the administration of the Council of the League of Nations (later replaced by the United Nations). The League of Nations mandated Australia to administer German New Guinea which Australia formally enforced in 1920 under the *New Guinea Act 1920* (Cth).

By 1945, Australia jointly administered the territories of Papua and New Guinea subject to the United Nations bequeathing all administration power over German New Guinea to Australia.[16] A Trusteeship Agreement soon followed between the United Nations and Australia, permitting Australia to administer German New Guinea as a Trust Territory. The Agreement recognised that

> Australia has the same powers of legislation, administration and jurisdiction over the Territory of New Guinea as it would have if that Territory were an integral part of Australia, including power to bring that Territory into an administrative union with other dependent territories under its jurisdiction or control...[17]

By 1949, Australia unified the two colonies into the Territory of Papua and New Guinea and ruled until 16 September 1975 when Papua New Guinea became Independent.[18] The impact of these changes on the development of the judicial system is discussed in Chapter 3.

Impacts of systems of administration

While the pre-colonial consensus-based system of government provided the consultative basis for constitution-making, the people's views on the design of the Constitution were greatly influenced by their experiences with the colonial systems of government.[19] In his reflection in assisting the native leaders during the transition to Independence, Narokobi described the effect of colonial laws in these terms:

> The colonial law was part of the colonial wave which came without invitation and without warning, toppling Papua New Guinean societies, destroying its laws and institutions.[20]

The implications of colonial institutions and administrations affect people in various way of which three were pivotal in providing the impetus for the rejection of the colonial constitutional arrangements and encouraged the desire for the 'home-grown' Constitution.

---

15 James Stuart Olson, *Historical Dictionary of European Imperialism* (Greenwood, 1991) 485.

16 *Papua-New Guinea Provisional Administration Act 1945* (Cth).

17 *Papua and New Guinea Act 1949* (Cth), Preamble.

18 *Papua-New Guinea Act* 1949 (Cth); Australia ceased control with the enactment of the *Papua New Guinea Act 1975* (Cth).

19 *House of Assembly Debates*, 23 May 1975, p 5811.

20 Bernard Narokobi, *The Melanesian Way: Total Cosmic Vision of Life* (1980) Boroko: Institute of Papua New Guinea Studies, 144.

(a) Powerful Central Government with limited political participation

The first set of experiences that influenced the people's view on the new Constitution were from interactions with the colonial political and bureaucratic system. The colonial system of government under Australia was highly centralised, compartmentalised and bureaucratic compared to many other developing countries.[21] It was completely opposite to the uneven but decentralised and consensus-driven system widely present in traditional Papua New Guinea society.

Australian patrol officers, and later district administrators, were authoritative colonial agents exercising the tripartite power of making, administering and enforcing laws.[22] There was significant lack of scrutiny from the Australian authorities in Canberra, leaving the colonial administration unaccountable 'to any political body in the exercise of its very considerable power'.[23]

The CPC would reflect on this in their 1974 Report to the House of Assembly for an independence constitution:

> Colonial rule has had an important impact upon the character and [lifestyles] of our people. It ignored our traditional forms of social organisation without proper consultation with our people. It deprived us of self-government, and even of self-respect. The proud independence of our local communities was replaced by dependence – upon the all-powerful representative of the colonial government, the *kiap*.[24]

This exercise of unchecked powers by the colonial institutions inspired thinking around the new 'home-grown' Constitution and how best to constrain the powers of government.

Both Germany and Britain had earlier imposed similar unrestrained authority, although less widespread; having started with a more 'indirect rule', they later moved to a more direct rule. The system of 'indirect rule' was predominantly used in Africa where the colonisers dealt only with singular traditional authorities such as *chiefs* to impose the will of the colonial power on the people.[25]

However, unlike the successful implementation of 'indirect rule' in Africa, its application in Papua New Guinea proved challenging due to the absence of authoritative figures with absolute and inherited authority. Instead, Germany, Britain, and later Australia identified selective individuals, to serve as intermediaries between the central administration and the local populace. These individuals, designated as 'village constables,' 'tultuls,' and 'luluais,' acted as access points for the colonial

[21] CPC Report 1974, Chapter 10 [5]–[6]; D Conyers, *The Provincial Government Debate: Central Control Versus Local Participation* (Institute of Applied Social and Economic Research, 1976), 9.

[22] Sinclair Dinnen, *Law and Order in a Weak State: Crime and Politics in Papua New Guinea* (University of Hawaii Press, 2001) 28.

[23] Yash Ghai and Anthony Regan, *The law, politics, and administration of decentralisation in Papua New Guinea* (National Research Institute, 1992), 8.

[24] CPC Report 1974, Chapter [1]–[3]. 'Kiap' is a word in Tokpisin language referring to Australian colonial officers. Kiap is discussed further in Chap. 3 in the context of 'Kiap justice'.

[25] Adiele E. Afigbo, *The Warrant Chiefs: Indirect Rule in South-eastern Nigeria, 1891–1929* (London, 1971) 129.

authorities.[26] These local colonial agents lacked formal authority, yet, their representation and alignment with the colonists elevated their status within their tribes to that of 'bigmen' with influential 'connections'.[27] This transformation deviated from the traditional consensus model of governance, prompting the need for a constitution capable of restraining both the colonists and the burgeoning influence of village 'bigmen'.

The central government further lacked any meaningful local representation. The *Territory of Papua Act 1905* (Cth) provided for members of the Legislative Council to be appointed.[28] However, appointees were only made from the white population, as locals were deemed incapable of performing representative duties at the Legislative Council.

It was not until 1951 when three indigenous members were nominated by the colonial administration to the inaugural combined Legislative Council of Papua and New Guinea.[29] The discrimination and denial of suffrage against the locals persisted for nearly 60 years until the enactment of the *Papua and New Guinea Act 1963* (Cth), which brought significant changes to electoral participation and representation. This Act replaced the Legislative Council with a House of Assembly, allocating sixty-four seats. Locals qualified for forty-four of the elected seats, while ten seats were reserved for the white population, and the remaining ten seats were designated for appointees of the colonial administration.[30]

At the local level, the colonial administration maintained a 'centralised and hierarchical' approach with little effort to govern the country through local leaders or institutions.[31]

The establishment of the Local Level Government Councils in 1949 aimed to enhance local representation, and by 1969, there were 156 councils covering nearly 90 per cent of the population.[32] However, their role in policy-making and advisory functions remained minimal, often overshadowed by colonial 'advisers'. This dominance extended to many local leaders elected to the national House of Assembly in the 1964 election.[33]

---

[26] Aaron Podolefsky, 'Mediator Roles in Simbu Conflict Management' (1990) 29 (1) *Ethnology* 67, 69–70, 72.

[27] M. Strathern, Sanctions and the Problem of Corruption in Village Courts' in Jean Zorn and Peter Bayne (eds), *Lo Bilong Ol Manmeri: Crime, Compensation and Village Courts* (University of Papua New Guinea, 1975) 48–54.

[28] *Territory of Papua Act 1905* (Cth) s 29.

[29] Ian Grossart, 'Members in the Legislative Council of Papua and New Guinea 1951–1963' (1966) 1 *The Journal of Pacific History* 147, 149.

[30] *Papua and New Guinea Act 1963* (Cth) ss 4, 35, 36.

[31] Yash Ghai and Anthony Regan, *The law, politics, and administration of decentralisation in Papua New Guinea* (National Research Institute, 1992), 6.

[32] *Native Village Government Councils Ordinance 1949* (Cth); The Ordinance also amended the *Papua New Guinea Act* 1949–1954 (Cth) ss 3, 6–9. The 1949 Ordinance was later renamed *Native Local Government Councils Ordinance 1954* (Cth).

[33] Ian Downs, *The Australian Trusteeship: Papua New Guinea* 1945–1975 (Canberra, 1980) 313.

During its consultation, the CPC noted widespread dissatisfaction among the people due to the limited opportunities for meaningful participation and representation in the management of their affairs under the colonial administrations:

> There is widespread discontent with the present distribution of power in our country, and a deep yearning among our people for a greater say in the conduct of their affairs…The present governmental structure, inherited from the colonial administration, is one of the most centralized in the world…and minimum opportunity [is provided] to our own people to be meaningfully involved in their own government.[34]

While the CPC Report acknowledged certain positive changes brought about by colonial rule, it contended that 'the price of these changes has been the establishment of a system of government that has not made adequate provision for local initiative'.[35] It viewed the colonial centralised system as elitist and reported that 'our people are firmly against elitism, which is both unjust and undemocratic'.[36] The sustained underrepresentation of natives in the government system stemmed from a deep reluctance on the colonial administration to relinquish the responsibility of government to a people considered incapable and threatening to the colonial interests.

The institutional deficit in authority and representation impacted the people's aspirations for self-government. This situation fueled secessionist movements in the early 1970s across regions such as the Gazelle Peninsula, Bougainville and Papua.[37] These anti-colonial micro-nationalist movements eventually pressured the CPC to recommend a constitution that provides for a decentralised government model, with substantial devolution of legislative, executive, and financial powers to the provincial governments.

(b) **Exploitation of land and resources**

The second significant factor shaping public perception of the new Constitution was the exploitation of land and natural resources. Beyond their initial strategic motivations, Britain, Germany, and Australia primarily pursued their economic interests, neglecting long-term social and political development in the country.

Germany, for instance, delegated administration of its New Guinea colony to the New Guinea Company of Berlin, a commercial entity. While ostensibly limited to domestic affairs, excluding foreign relations and the justice system, the company wielded considerable influence over these crucial aspects, prioritizing economic gains over the well-being of the local population.[38]

---

[34] CPC Report 1974, Chapter [1]–[3]; Chapter 2[43].

[35] CPC Report 1974, Chapter 10 [1]–[3].

[36] CPC Report 1974, Chapter 2 [50].

[37] Ron May, *Micronationalist Movements in Papua New Guinea* (Australian National University, 1982).

[38] Emma Thomas, 'Rape, Indenture and the Colonial Courts in German New Guinea' in Hartmut Berghoff, Frank Biess, Ulrike Strasser (eds), *Explorations and Entanglements: Germans in Pacific Worlds from the Early Modern Period to World War I* (Berghahn Books, 2018) 255.

Similarly, executives of private Australian companies were influential in the administration of New Guinea. Historian Hank Nelson observed that this influence made the Australian administration more concerned with 'the well-being of Australian businesses' rather than the 'welfare and advancement of the territory'.[39]

The findings of a United Nations Visiting Mission to New Guinea also referred to Australia's neglect of the colony.[40] Reporting on the UN-Australia Trustee Agreement, the Visiting Mission found that the Australian colonial administration in New Guinea prioritised 'dealing with the conditions arising from the expansions of the European commercial activity, rather than to any constructive attempt to deal with the needs of the native community'.[41]

In New Guinea, it became increasingly apparent to the locals that the Australians were upholding the old German priorities: 'business first, and all else afterwards.'[42] This approach, some argued, seemed to permeate 'every aspect of the Australian presence in New Guinea'.[43] Prioritising business interests meant that colonial administrators often disregarded the socio-economic and political development needs of the people and the customary landowners of natural resources.

Australian historians further noted that most Australians viewed the New Guineans, during that period, as an 'undifferentiated mass of "*kanakas*"',[44] a derogatory term characterising the native people as a 'backward branch of the human race marked by deceitfulness, cowardice, avarice and laziness'.[45] Such degrading perceptions perpetuated exploitation. Additionally, deliberate policy measures were undertaken by the Australian colonial government to hinder economic development in Papua and New Guinea, forcing the colonies to deepen their reliance on Australia.[46]

The expropriation of land and its resources emerged as a central concern for the CPC during its consultation on the new Constitution. Recognising sovereignty over natural resources as fundamental to nationhood, the CPC recommended asserting this principle in the Constitution. The CPC reported on these concerns:

> Because sovereignty over our natural resources is so basic to a nation, we recommend that this be asserted as a fundamental constitutional provision...Land being the most basic resource of our people, the use of which we should strictly control in the interests of our citizens...no foreigner should have a freehold interest in the land.[47]

---

[39] Hank Nelson, Stewart Firth and James Griffin, *Papua New Guinea: A political history* (Pearson Education, 1979), 49–50.

[40] A.M. Healey, 'The Foot Report and East New Guinea' (1962) 34(2) *The Australian Quarterly* 11.

[41] Lord Hailey, cited in Lucy Mair, *Australia in New Guinea* (Christophers, 1948) xvi.

[42] Nelson et al, above n 39, 54.

[43] Ibid.

[44] 'Kanakas' is a word in the Tokpisin language to describe a person or group of people considered as uncivilised and primitive.

[45] Nelson et al, above n 39, 46.

[46] Peter Fitzpatrick, *Law and State in Papua New Guinea* (Academic Press, 1980) 54-6.

[47] CPC Report 1974 Chapter 15 [21]–[22].

The Papua New Guinea Constitution addresses these concerns through its fourth goal—to protect natural resources and the environment—and in Section 53, which safeguards against unjust deprivation of property. These conditions fueled nationalist sentiments and aspirations for self-government.

(c) **Human rights violations**

The third significant influence on the people's perception of the new Constitution was the violations of their rights and privileges. Part of the economic exploitation mentioned earlier involved the exploitation of the locals as cheap labourers.

Historians noted that among colonists, the prevailing sentiment was a 'New Guinean was useless unless he was a labourer'.[48] Some forced labourers were even shipped to other parts of the Pacific to toil on plantations, where they often succumbed to diseases and neglect. They were grossly underpaid, and deserters faced severe punishment. Lieutenant-Governor Hubert Murray of the Australian Territory of Papua even conceded that the colonial system operated 'really rather like slavery'.[49]

In German New Guinea, German colonists evaded accountability for brutal conflicts with locals over land. Driven by commerce, the German Imperial Government and the New Guinea Company of Berlin reportedly employed a policy of 'overwhelming force against any New Guineans who objected'.[50]

Similar practices were seen in British New Guinea, later governed by Australia as the Territory of Papua. Peter Fitzpatrick described the colonial agents' violations of law as 'flagrant, widespread and usually uncorrected'.[51]

The Australian administration reintroduced the head-tax system previously implemented by the Germans in New Guinea. Those unable to pay the tax were compelled to work as laborers instead. Forced labor recruitment thrived, while educational and training opportunities were deliberately suppressed out of fear that an educated Papua New Guinean 'would no longer be the manageable unit of labour he was'.[52]

In contrast to the Territory of Papua, most colonial officers in the Territory of New Guinea were former Australian military personnel who remained in the colony after the First World War. It meant their administrative practices were often militaristic.[53] Access to the colonial court systems was limited for the people of New Guinea, and the colonial judges and magistrates were viewed with suspicion as agents of colonialism, considering their position as appointees of the colonial administration. Chapter 3 discusses this further in the context of the development of the liberal judiciary.

These experiences both mirrored and contradicted the systems of government and accountability in the colonising powers' countries. Progress made in England

---

[48] Nelson et al, above n 39, 42.

[49] Hubert Murray, *The Scientific Mode as Applied to Native Land Problems in Papua* (Government Printer, 1931) 9.

[50] Nelson et al, above 39, 42.

[51] Fitzpatrick, above n 46, 57.

[52] Ibid 55.

[53] Donald Denoon and Kathleen Dugan, *Public Health in Papua New Guinea: Medical Possibility and Social Constraint, 1884-1984* (Cambridge University Press, 2002) 45.

and Australia toward promoting the rule of law and establishing constitutional and accountable governments was not reflected in the colonies.

These injustices and accountability shortcomings in the colonial system strongly influenced the people of Papua New Guinea's desire for a constitution that could address these concerns.

3 The Making of a 'Home-Grown' Constitution

The amalgamation of pre-colonial and colonial experiences shaped a unique and unparalleled process of constitutional development. This endeavor, as emphasized by the drafters and the Supreme Court of Papua New Guinea, culminated in a Constitution that was deemed 'truly autochthonous' or 'home-grown'.[54]

A 'home-grown' constitution is one that is enacted within the country through processes developed and administered by the indigenous people, distinct from colonies with constitutions that were either enacted by the parliament of the colonial power or influenced by its constitution-making mechanisms. The latter was the case for most of the countries in the Pacific region, including Australia.

The Australian colonial judges described the unique 'home-grown' nature of the Papua New Guinea Constitution in these terms:

> The Constitution itself is a truly autochthonous Constitution established, as the preamble recites, by the will of the people, to whom 'all power belongs'. It is not a Constitution given to the country by somebody else, as in the case of Australia. It derives from the people of Papua New Guinea, it grew here and is given to Papua New Guinea by her own people.[55]

These observations align with the findings of the CPC, which noted that 'many of [our] recommendations are novel [and] [t]heir impetus springs strongly from the needs and hopes of our people [who] have accepted the possibility of devising a truly home-grown Constitution'.[56]

The CPC went on to provide the rationale for adopting a 'home-grown' Constitution:

> What has influenced us in framing our recommendations has been the desire to meet Papua New Guinean needs and circumstances...Having done our best to incorporate the views of the people in these proposals for the Constitution of our nation and to make adequate provision for what we believe are their needs and aspirations, and taken due account of their fears, we believe the Constitution itself should be legally, as well as politically, 'home-grown'. In legal terms, it should be 'autochthonous'. By this we mean that it should have its legal origin

---

[54] *The State v Wonem* [1975] PNGLR 311 (unnumbered judgment); *Re Rights of Person Arrested or Detained* [1977] PNGLR 362 (unnumbered judgment) (Frost CJ); *Peter v South Pacific Brewery Ltd* [1976] PGLawRp 537 (unnumbered judgment); Frost CJ.

[55] *The State v Wonem* [1975] PNGLR 311 (unnumbered judgment) (Frost CJ, Raine J).

[56] CPC Report 1974, Chapter 10A [259].

in a law of Papua New Guinea, not in an external source, such as the laws of Australia or of any other country.[57]

As the rest of this Chapter will elaborate, three distinct features underscore the 'home-grown' nature of the Papua New Guinea Constitution. First, exhaustive consultations were conducted with the people to ascertain their preferences for the type of constitution they desired. Second, the constitutional frameworks were crafted through a public consultation process rather than being copied or imposed. Third, the institutions responsible for formalising the Constitution operated independently from those established under Australian laws, ensuring that the Constitution was 'home-grown' both in drafting and enactment.

3.1 Drafters of the Constitution

The endeavor to craft a 'home-grown' Constitution commenced with the establishment of the Select Committee on Political Development in 1962. Consisting of two senior Australian public servants, two Australian settlers, and two Papua New Guineans—all members of the Legislative Council—the Committee's mandate was to discern the appropriate framework of government and chart the future course of the country amid mounting pressure, notably from the United Nations, for indigenous representation and gradual decolonisation.

Following the inaugural elections in 1964 and the formation of the first House of Assembly, the Select Committee on Political Development was succeeded by the Select Committee on Constitutional Development in 1965. According to historian Clive Moore, the impetus for the second Select Committee stemmed from skepticism regarding the Australian government's commitment to further constitutional change and political progress.[58]

Comprising fifteen members, including nine indigenous political leaders and six foreigners (four of whom were officials from the Australian colonial administration), the second Select Committee was tasked with investigating and presenting proposals 'for future constitutional development in Papua New Guinea'.[59] Though the Committee clarified that it 'does not see its recommendations as committing the country or attempting to commit the country to any particular course',[60]

---

[57] CPC Report 1974, Chapter 15 [2]–[3].

[58] Clive Moore and Mary Kooyman (eds), *A Papua New Guinea Political Chronicle* 1967–1991 (Crawford House Publishing, 1998) xxvi.

[59] Edward Wolfers, *January-April 1967* in Clive Moore and Mary Kooyman (eds), Ibid 13.

[60] House of Assembly, Territory of Papua and New Guinea, *Final Report from the Select Committee on Constitutional Development together with Minutes of Proceedings*, Port Moresby, June 1967, 10.

the Committee's final report in 1967 'represented a cautious advance towards the territory's self-government'.[61]

The second Select Committee was replaced with the third Select Committee on Constitutional Development in 1969, predominantly composed of indigenous political leaders. Unlike its predecessors, this Committee's objective was not to achieve self-government or independence but rather to gauge public sentiment on the matter.[62] After undertaking extensive consultations domestically and in other decolonised regions, such as Africa, South-West Pacific, and South-East Asia, the Committee reported to the House of Assembly in 1971 that the majority of the people felt internal self-government should materialise during the tenure of the 1976–1980 House of Assembly.[63]

In response to this report, the colonial House of Assembly replaced the third Select Committee with the Constitutional Planning Committee (CPC) after the 1972 elections. The CPC was chaired ex officio by Chief Minister Michael Somare and led by Deputy Chairman John Momis. Momis was a particularly significant member of the CPC as his libertarian theological training in his former role as a Catholic priest, before being a member of the colonial House of Assembly, became influential in the liberal formulations of the Constitution.

The CPC purposed to respond to the increasing demand for self-government with a view that the timeframe might be sooner than that proposed by the third Select Committee. Comprising entirely of indigenous Papua New Guineans, the CPC, assisted by advisors—both Papua New Guinean and expatriate, among whom only one, Professor Edward Wolfers, was Australian—eschewed external influence, insisting on drafting a constitution tailored to the needs and circumstances of Papua New Guinea.[64] This commitment to indigenous agency in constitution-making marked a departure from the colonial order and its constitutional paradigms, reflecting the people's aspiration for self-determination.

The CPC reasoned that 'what has influenced us above all in seeking formulations and adapting them, has been the desire to meet Papua New Guinean needs and circumstances.'[65] Therefore, it argued, we would not 'merely follow some firm precedent, Westminster or otherwise' or allow the Constitution to be drafted in 'Marlborough House in London or in Paris' or even be seen to 'merely rubberstamp prefabricated ideas from Canberra'.[66] Instead, the members of the CPC were adamant that 'we

---

[61] Wolfers, above n 59.

[62] The Commonwealth, 'Australian Political Chronicle May–August 1969' (1969) 15 *Australian Journal of Politics & History* 81, 122.

[63] Don Aitkin and Edward P. Wolfers, 'Australian Attitudes Towards Papua New Guinea Since World War II', (1973) 27 *Australian Outlook* 202, 209.

[64] Don Woolford, *Papua New Guinea: Initiation and Independence (*University of Queensland Press, 1976) 158–59.

[65] CPC Report 1974, Chapter 1 [9].

[66] CPC Report, Chapter 1 [9]; Bernard Narokobi, 'Experiences in constitutional development in post-independence Papua New Guinea' in Rick Gray, David Lea and Sally Roberts (eds), *Constitutional changes in the 1990s: Proceedings of the 1990 Constitutional Conference, Darwin* (Australian

must write our own constitution'.[67] The refusal to have the Constitution drafted or influenced by the colonial powers marked a rejection of the colonial order and its constitutional designs and expectations.

Chief Minister of the Territory Michael Somare, who would later become the first Prime Minister of PNG, attested to the importance of this 'home-grown' constitution drafting endeavour in his address to the House of Assembly:

> It is important that the fullest consideration be given to the type of future government we shall have. It is for our people that a constitution will be made. It is our people who shall have to live under the system of government that is established. *We must ensure therefore that the constitution is suited to the needs and circumstances of Papua New Guinea and is not imposed from outside. In short, it should be a home-grown constitution.*[68] (emphasis added)

Somare's resolve that the Constitution respond to the 'needs and circumstances of Papua New Guinea' and 'not [be] imposed from outside' supported the CPC's and the people's rejection of the colonial model of constitutional arrangements.

The 'needs and circumstances' of Papua New Guinea that justified a departure from the colonial model included the complexity of Papua New Guinea's societal fabric, characterised by linguistic diversity with over 836 languages and the over 5000 myriad clan groups. Against a backdrop of state fragility, abuse of power, and corruption, the CPC faced the formidable task of garnering public consent in a highly heterogeneous and fragmented society.

These challenges were unlike constitution-making in many other Commonwealth countries that sought 'to secure the assent of the peoples…with their diverse interests, sentiments, prejudices, ambitions and apprehensions'.[69] The assignment for the CPC was more than merely fulfilling a requirement of constitution-making—they had to secure the assent of the people who were inherently distrustful of public power—in a manner that reflected the model of consultation and decision-making deemed legitimate among the people. These challenges underscored the significance of the CPC's endeavour to establish a 'home-grown' Constitution.

National University, 1994) 37; Father John Momis (CPC Deputy Chairman), 'The Constitutional Planning Committee and the Constitution' in Anthony Regan, Owen Jessep and Eric Kwa (eds), *Twenty Years of Papua New Guinea Constitution* (Law Book Co, 2001) 19.

[67] Ibid, John Momis.

[68] House of Assembly Debates, Third House, Second Meeting of the First Session (23 June 1972) 279.

[69] *Spratt v Hermes* (1965) 114 CLR 226, 250.

3.2 The People's Constitution

The need for the Constitution to be the product of a consultative process and 'home-grown' meant the document must be derived from the people. This led the CPC to undertake a comprehensive consultation process, described earlier as 'unparalleled in comparative constitutional law history'.[70]

The consultation took three years and involved over 2000 written submissions, 500 discussion groups, each of about twenty people, set up throughout the Territory and 110 public meetings attended by an estimated 60,000 people.[71] While the attendance at the public meetings was only 2.4% of the 2,520,000 estimated total population at the time, it was still significant considering over 98% of the population lived in rural areas which were remote and largely inaccessible. Father John Momis, the CPC Deputy Chairman, would later recall that they tried to reach 'every remote village' in the country.[72] Australian jurist Justice Barnett described the significance of the CPC's consultation as an undertaking to 'tap the will and spirit of the people'.[73]

The CPC was able to conduct meetings in many of the remote communities as well as accept submissions from representatives of other isolated areas that were unable to attend but were informed by discussion papers and questionnaires that were widely distributed and publicised in the three main languages—English, Tokpisin, and Motu.[74] This inclusive approach resulted in a remarkable level of awareness among village residents about the constitutional process, surprising many observers.[75] This surprise stemmed from the initial assumption that such a diverse, largely illiterate, and geographically dispersed society might struggle to comprehend the complexities of constitution-making.

In addition to the extensive consultations, the drafters also drew upon recommendations of the 1960s Select Committee on Constitutional Development, which conducted visits to thirteen countries and territories across the Pacific, Africa, and Asia such as American Samoa, Fiji, India, Sri Lanka, Kenya and Tanzania, aimed at studying the social and political conditions under their post-colonial independence constitutions.

Until that point, the waves of decolonisation among former British colonies, including the Pacific Island states and Australia, had not witnessed such a breadth of consultation for constitution-making. Joe Lynch, the Constitutional Draftsman involved with the CPC, highlighted that the consultation on the draft framework of the new Constitution generated 'more than 550 recommendations' covering a wide spectrum of governmental activities, structures of accountability mechanisms,

---

[70] Goldring, above n 1, 15.

[71] CPC Report 1974, Chapter 1; Goldring, above n 1, 21.

[72] John Momis, 'The Making of the Papua New Guinea Constitution' (Paper presented at the 2nd Pacific Constitutions Conference, Emalus Campus, University of South Pacific, 5 December 2017).

[73] *Ref by Simbu Provincial Executive* [1987] PNGLR 151 (Barnett J) (unnumbered judgment).

[74] Rory Ewins, 'The Papua New Guinea Constitution: Australia's Role in its Development, 1960–75' (1990 Excerpt from an Honours Essay) (online accessed).

[75] Goldring, above n 1, 21-22.

and protection and preservation of natural resources, environment and cultures.[76] Lynch further noted that an initial draft of the Constitution, following the extensive consultation, exceeded 300 pages in length, which would have made Papua New Guinea have 'the longest Constitution in the world'.[77]

This extensive consultation process firmly mirrored the consensus-based model of government that prevailed before the imposition of the centralised colonial government. As later sections of this book will illustrate, the active involvement of the populace in crafting the Constitution not only provided a chance to address past injustices under the colonial regime but also enabled the creation of some novel constitutional frameworks distinct from colonial models.

Enactment of the Constitution

The process of enacting the Constitution was also critical in shaping its 'home-grown' or autochthonous nature. Unlike the typical legislative route through the House of Assembly, the Constitution was enacted by a Constituent Assembly, established by and predominantly composed of indigenous members of the House of Assembly. However, the Constituent Assembly lacked formal legislative authority under colonial statute, essentially rendering it a self-appointed body.[78]

Despite lacking legal mandate, the Constituent Assembly asserted its legitimacy as a representative body of the people. The Speaker of the House of Assembly emphasised the necessity of forming the Constituent Assembly to 'break any ties that may exist between Papua New Guinea and Australia', ensuring the independent Constitution was truly indigenous in origin.[79] The rationale was that since the House of Assembly was a creature of the Australian Parliament established under Australian laws, allowing it to enact the Papua New Guinea Constitution and the provisional legislation in preparation for Independence would mean 'the links to Australian law would not be clearly broken'.[80] That is, Papua New Guineans in the House of Assembly did not want Australia or its institutions to grant their independence Constitution—the Constitution had to be 'home-grown' and 'home-delivered'.

Australia refrained from contesting the legality of this action, partly due to its disinterest in maintaining Papua New Guinea as a colony. Furthermore, the members of the Constituent Assembly, perceived as elected representatives of the people, rejected the notion of being bounded by colonial institutions that hindered the creation of a 'home-grown' Constitution. Consequently, Papua New Guinea severed its ties with Australia decisively, paving the way for the emergence of a genuinely autochthonous constitution.

The case of Papua New Guinea differs markedly from other countries in the Pacific region including Australia. Unlike these nations, which either had their constitutions

---

[76] C. J. Lynch, 'The Achievement of Independence in Papua New Guinea' (1980) 15 The Journal of Pacific History 175, 191; CPC Report 1974, Chapters 1 & 2.

[77] Ibid.

[78] Ibid 179; *Papua and New Guinea Act 1945* (Cth).

[79] Papua New Guinea, *House of Assembly Debates*, House of Assembly, 23 May 1975, 5811.

[80] Lynch, above n 76, 185.

enacted by colonial parliaments or were guided by colonial advisors in the drafting process, Papua New Guinea's path to independence was distinguished by its own agency and autonomy in crafting and delivering the Constitution.

4 Resulting Constitution: A 'Home-Grown' Judiciary

While many of the fundamental structures of the resulting Constitution remained largely transplanted, their functions and purposes were extensively tailored to meet the needs and circumstances of Papua New Guinea.[81] In other areas, the CPC was markedly innovative, inserting new constitutional structures in contrast to existing models at the time. The CPC was adamant that the constitutional arrangements were not simply 'a mere continuation of the old colonial system', emphasizing the necessity for change and the disruption it was intended against entrenched interests:

> [T]o build a constitutional framework uniquely suited to Papua New Guinean needs…meant changes from a number of institutions and procedures we have inherited from our recent colonial past. And this in turn, means some disturbance to entrenched interests.[82]

A notable change evident in the CPC's formulations was alteration to the conventional understanding of the doctrine of the separation of powers. Instead of adhering strictly to conventional norms, the doctrine appeared reconfigured, featuring a liberal judiciary endowed with broad social engineering powers alongside a constitutionally entrenched independent integrity system referred to as the 'fourth arm' of government. The enhanced powers of the judiciary, in particular, described by Australian jurist Deputy Chief Justice William Prentice as 'frightening,'[83] signaled a departure from the colonial model towards a 'home-grown' judicial framework. Further elaboration on these findings is presented in the preceding chapters.

The drafters of the Constitution were resolute in their aim to differentiate Papua New Guinea's judicial system from that of Australia, emphasising the need for judicial functions and laws under the Papua New Guinea Constitution to better reflect the nation's 'own values and circumstances'.[84]

The CPC's determination did not stem from a nationalistic or reckless inclination to revolt against the establishment, although some members were considered zealous. The drafters recognised the challenges involved in deviating from the conventional colonial model. However, they deemed the existing system inadequate and unjust, prompting them on a path of constitutional ingenuity to establish structures more attuned to the needs and circumstances of Papua New Guinea.

---

[81] *Ref by Simbu Provincial Executive* [1987] PNGLR 151 (Barnett J) (unnumbered judgment).

[82] CPC Report 1974, Chapter 1 [10] [13].

[83] *Peter v South Pacific Brewery Ltd* [1976] PGLawRp 674 (Prentice DCJ) (unnumbered judgment).

[84] CPC Report 1974, Chapter 8 [12].

5 Conclusion

The Constitution of Papua New Guinea emerged from an exhaustive process of constitution-making aimed at addressing the injustices of colonial systems and responding to contemporary challenges. Specifically, the adverse colonial experiences, including the working of highly centralised government, exploitation of resources and human rights violations, inspired the rejection of the colonial state structures and its constitutional systems that failed to remedy. While these experiences may not encapsulate the entirety of colonial rule, they significantly influenced the desire for self-government.

Both pre-colonial legacies and colonial experiences, alongside a transformative vision for Papua New Guinea, shaped the 'home-grown' constitutional designs, which advocated for a liberal judiciary among other innovative constitutional designs. There was a deliberate effort to distance Australia and its ideologies from the drafting, enactment, and implementation of the constitutional frameworks. The factors underpinning the 'home-grown' constitutional undertaking are not merely of historical significance. As will be contended in the preceding chapters, they should be indispensable in informing the interpretation and application of the Constitution, including understanding the nature and role of the judiciary in Papua New Guinea. Chapter Three elaborates on this theme by examining the evolution of the judiciary before Papua New Guinea's independence, illustrating how it has acquired a distinct character under the 'home-grown' Constitution.

Chapter 3
The Colonial Justice Systems: Methods and Influence

Abstract This Chapter examines the development of the court system in Papua New Guinea under colonialism leading up to the Independence in 1975 to understand the formation of the modern judiciary and its distinguishing features from those of the colonial designs. It demonstrates that under both German and Britain, and later Australia colonial administrations, the impetuses and approaches that defined the judicial culture largely supported the objects of colonialism. Impartiality and judicial independence were compromised for the natives of Papua New Guinea as their justice needs became secondary. The people responded in their consultation on the post-Independence Constitution, desiring a judiciary that departs from the colonial models. This departure includes from uncritical adherence to legalism and the narrow functions of the courts that were propagated by the domineering influence of the Australian High Court.

Keywords Colonial justice · Colonial courts · Village courts · Native affairs · German colonialism · British colonialism · Australian colonialism · Legalism

1 Introduction

The systems and models of justice in the pre-colonial and colonial periods significantly influenced the views of the people of Papua New Guinea regarding the character of the judiciary under the Independent Constitution. Those involved in the exhaustive consultation processes led by the Constitutional Planning Committee (CPC) drew from their own experiences with these justice models as well as their observations of the operations and inadequacies of these models, leading them to desire a judiciary with a different character.

The assessment of the various pre-independence models of justice, which were determinant to the design of the liberal judiciary argued in this book under the Papua New Guinea Constitution, unfolds in two parts. The first part concerns the various judicial institutions at pre-independence, while the second part focuses on the judicial methods of the superior courts. The analysis of the latter, particularly drawn from

B. Kama, *Rethinking Judicial Power in Papua New Guinea*,
https://doi.org/10.1007/978-981-97-2946-3_3

the judgements of the Supreme Court of the Territory of Papua and New Guinea and the High Court of Australia, aims to ascertain the underlying ideologies informing judicial governance and the judiciary's role as understood by the colonial courts before the enactment of the 'home-grown' Constitution.

This discussion will demonstrate that the liberal judiciary contended in this book for Papua New Guinea had its early influence from a range of informal and formal judicial systems, the agendas and conceptions of justice of which remain contested in the post-independence era.

2 Pre-colonial and Colonial Judicial Systems

2.1 Pre-colonial Judicial System

The people of Papua New Guinea lived in settled rather than nomadic communities before the advent of colonialism, and had an ordered system that governed their societies. This structure, rooted in tightly woven kinship relations of interdependence and communalism, extended across jealously guarded territories. Although the notions of 'justice' and the way it was applied differed among the self-governing societies, they had a form of judicial system based on indigenous laws and customs that governed their settled communities.

The precolonial judicial system was characterized by two primary dispute resolution methods. First was a revenge-oriented system wherein disputing factions engaged in warfare, sorcery, or other retaliatory actions to settle grievances.[1] Societal warfare and payback killings, although outlawed, continue to this day in many parts of Papua New Guinea. Traditionally, the revenge-oriented system was practised to maintain the respect and honour of the society. It was perceived that failure to take revenge made a society weak, thereby, availing it to further incursions. Despite being outlawed, societal warfare and retaliatory killings persist in modern Papua New Guinea among some communities.

The second primary method for dispute resolution was mediation. It was driven by increasingly interdependent communities seeking to restore relations. Mediation focused on preserving community harmony over individual needs, with the drastic costs of societal warfare eventually elevating mediation above retributive justice.

Mediation resonated with Papua New Guinea's values of communalism, respect, and consensus-building, with settlements of disputes often involving material compensation and other reconciliatory gestures such as the exchanging of brides.[2]

---

[1] Richard Scaglion, 'Legal Adaptation in a Papua New Guinean Village Court' (1990) 20 *Ethnology* 17, 21–2.

[2] Michael Goddard, *Substantial Justice: An Anthropology of Village Courts in Papua New Guinea* (Berghahn Books, 2009) 14.

Early European contact in the sixteenth century, along with the influence of Christian missionaries and colonialism in the early nineteenth century, encouraged greater adoption of community mediation and discouraged retribution.[3]

The concepts of fairness and justice among the people were influenced by a range of factors including historical events, local belief systems, customary norms, and shared values. The indigenous judicial system operated autonomous and was community-oriented, with mediators typically being community elders or traditional 'bigmen' well informed about local circumstances. As local leadership was largely merit-based as discussed in Chap. 2, the leaders appointed to lead the mediations used their influence to prioritise community's interests for conciliation and harmony.

2.2 Colonial Judicial Systems

As colonial influence permeated indigenous communities, local justice institutions were absorbed into or coexisted alongside various iterations of the colonial judicial system. Imposing itself on the traditional societies, the colonial judicial systems not only disregarded the strengths of the traditional judicial systems, but also exacerbated its weaknesses. The colonial judicial systems became largely an extension of colonial control over the people. It disrupted the harmony between communities and their leaders, replacing the consensus-based values of mediatory justice with a hierarchical structure, often neglecting local initiatives and autonomy.

Luluais, tultuls and village police constables

The first form of colonial justice mechanism was the system of *luluais, tultuls,* and village police constables. Established by Germany and Britain shortly after claiming the territories of New Guinea and Papua, respectively, in 1884, the system involved recruiting influential men from the local population to enforce colonial rule.

Albert Hahl, a German judge, initiated the system of *luluais* and *tultuls* in New Guinea in 1896 by recruiting local clan elders (*luluais)* and their assistants (*tultuls)* to assist in settling disputes.[4] They were granted formal magisterial powers to resolve minor criminal and civil disputes.[5] Hahl's program initially proved a success because it enabled locals, who were well-versed in the social and cultural contexts, to adjudicate disputes among the people.

The *luluais* and *tultuls* were also tasked by the German administration with overseeing the implementation of administrative programs in their local communities, such as collecting taxes, organising community efforts to build roads, and administering disease control measures. However, their dual function in administering justice and serving as agents of the executive government undermined the impartiality of

[3] Aaron Podolefsky, 'Mediator Roles in Simbu Conflict Management' (1990) 29 (1) *Ethnology* 67.

[4] Goddard, above n 2, 28.

[5] Peter Sack and Dymphna Clark (eds), *Albert Hahl: Governor in New Guinea* (Australian National University, 1980) 18.

their judicial role.[6] The German administration, heavily influenced by the commercial entity, the German New Guinea Company, faced resentment among the people due to its exploitation of resources and human rights abuses.[7] Similar to Hahl and his fellow judges, the *luluais* and *tultuls* ultimately functioned as agents of the colonial enterprise than independent arbiters of justice.

In British Papua, the British government instructed the establishment of a native juridical system that was 'summary in its operation and free from technicalities of procedure'.[8] Consequently, a Native Magistrates Court was established with the aim of training selected locals in magisterial duties. However, the locals were considered incapable of impartial judgment due to their extended kinship and tribal networks and were instead relegated to being village police constables with no official magisterial functions.[9]

The assumptions against the village police constables in British Papua contrasted with the *luluais* in German New Guinea. It overlooked the ability of the Papuans to provide a more considered judicial outcome compared to a European magistrate uninformed by local realities and conceptions of justice. The police constables in British Papua, however, often used their association with the colonial administration as license to exercise magisterial functions within their communities.[10] The dual functions of *luluais, tultuls* and police constables as agents of the executive government with judicial power resulted in many of them being local despots.[11]

This introduced system of local governance elevated the local authorities above the traditional leadership and accountability structures and distorted the conception of justice as something to be only horizontally applied. Notwithstanding this implication, people were more responsive to the exercise of judicial power by the *luluais, tultuls,* and police constables than to the colonial officials. John Guise, a native representative in the colonial House of Assembly and the first Governor-General of Papua New Guinea, complained in 1968 that 'the breakdown of law began when the *village constable,* the luluai and the tultul system was abolished'.[12]

Courts for Native Matters and Native Affairs

The second influence that impacted the people's conception of a judicial system was the Courts for Native Matters and Native Affairs. Australia established both courts

---

[6] *Native Administrative Regulation 1924* (Cth) s 90; Goddard, above n 3, 29.

[7] Stewart Firth, 'The Transformation of the Labour Trade in German New Guinea, 1899–1914' (Part I) (1976) 11 *Journal of Pacific History* 51, 52–3, 56.

[8] R. B. Joyce, *Sir William McGregor* (Oxford University Press, 1971) 182.

[9] A. M Healy, 'Paternalism and Consultation in Papua, 1880–1960' (1967) 4 *ANU Historical Journal* 19, 21.

[10] Donald Denoon and Malama Meleisea, *The Cambridge History of the Pacific Islanders* (Cambridge University Press, 2004) 275.

[11] *Queen v Pamboa-Taka* [1962] PGSC 29.

[12] Papua New Guinea, *House of Assembly Debates*, House of Assembly, 09 March 1967, 2318 (John Guise).

after assuming control of the territories of British Papua and German New Guinea respectively in 1905 and 1920.[13]

There was a direct right of appeal from the Courts for Native Matters and Native Affairs to the Central Court of each of the colonies (later to become the Supreme Court of the combined territories) and to the High Court of Australia.[14] The purposes and practices of these two court systems raised three important issues that appeared to influence the design of the judicial system in the post-independence era.

First, both courts were established to deal only with disputes among the local people.[15] While this exclusivity may have been intended to localise the colonial judicial system, it reinforced the discrimination and segregation of locals already visible in other aspects of the society under the Australian rule.[16] It also created confusion and inconsistencies, as disputes between the people and the Europeans were prosecuted in other courts unfamiliar to the people.

Second, although the courts were established for the locals, they were administered by 'low-level' and legally untrained Australian colonial government officials.[17] This mirrored the lesser priority placed on the judicial needs of the people. While these 'magistrates' asserted themselves as the ultimate arbiters of all disputes, their lack of local knowledge and cultural awareness often meant they were uninformed about the underlying socio-cultural factors underpinning disputes and the appropriate ways of dispute resolution. Their judicial conduct was more reflective of the colonial objective for control rather than the need for substantive justice.[18]

Third, while the legislative framework provided for appeals to the superior courts,[19] such an appeal was inaccessible and costly for the people with little effort made by the colonial government to overcome this barrier. This disempowered litigants and forced them to either accept the decisions of the colonial courts or resolve their grievances in other unofficial ways.

Kiap 'justice'

The colonial administrative officials who operated in the native communities and local districts were collectively known as *kiaps* in the Tok Pisin language.[20] The *kiaps*

---

[13] *Papua Act 1905* (Cth); *New Guinea Act 1920* (Cth); *Native Regulation Ordinance 1908–1930* (Cth) s 3.

[14] *Papua Act 1905* (Cth) s 43; *Native Administrative Ordinance 1921* (Cth) s 2–3.

[15] *Native Regulation Ordinance 1908* (Cth) ss 3–4; *Judiciary Ordinance 1921–1938* (Territory of New Guinea) (Cth) s 7A.

[16] Edward Wolfers, *Race Relations and Colonial Rule in Papua New Guinea* (Australia and New Zealand Book Company, 1975) 153.

[17] *Native Administrative Ordinance 1921* (Cth) s 2(3); *Native Administration Regulation 1924* (Cth) s 11; Goddard, above n 2, 43.

[18] Hank Nelson, *Taim Bilong Masta: The Australia Involvement with Papua New Guinea* (ABC, 1990) 187.

[19] *Judiciary Ordinance* 1921–1938 (Territory of New Guinea) (Cth) s 24.

[20] Tokpisin is the only nationally spoken language apart from Motu and English, which are not widespread. 'Kiap' is the Tokpisin translation of the German word for 'captain' which is 'kapitan'. Colonial legislation referred to these officials with various titles including 'district officers', 'patrol

were non-indigenous, mostly Australians, and played a significant role in Australian colonialism. Unlike those in the Territory of Papua, the first *kiaps* in the Territory of New Guinea were typically former Australian military personnel who remained in the colony after the First World War.

A *kiap* embodied the powerful colonial institution and had the ultimate tripartite power of making, executing, and judging the exercise of the colonial laws. As anthropologist Michael Goddard described it, 'the kiap was the investigator, arrester, magistrate and gaoler'.[21] This was evident in the various colonial legislative instruments. For instance, *kiaps* could sit as magistrates on the Court of Native Affairs,[22] administer the whipping of offenders,[23] and represent the people in appeal cases.[24] According to Australian historian Professor Hank Nelson, the Kiaps used the Courts of Native Affairs to dispense 'rough and ready justice'.[25]

Their powers extended to regulating any matter having a 'bearing or affecting the good government and wellbeing of natives'.[26] This included making regulations for marriage, property ownership, observance and relevance of local customs, what food people should plant on their land, and the type of clothes to be worn.[27] Heralded as instruments of the civilising mission, these regulations constituted an intrusive body of restrictions that systematically disempowered the social, economic and political autonomy of the people.

The *kiaps* performed their 'judicial work with an executive mind,' raising concerns about their impartiality.[28] Grievances against the *kiaps* were suppressed or summarily dealt with by the *kiaps* themselves, discouraging people from readily exploring appeals to superior courts due to a general distrust of the judicial system and inherent structural barriers discussed earlier.

Characterised by inflexibility, *kiap* justice asserted the supremacy of colonial laws over indigenous ones, exerting significant control over the local judicial system 'with little or no oversight'.[29] As later discussed in the book, experiences with *kiaps* significantly influenced the development of a more liberal judiciary aimed at curbing governmental authority.

---

officers' or 'commissioned officers', see *Native Administrative Ordinance 1921* (Cth) s 2(2); *Native Administration Regulation 1924* (Cth) s 80; *Native Regulation Ordinance 1908–1930* (Cth) s 3.

[21] Goddard, above n 2, 43.

[22] *Native Administration Regulation 1924* (Cth) s 11.

[23] *Native Regulation 1939* (Cth) s 92(2).

[24] *Judiciary Ordinances 1921* (Cth) s 23(1).

[25] Nelson, above n 18, 185.

[26] *Native Regulations Ordinance 1908–1939* (Cth) s 5.

[27] *Native Administrative Regulation 1924* (Cth) s 5 (1) (6)-(8); N*ative Administrative Regulation 1924* (Cth) ss 57, 79A and 110.

[28] Peter Bayne, 'Legal Development in Papua New Guinea: The Place of Common Law' (1975) 3 *Melanesian Law Journal* 9, 14.

[29] Tristan Moss, *Guarding the Periphery: The Australian Army in Papua New Guinea, 1951-75* (Cambridge University Press, 2017) 18.

Councillor 'justice'

The fourth judicial development was the establishment of the Native Village Council system in 1949.[30] It was one of the many reforms initiated by the Australian Labour government between 1945 and 1950 in the aftermath of the Second World War and in response to pressure from the United Nations to develop the Trust Territory of New Guinea. Councillors were initially appointed by the colonial administrator and later through election from a list of intending candidates. They were often traditional leaders or persons already in position of respect and standing within their communities.

Councillors had three main functions: first, to maintain peace and order among their people; second, to intervene and prevent offences from being committed; and third, to perform the responsibilities imposed on them by any colonial laws.[31] However, the councillors perceived their authority to be broader, including having magisterial powers. As a result, councillors appointed selected group of people known as 'komiti' in their council ward area to resolve smaller disputes while larger or intractable matters would proceed to them before reaching the *kiaps*.[32] While *kiaps* were at the apex of the councillors' justice, the people preferred councillors to resolve their complex cases because of their ability to consider local circumstances, including customs.[33]

However, the sense of hope in councillors as an independent local authority was temporal as councillors, fearing repercussions from the *kiaps* given their dominant position in the local government,[34] increasingly deferred their judicial role to the *kiaps*. Similar to the *luluais, tutuls* and village constables, councillors eventually became enforcers of colonial laws. Anthropologist Andrew Strathern aptly described the kiap-councillor relations:

> Kiaps saw themselves as generalist field officers with very wide powers of command administratively and also combining magisterial and police powers. They saw councillors as largely there to carry out their own directives... not as leaders in their own right.[35]

Injecting the councillors who are already local leaders into the colonial judicial system not only undermined their autonomy and traditional leadership roles, but also marked a shift in dispute resolution among the people from being locally led, mediatory and autonomous to being legalistic and externally directed. The unchecked authority of the *kiaps* over the councillors further eroded the trust of the people in their councillors to make any meaningful representation on their behalf.

---

[30] *Native Village Councils Ordinance 1949* (Cth).

[31] *Native Village Councils Ordinance 1949* (Cth) s 10 (a)(b)(c). This was incorporated into the *Papua-New Guinea Act 1949* (Cth) ss 15 & 29.

[32] Podolefsky, above n 34, 67, 77–8.

[33] Goddard, above n 2, 37.

[34] *Native Local Government Councils Ordinance 1949* (Cth) ss 7(3), 14.

[35] Strathern, Andrew and Pamela J. Stewart, *Arrow Talk: Transaction, Transition, and Contradiction in New Guinea Highlands History* (Kent State University Press, 2000) 87; Fenbury, David, *Practice without policy: genesis of local government in Papua New Guinea* (Australian National University, 1978) 12.

The *kiaps*' behaviour also portrayed a model of authoritarian leadership, which, up to that time, was alien to the people accustomed to the traditional consensus and consultative style of leadership. This profoundly influenced the behaviour of the local councillors to act like *kiaps*, giving rise to the need under the 'home-grown' Constitution to prevent despotic power.[36]

Derham Report: reforms for Judiciary

The failings of colonial judicial initiatives led, for the first time, to a holistic review of the entire colonial justice system in 1959 commissioned by Paul Hasluck, the Minister for Territories in the Menzies government. Hasluck rejected the dual agency of the councillors and the tripartite functions of the *kiaps* as concentrating the governmental power in a privileged minority and insisted on the introduction of the doctrine of the separation of powers into the colonial government. Hasluck advocated for a non-discriminatory court system to administer a single body of law applicable equally to both locals and Europeans:

> What I was mainly concerned about in the short term…was to familiarise the people with the idea of justice as a principle to be applied without discrimination in all situations, the idea of law as a code that applied evenly and justly to all citizens, and the idea of justice as institutions that were independent, not subject to, the direction of those in authority, not to be used as one of the agencies of governmental administration, and equally accessible on the same terms to all peoples.[37]

Hasluck commissioned David Derham, an Australian jurist and Professor of Jurisprudence at the Melbourne University, to undertake the review and make recommendations consistent with Hasluck's vision. The Ministerial direction was

> to inquire into the existing system of the administration of justice in the Territory of Papua and New Guinea, report thereon to the Minister for Territories, and make suggestions for its improvement having regard to both the present and future requirements of the Territory.[38]

The inquiry began on 31 July 1960 and ended on 05 September 1960 resulting in what would become the Derham Report.[39] Having realised the practical shortcomings of the colonial judicial order, Derham prefaced in his Report that

> [i]t was necessary to understand not only the laws establishing the legal and judicial system in the Territory but also the way the system works in fact, and the degree to which it satisfies the needs of the population both indigenous and expatriates.[40]

---

[36] Strathern A. J, 'Kiap, Councillor, and Big Man: Role Contrasts in Mount Hagen' in M. Ward, *The Politics of Melanesia* (Australian National University, 1970) 549–67.

[37] Paul Hasluck, *A time for Rebuilding: Australian administration in Papua and New Guinea, 1951–1963* (Melbourne University Press, 1976) 348.

[38] David P. Derham, *Report on the System for the Administration of Justice in the Territory of Papua and New Guinea* (Department of Territories, 1960) 1 [2].

[39] Ibid.

[40] Ibid.

Derham found that '[t]he basic weakness in the system of administration of justice at present lies in the relations between the executive and the judicial arms of government at all levels'.[41] Observing tripartite functions of the *kiaps* and the dual agency of the councillors, Derham recommended that 'in a country where the legislature is effectively controlled by an official executive, it is even more important to provide that the judicial system serves the law free from executive interference'.[42]

Derham rebuked what he described as 'the divine right of the kiaps' where

> many powers were exercised indiscriminately and without formal check...and the rights and interests of native subjects were at the mercy of the personal rule uncontrolled by any effective law.[43]

On the separation of judicial power from the executive branch, Derham insisted that a society expected

> to live according to a "rule of law" [is] not merely according to the directions of an executive power [but] a Magistrate freed from duties which conflict with his judicial duties...[Magistrates] cannot decide cases so as to further some government or executive policy of a particular kind.[44]

The Derham Report was written five years after the landmark decision of the Australian High Court in 1956 in the *Boilermaker's Case* that affirmed separation of judicial powers as critical to rule of law and democratic government in Australia.[45] Following from that case, the Derham Report became the first major attempt by an Australian jurist at endorsing developments in Australian constitutional law into the colony. It provided a grim assessment of the serious inadequacies of the colonial judicial system as well as the blueprint for judicial independence, rule of law and the doctrine of separation of powers in Papua New Guinea.

Local Court

The three main recommendations in the Derham Report of 1960 were to abolish the Courts for Native Matters and Native Affairs, withdraw the magisterial powers of the *kiaps* and councillors to independent judicial personnel and to remove the police force from the control of the Administrator of the colony.[46] The ensuing reforms led to the establishment of a non-discriminatory lower court system, the Local Court, in 1963, along with the training of Papua New Guineans as interpreters, clerks of courts, and magistrates.[47] While the Local Court was structurally subordinate to the District Court, their jurisdictions were streamlined and identical in some areas, thus easing

---

[41] Ibid 5 [3].

[42] Ibid [4].

[43] Ibid 20.

[44] Ibid 27.

[45] *R v Kirby; Ex parte Boilermakers' Society of Australia* (1956) 94 CLR 254.

[46] Derham, above n 38, 7–8.

[47] Ibid; *Local Courts Ordinance 1963* (PNG); C.J. Lynch, 'A Description of Aspects of Political and Constitutional Developments and Allied Topics' in B. J. Brown (eds), *Fashion of Law in New Guinea* (Butterworths Australia, 1969) 55.

access to justice for the people and providing a direct appeal pathway to the Supreme Court.[48]

Another significant reform was the enactment of the *Customs Recognition Act 1963* (PNG) which provided for traditional customs to be recognised and pleaded in 'all courts,' as well as a formal recognition of native customs previously overlooked.[49]

The independence of the Local Court and its equitable approaches led to a significant improvement in the involvement of indigenous people at the Local Court.[50] Although the magistrates continued to be Australians, the emphasis in the Derham Report for indigenous involvement in the justice system allowed for Papua New Guineans to be trained, eventually leading to the appointments of four Papua New Guinean magistrates in 1972.[51]

These reforms were further complemented by the enactment of the *Local Government Ordinance* 1963 (PNG) which replaced the Village Council system and reduced the functions of the village councillors to only political representation and participation. This was an important precursor to the 1964 elections where Papua New Guineans, for the first time, had formal and direct opportunity to stand for national public office.[52] The 1960 Derham Report contributed to the momentum for reform not only in legal but also in the political arena.

While the various reforms brought about some significant improvements in access to justice and integrity in judicial administration, they also introduced new challenges in dealing with the rigidity of the formal legal structure. The emphasis placed by the Derham Report on establishing a rules-based society assumed that the diverse local practices, customs and expectations could be codified into rules and applied by independent adjudicators. However, no such codification took place. It proved challenging for Australian magistrates at the Local Courts to adhere strictly to a rigid system and enforce strict procedural requirements. Language difficulties and the adversarial methods of litigation, which often resulted in winners and losers contrary to the traditional mediatory outcomes, were amongst the persisting challenges at the Local Court. Consequently, people continued to readily resort to their informal courts and traditional dispute resolution mechanisms.

Village courts

By the late 1960s, the shortcomings of the Local Court system became a political issue among the educated Papua New Guineans, some of whom have been elected to the newly formed House of Assembly after the inaugural national election in 1964.

---

[48] Although it was rarely used due to the unaffordability of skilled legal assistance and other structural barriers; *Local Court Ordinance 1963* (PNG) s 43; T. E. Barnett, 'The Local Court Magistrate and the Settlement of Disputes' in B. J. Brown (eds), above n 99, 175.

[49] *Customs Recognition Act 1963* (PNG) s 6.

[50] Goodard, above n 2, 46.

[51] Ibid.

[52] C. J. Lynch, 'Parliamentary and Executive Control of Delegated Legislation under the Legislative Council for Papua and New Guinea 1951–63' (1966) 5 *Melbourne University Law Review* 329, 357.

They advocated for a judicial system that would better acknowledge local customs and methods of dispute resolution.[53]

This advocacy promoted a review of the Local Court system from 1971–1972, led by L. J. Curtis, an Australian who was the Secretary for Law in the colonial administration.[54] Curtis tasked his review team, consisting of two magistrates, Neil Desailly (Australian) and Francis Iramu (Papua New Guinean), with assessing the effectiveness of the lower courts and proposing the implementation of a system of village courts.[55]

The review confirmed the deficiencies of the local courts and highlighted the effectiveness of customary dispute resolution through mediation and reconciliation.[56] Although the review cautioned against the application of 'strict customary rules…which would perpetuate old ideas in times of change', it recommended for a village court system that was to be 'strongly influenced by the customs of the area and by local attitudes and mores'.[57]

By 1973, the discussion around a custom-oriented court system became integral to the broader discourse on decolonisation. Indigenous politicians, now the majority in the House of Assembly following the 1972 national election, enacted the *Village Courts Ordinance 1973* (PNG). According to this legislation, village courts were to be situated within communities, guided by local customs and practices, with magistrates selected from the village itself.[58]

The primary function of a Village Court, as outlined in the legislation, was to promote peace and harmony in its designated area through mediation and the fair resolution of disputes.[59] The courts were charged 'to apply any relevant native custom' and to 'attempt to arrive at a settlement by mediation…in all matters before it' except certain criminal offences.[60]

The establishment of the village court system held significant implications, representing a departure from traditional Australian colonial practice by granting official magisterial powers to untrained locals. It also underscored the importance of local dispute resolution—a departure from the adversarial and zero-sum approach to justice under colonialism.[61] As the 2001 Papua New Guinea Magistrates Manual

---

[53] Goddard, above n 2, 48.

[54] Ibid.

[55] R.N. Desailly and F. Iramu, *Report of Inquiry into the Need for Village Courts and Village Constables* (Port Moresby, 1972) 2.

[56] Ibid 3-4, 8.

[57] Ibid 8.

[58] *Village Court Ordiance* 1973 (PNG) ss 8, 9, 17; Abdul Paliwala, 'Law and Order in the Village: The Village Courts' in David Weisbrot, Abdul Paliwala and Akilagpa Sawyerr (eds), *Law and Social Change in Papua New Guinea* (Butterworths, 1982) 191.

[59] *Village Courts Ordinance 1973* (PNG) s 19; *Village Courts Act 1989* (PNG) s 52.

[60] *Village Courts Ordinance 1973* (PNG) s 29; *Village Courts Act 1989* (PNG) ss 52, 53, 57.

[61] Chalmers. D, 'The Village Courts of Papua New Guinea: Their Introduction, History and Operation Until 1976' (1978) 6 *Melanesian Law Journal* 56.

attested, the village court system marked a shift 'away from a winner/loser determination of disputes' to facilitate 'compromise in a way that is acceptable, not just to the parties of a dispute, but also to the wider community'.[62]

Despite these advancements, the village court system faced constraints during its development in the late colonial and early independence period. *Kiaps* were still dominant as representatives of the central colonial administration in villages, wielding considerable influence and often exercising a de facto veto power over village court proceedings. Additionally, village court magistrates were aware of their vulnerability under the *Village Court Ordinance*, which provided a nominal three-year tenure but left them susceptible to suspension or dismissal by influential kiaps.[63]

This indirect control over the native magistrates by the *kiaps* hindered the realisation of the emancipatory expectations afforded on the village court during its formative years. The native magistrates applied the colonial laws and common law's rigid adversarial methods with 'little scope for community involvement and party consensus'.[64] The persistence of colonial influence over the operation of the Village Courts underscored the preference for an Australia-centric judicial system, where courts remained entrenched in Australian 'personnel, principles and procedures'.[65]

Superior courts

The *Papua Act 1905* (Cth) provided the overarching governing framework for Australia's governance of Papua, establishing the Australian High Court as the highest judicial authority, followed by the Central Court of Papua.[66] In 1971, after assuming administration of New Guinea, Australia established the Supreme Court of New Guinea.[67] These two courts merged in 1945 to form the Supreme Court of the Territory of Papua and New Guinea.[68]

Before the merger, all judicial officers in Papua, including judges of the Central Court, were appointed by the Lieutenant-Governor, head of the colonial administration.[69] The Commonwealth Government had minimal oversight, except that appointments were made "in the name" of the Commonwealth Governor-General.[70] The

---

[62] Edward Hills and Guy Powles, 'Magistrates Manual of Papua New Guinea' (University of Papua New Guinea Press, 2001) Chapter 18 [18.2.1].

[63] *Village Court Ordinance 1973*s 10; Joseph A. Peasah, *Local-level Government in Papua New Guinea: A Study in Change and Continuity in the Development of Liberal-democratic Self-determination at the Local Level* (PNG National Research Institute, 1994) 79.

[64] Abdul Paliwala, above n 58.

[65] Donald Denoon, *A Trial Separation: Australia and the Decolonisation of Papua New Guinea* (ANU Press, 2012) 75.

[66] *Papua Act 1905* (Cth) s 43.

[67] *Judiciary Ordinance 1921–1938* (Cth) s 7.

[68] *Papua-New Guinea Provisional Administration Act 1945* (Cth) s 16; *Supreme Court Ordinance 1949–1959* (Cth) s 12.

[69] *Papua Act 1905* (Cth) s 17; *Judiciary Ordinance 1912–1940* (Cth) Part II.

[70] *Papua Act 1905* (Cth) s 17.

Lieutenant-Governor had sole discretion in appointments, which were for fixed term set by the colonial administration.[71]

In contrast, when Australia took control of the Territory of New Guinea in 1921, judges were appointed by the Commonwealth Governor-General.[72] Supreme Court judges had tenure up to age sixty-five with fixed remuneration and the same 'jurisdiction, power and authority as the [judges of the] Supreme Court of Queensland'.[73] Unlike in Papua, only the Commonwealth Governor-General could remove judges in New Guinea for proven misconduct or incapacity, similar to the process for removing High Court judges under the Australian Constitution.[74]

The difference in governance between Papua and New Guinea stemmed from New Guinea being a Mandated Territory of the League of Nations, prompting greater sensitivity from the Australian Parliament in administration.[75]

Initially, the Supreme Court of the Territory of Papua and New Guinea served as a court of first instance in certain prescribed matters with appeals to the High Court. It later adopted an appellate jurisdiction as the Full Court of the Supreme Court of the Territory of Papua and New Guinea in 1966 to limit appeals to the High Court.[76] Beneath the Supreme Court was the District Court and the Court of Petty Sessions followed by the courts of Native Matters and Native Affairs.[77] The latter courts were replaced by the Local Court system in 1963 and eventually the Village Courts in 1973.[78]

The Supreme Court comprised legally trained Australian judges appointed by the Commonwealth Governor-General, unlike the lower courts where magistrates were appointed by the colonial administration. However, unlike the High Court where the judges at the time had a life tenure (reduced to a mandatory retirement age of seventy as of 1977),[79] the colonial Supreme Court judges were appointed to the age of sixty-five for full time judges and a term of twelve months for acting judges.[80] While political leadership for Papua New Guineans began with the inaugural 1964 national elections, the judicial system remained an exclusively colonial institution until the establishment of the Village Court in 1973. Noting that the *Village Court Act* came into force in November 1974, the locals were formalised to serve in the

---

[71] *Central Court Ordinance 1925* (Territory of Papua) (Cth) ss 5, 7; *Justices Ordinance 1940* (Cth).

[72] *Judiciary Ordinance 1921–1938* (Territory of New Guinea) (Cth) s 8.

[73] *Judiciary Ordinance 1921–1938* (Territory of New Guinea) (Cth) ss 8, 10-11.

[74] *Judiciary Ordinance 1921–1938* (Territory of New Guinea) (Cth) s 8; *Australian Constitution* 1900 (Cth) s 72(ii).

[75] *New Guinea Act 1920* (Cth) s 15.

[76] *Papua and New Guinea Act 1966* (Cth) s 8.

[77] *Native Regulations Ordinance 1908–1930* (Cth) s 3; *Native Administrative Ordinance 1921–1938* (Cth) s 2; *Justice Ordinance 1920* (Cth) s 2.

[78] *Local Courts Ordinance 1963–1966* (Cth); J.R Mattes, 'The Court System' in David Weisbrot, Abdul Paliwala and Akilagpa Sawyerr (eds), above n 58, 71, 76.

[79] See *Constitution Alteration (Retirement of Judges) Act* 1977 (Cth).

[80] *Papua and New Guinea Provisional Administration Act* 1945 (Cth) s 16(2); *Papua-New Guinea Act* 1949 (Cth) s 59–60.

colonial judicial structure only a few months before Independence of Papua New Guinea on 16 September 1975.

3 Character and Methods of the Colonial Courts

The character and methods of the various colonial courts outlined above became highly influential in shaping how people perceived the role of the judiciary in the post-independence era. While these courts evolved in diverse forms under the Australian colonial administration, their judicial approaches to addressing issues and perceptions of their users remained largely consistent with the broader colonial objectives. The colonial courts are categorised into lower courts and superior courts to facilitate the assessment of their judicial approaches, methods and perceptions.

3.1 Lower Courts

The populace engaged more with the lower courts than the superior courts, given their role as courts of first instance and their greater accessibility. However, the absence of court case records impedes the ability to properly evaluate their character. An analysis of broader literature, encompassing accounts from magistrates and appeal cases, reveals at least four significant insights about these lower courts.

First, observations from cases involving interactions between the white population and native Papua New Guineans suggest an inherent expectation for bias favouring the white population in judgements.[81] Hubert Murray, the Lieutenant-Governor of the colony of Papua in 1908, acknowledged that it was ‘quite impossible to administer even-handed justice [because] public opinion [among the white population] is so strong against’ ruling in the favour of natives.[82] Murray observed that ‘a native must have a very strong case indeed to get a conviction against a white man’.[83]

Similarly, Justice Winter, a colonial judge in British Papua in 1902, lamented this systemic bias, stating that ‘racial feeling [against natives] is so great and so strong in this country that I cannot regard the defendant (European) morally culpable in taking the life of a native’.[84] Native Papua New Guineans struggled against a pervasive perception, both in the community and institutions, that they were disposed to

[81] Fitzpatrick, above n 46, 66.

[82] Hubert Murray cited in A. Inglis, *Not a White Woman Safe: Sexual Anxiety and Politics in Port Moresby 1920–1934* (ANU Press, 1974) 79.

[83] Ibid.

[84] Justice Winter (1902), cited in Fitzpatrick, above n 46, 66.

unlawful behavior.[85] Although the judicial system evolved over time, initial prejudices persisted due to various discriminatory laws enacted during the colonial period, perpetuating biases within the European community up until Independence.

Second, available literature indicates a strict adherence to colonial laws and procedures in the lower courts.[86] Attempts at liberalising judicial methods and procedures were met with resistance. For instance, Australian Magistrate A.H. Germain cautioned against 'depart[ing] from current established practice in the English and Australian Courts' and for greater 'precision in procedure [if] the concepts of law prevailing in Australia is to take root in this country'.[87] Such an approach enhanced colonial control and weakened the ingenuity and autonomy expected from the Village Court magistrates.

Third, there was a significant emphasis on punishment-oriented justice.[88] The 1960 Derham Report uncovered a widespread misconception among the colonial magistrates that a native 'likes going to gaol or at least does not mind going to gaol [because] in gaol, they are well fed, housed adequately and their health is cared for'.[89] Derham described it as 'an erroneous belief' and 'a dangerous one'.[90] Magistrates, mostly appointed by the colonial administration and predominantly kiaps or former kiaps, were responsible for enforcing this approach, which often bypassed legal limits and subjected Papua New Guineans to a repressive judicial system.[91]

The fourth, and less common but more constructive, development in the local court was the use of local customary laws and practices.[92] Informal judicial pathways established by the people occasionally conflicted with the colonial structure, necessitating compromises. This situation prompted various reforms outlined in the 1960 Derham Report, including the enactment of the *Custom Recognition Act* 1963.

3.2 Superior Courts

The judicial character and approaches of the superior courts were among the most influential factors in determining the extent of power these courts would wield post-independence and the role of the judges. A study of 913 reported judgments available online from the Supreme Court of the Territory of Papua and New Guinea and the

[85] B. Jinks, P. Biskup and H. Nelson, *Readings in New Guinea history* (Angus and Robertson, 1973) 38.

[86] T.E. Barnett (eds), *Magistrates' Note* (Australian National University, 1967) 10.

[87] Ibid.

[88] For instance, see *Tago v Arura* [1950] PGSC 10; *Malagigi v Geelan* [1953] PGSC 11.

[89] Derham, above n 38, 20.

[90] Ibid.

[91] For instance, see *Re Appeal by Stanislaus Toboromilat* [1953] PGSC 15; Derham, above n 38, 22.

[92] For instance, see *Director of District Services v Coconut Products Ltd* [1954] PGSC 4.

High Court of Australia from 1945 to 1974 highlighted three key judicial character and approaches.[93]

First, the cases demonstrated that many colonial judges haboured adverse preconceptions against Papua New Guineans. For example, there was a prevailing perception that Papua New Guineans were unintelligible and untrustworthy, leading to their testimonies as victims or witnesses being afforded low credibility. In the case of *Re The King* (1950),[94] a 13-year-old girl accused her Australian school principal of sexual abuse. The judge, after warning himself of 'the terrible consequences of conviction in cases of this nature', doubted her testimony primarily because her demeanor and engagement in Court were considered 'weak', resulting in the acquittal of the accused.[95]

These judgments often failed to consider that the victim's demeanor, displaying a lack of confidence, was rooted in cultural norms of respect for authority figures and reflected her own shame and immaturity. Similar judgments were observed in other sexual abuse cases involving Australians and other members of the white population.[96]

Another adverse preconception was that to instill discipline and order among what colonial judges described as 'savage' locals, judicial outcomes needed to be punishment oriented. This sentiment was particularly emphasised in criminal cases involving white women and locals.[97] While special legislation, such as the *White Women's Protection Ordinance 1926* (Cth), was enacted to specifically protect white women against locals with harsher penalties, similar legislative protection was not provided for Papua New Guinean women against European men.[98]

The landmark case of *Queen v Creighton* (1952) marked the first attempt by the Supreme Court to challenge some of these adverse preconceptions. It involved a rape allegation against a European by a Papua New Guinean woman and resulted in the first jury trial in the Territory of Papua and New Guinea. Acting Chief Justice Ralph Gore instructed the all-male white jurors that:

> You have, on the one side, a native complainant and native witnesses. You have, on the other, the accused and his witnesses, some white, some native. The woman is a native and her witnesses are natives, but because their skins are black, it does not necessarily follow that they should not be believed. They may lie; natives do lie – so do whites. It seems to me that the same tests of truth should be applied to them as in the case of Europeans.[99]

---

[93] Judgments can be found on the website of the Pacific Islands Legal Information Institute (PacLii) http://www.paclii.org/pg/cases/PGSC/ . This is used as printed case law reports were not readily available.

[94] *Re The King* [1950] PGSC 3 (Bignold J) (unnumbered judgement).

[95] Ibid.

[96] For instance, *Queen v Mumford* [1953] PGSC 7; *Queen v Evans* [1954] PGSC 1.

[97] See for instance, *Queen v Ofu-Koloi* [1956] PGSC 29.

[98] *White Women's Protection Ordinance 1926–1934* (Cth). *The Native Women's Protection Ordinance* 1951 restricted the movement of native women as opposed to providing penalties for their abuse was the case of *White Women's Protection Ordinance 1926–1934*.

[99] *Queen v Creighton* [1952] PGSC 1 (Gore ACJ) (unnumbered judgment).

This instruction was significant as it addressed the inherent assumptions about the credibility of locals and affirmed their equal right to due process. The jury subsequently returned a guilty verdict.

By 1960s, the superior courts actively challenged the negative preconceptions against Papua New Guineans. In the case of *Kwale-Tauwan v Iwas* (1960), the Court emphasised that 'it must be remembered that these people are not only natives, and are not only required to obey the law; but are entitled as citizens to the full protection of our legal system'.[100] This change in judicial attitude was partly attributed to the various legal and political reforms at the time, including those recommended in the 1960 Derham Report.

The second important development in the superior courts was the emphasis on the independence of the judiciary. Although the Supreme Court was granted independent status at the amalgamation of the two colonies of Papua and New Guinea in 1945,[101] officials at the lower courts continued to perform dual judicial and executive functions. This issue was addressed in the case of *Tago v Arura* (1950), where the Court overturned a decision by a colonial magistrate who had acted on his own volition to imprison a native for failing to take his sick child to the hospital. The magistrate was performing the role of a community health inspector. The Court held that magistrates, as members of the judiciary, cannot exercise both executive and judicial functions.[102] This decision, reiterated in the 1960s following the Derham Report, reflected the evolving jurisprudence in Australia, focusing on the separation of judicial power from the executive arm of government.[103]

The third significant development stemmed from the judgments of the Australian High Court as the final appellate court.[104] Led by Chief Justices Owen Dixon and later Garfield Barwick between 1945 and 1974, when the colonial Supreme Court was operational, the High Court adopted a firmly legalistic or black-letter law approach to judicial decision-making.[105] Dixon, for instance, staunchly advocated that '[t]here is no other safe guide to judicial decisions in great conflicts than a strict and complete legalism.'[106] Dixon insisted that judges should not be 'conscious judicial innovator[s]'.[107] Stephen Gageler SC (currently the Chief Justice of the High Court) later asserted that legalism was 'the dominant theme of the judicial style of the

---

100 *Kwale-Tauwan v Iwas* [1960] PGSC 4 (unnumbered judgment).

101 *Papua and New Guinea Provisional Administration Act 1945* (Cth) s 16.

102 *Tago v Arura* [1950] PGSC 10 (Kelly J) (unnumbered judgment); See also *Loa v Safe* [1963] PGSC 42.

103 *Loa v Safe* [1963] PGSC 42; *Huddart, Parker & Co Pty Ltd v Moorehead* (1909) 8 CLR 330; *R v Kirby; Ex parte Boilermakers Society of Australia* (1956) 94 CLR 254.

104 *Supreme Court Ordinance 1949* (Territory of Papua and New Guinea) (Cth) s 12.

105 Rachel Gray, *The Constitutional Jurisprudence and Judicial Method of the Australian High Court* (Presidian Legal Publications, 2008) 2; Leslie Zines, 'The Australian Constitution 1951–1976', (1976) 7 *Federal Law Review* 89, 90.

106 Sir Owen Dixon, Address upon taking the oath of office in Sydney as Chief Justice of the High Court of Australia on 21st April, 1952 cited in Woinarski J (eds), *Jesting Pilate and Other Papers and Addresses* (Law Book Co, 1965) 247.

107 Owen Dixon, 'Concerning Judicial Method' (1956) 29 *The Australian Law Journal* 486, 472.

[High] Court for much of the twentieth century'.[108] Chapter 5 of the book discusses how legalism was rejected by the drafters of the Constitution as unsuitable for Papua New Guinea's its context.

Turning to the 913 cases available online that were adjudicated by the superior colonial courts, only twelve were High Court cases.[109] These twelve cases offer three important insights into the judicial methods and thinking of the High Court, which became considerations when designing Papua New Guinea's post-independence judiciary.

First, the High Court's commitment to legalism appeared to restrict judges on the Territory's Supreme Court from exercising their judicial power more broadly. This constrain was evident, for instance, in *Queen v Creighton* (1952), which was discussed earlier concerning the jury conviction of a European man for the rape of a native woman. The instruction of Acting Chief Justice Gore to the jury aimed to address a social issue of inherent prejudice against Papua New Guineans.

However, the High Court overturned the decision, arguing that the instruction was intended to address a social rather than a legal issue, constituting a miscarriage of justice.[110] In reaching this decision, the High Court not only disregarded the propriety of the entire instruction[111] but, significantly, overlooked the social context underlying the justice issue before the trial judge.

The case of *Kristeff v Regina* (1967) provides another example of the influence of legalism exerted by the High Court on the Supreme Court of the Territory of Papua and New Guinea.[112] The High Court overturned a conviction for manslaughter that was based on a voluntary investigation conducted by a Supreme Court judge, which found evidence contrary to the sworn statement of the accused. The High Court held that the judge of the Supreme Court had 'overstepped limits and substituted for sworn evidence inferences which, rightly or wrongly,' influenced the judgment.[113]

The judge undertook the investigation to inform his judgment upon discovering discrepancies in the statement of the accused and due to the inefficiencies of the parties to correct the discrepancies. However, by applying a legalistic view of the role of the judiciary, the High Court disregarded necessary extra-legal considerations and the need for broader judicial role required to attain justice.

The second insight drawn from cases brought before the High Court is that, like some of the Supreme Court judges, the High Court judges also held adverse preconceptions about native Papua New Guineans. Descriptions such as 'primitive,'[114]

---

[108] Stephen Gageler, 'Legalism' in Tony Blackshield, Michael Coper and George Williams (eds), *The Oxford Companion to the High Court of Australia* (Oxford University Press, 2001) 429.

[109] The cases were accessed on Pacific Islands Legal Information Institute (PacLii) http://www.paclii.org/pg/cases/PGHCA/.

[110] *Creighton v Queen* [1952] PGSC 4 (Dixon CJ, Webb and Taylor JJ) (unnumbered judgement).

[111] *Queen v Creighton* [1952] PGSC 1 (Gore ACJ) (unnumbered judgment).

[112] *Kristeff v Regina* [1967] PGHCA 2 (Barwick CJ, Menzies & Owen JJ) (unnumbered judgment); See *Evgeniu v Reginam* [1964] PGHCA 1 (McTiernan, Taylor, Menzies, Windeyer & Owen JJ) (unnumbered judgment).

[113] Ibid.

[114] *Gaio v The Queen* (1964) 104 CLR 419.

'warlike,' and 'completely unsophisticated,'[115] with 'savage disposition,' were used to characterised the people.[116] These preconceptions reinforced colonial notions, disregarded local autonomy and initiatives, and underscored the overarching attitude that externally developed principles of law and justice needed to be imposed as part of a civilising and paternalistic intervention.

Third, the judgments indicate that accessing the High Court served as a positive restraint on punishment-oriented judges of the colony's Supreme Court.[117] Being based externally in Australia, the High Court presented itself as more objective than the Territory's Supreme Court.[118] However, as discussed earlier, the High Court decisions were not always well-received by the colonial judges who increasingly viewed the distant judgments as out of touch with the local context and social dynamics.[119]

In response to this discontent, the Derham Report recommended an appellate court within the Territory, leading to the establishment of the Full Court of the Supreme Court in 1966.[120] These reforms resulted in a reduction of appeals to the High Court between 1967 and 1973. Chapter 5 of the book delves into how, having been liberated from the High Court's binding jurisprudence, the liberal judges of the colony's Supreme Court rejected the legalistic approaches of the High Court in some of the early post-independence Supreme Court judgments.

4 Conclusion

The justice institutions throughout much of colonialism primarily functioned as tools of colonial control rather than impartial dispensers of meaningful justice. The judicial initiatives implemented by Germany, Britain, and largely by Australia, often failed to address local needs, and instead, perpetuated discrimination and injustice. The people's traditional, mediation-based concepts of justice were replaced by inflexible judicial systems that offered little room for indigenous initiatives and autonomy. Papua New Guineans were integrated into the colonial judicial apparatus solely as agents of the colonial powers, serving as *luluais, tultuls*, village constables or councillors. While their involvement brought some semblance of order to a previously ungoverned society, it distorted the notion of justice from a community-oriented undertaking to one of command and externally-driven.

---

[115] *Wendo v Regina* (1963) 109 CLR 559 [5].

[116] *Papua and New Guinea v Daera Guba* (1973) 130 CLR 353 [38], [54], [60]-[61].

[117] *Timbu-Kolian v The Queen* [1967] PGHCA 5.

[118] *Benggong v Bougainville Copper Pty Ltd* [1971] PGHCA 1; *Administration of the Territory of Papua and New Guinea v Doriga and Guba* [1973] PNGLR 603.

[119] This sentiment among some of the colonial judges became more evident straight after Independence, for instance, in *The State v Wonem* [1975] PNGLR 311 (unnumbered judgment). Raine J declared that the Papua New Guinea Constitution 'was not given to the country by somebody else, as in the case of Australia. It derives from the people of Papua New Guinea, it grew here' and therefore deserved a 'home-grown' and liberal interpretative approach.

[120] Derham, above n 38, 53; *Papua and New Guinea Act 1966* (Cth) s 8.

The 1960 Derham Report provided some acknowledgement and a blueprint for salient democratic and constitutional principles such as the doctrines of separation of powers, judicial independence, and the rule of law in Papua New Guinea. However, despite addressing issues such as systemic discrimination and partiality in the justice system, and advocating for increased participation of Papua New Guineans in the justice delivery, the resulting mechanisms remained undermined by the pervasive influences of colonial administration.

Moreover, the commitment of the Australian High Court to legalism further entrenched conservatism within the Territory's Supreme Court, rendering it largely insensitive to local needs and circumstances. The judicial developments, coupled with the adverse social and political environment of colonialism, provided an impetus for a 'home-grown' Constitution aimed at fostering change and transformation, as will be explored in the following chapter.

Chapter 4
A Transformative Constitution for Papua New Guinea

Abstract This Chapter argues that properly characterising the Constitution is important to fully appreciate its intents and unique structures, especially the liberal and interventionist role of the judiciary. It contends that the resulting constitution from the 'home-grown' process of constitution-making was 'transformative' in intent and character. By analysing examples of transformative constitutions elsewhere, such as India, South Africa and Kenya, it asserts that the transformative nature of the Papua New Guinea Constitution is marked by the Constitution's intent for change from past conditions, its constitutionally entrenched human rights charter, and the highly liberal role of the judiciary. The analysis also introduces the doctrine of transformative constitutionalism as a framework for the constitutional study of Pacific constitutions and refutes alternative descriptions of Papua New Guinea Constitution, such as 'aspirational' or 'programmatic,' as failing to accurately reflect the 'home-grown' Constitution.

Keywords Transformative constitution · Constitutionalism · Papua New Guinea constitution · Pacific constitutions

1 Introduction

The adverse colonial experiences and the impetuses that propelled the 'home-grown' constitutional project resulted in the Papua New Guinea Constitution being one of the most detailed and lengthiest constitutions in the Commonwealth. Some have loosely described the Constitution as an 'aspirational' or 'programmatic' constitution.[1] However, these descriptions fail to reflect its true character and intent. Instead, a closer assessment of the various aspects of the Constitution indicates that it is a 'transformative constitution'.

---

[1] Yash Ghai, 'Establishing a Liberal Political Order through a Constitution: The Papua New Guinea Experience' in Anthony Regan, Owen Jessep and Eric Kwa (eds), *Twenty Years of Papua New Guinea Constitution* (2001) 43.

B. Kama, *Rethinking Judicial Power in Papua New Guinea*,
https://doi.org/10.1007/978-981-97-2946-3_4

Identifying the proper character of the Papua New Guinea Constitution is important firstly because it provides the theoretical basis for understanding the unusual features of the 'home-grown' Constitution, some of which, namely, the liberal character of the judiciary and the modified doctrine of separation of powers, are discussed in this book. An elevated and liberal role of the judiciary is the foremost characteristic of a transformative constitution. Secondly, a proper identification of a constitution assists those charged with interpreting and applying it to do so with a different perspective on the forces and intentions behind it.

Arguing that the Papua New Guinea Constitution should be considered a 'transformative constitution' is not merely a linguistic or descriptive exercise. It is a substantive undertaking in constitutional history, as well as an effort to discover the identity and place of the 'home-grown' Constitution in broader constitutional law thinking and jurisprudence.

The chapter begins with a brief discussion of the evolution of the concept of transformative constitutionalism and then identifies its key distinguishing features before concluding with its application to the 'home-grown' Constitution of Papua New Guinea.

2 What is a Transformative Constitution?

An analysis into the background of transformative constitutionalism and of the existing models is essential to establish its defining features that can be applied to the case of Papua New Guinea.

2.1 Early Development

The notion of transformative constitutionalism has not yet been studied in the context of constitutions in the Pacific, including Australia and New Zealand. The concept was first introduced by Professor Karl Klare in his seminal paper, *Legal Culture and Transformative Constitutionalism* (1998).[2] Klare conceptualised:

> By transformative constitutionalism I mean a long-term project of constitutional enactment, interpretation, and enforcement committed (not in isolation, of course, but in a historical context of conducive political developments) to transforming a country's political and social institutions and power relations in a democratic, participatory and egalitarian direction.[3]

Klare made the observation while studying the newly enacted South African Constitution that came into effect in 1997. Klare argued that the intents of the South African Constitution to achieve 'large-scale social change,' after the horrors

---

[2] Karl E. Klare, 'Legal Culture and Transformative Constitutionalism,' (1998) 14 *South African Journal of Human Rights* 146.

[3] Ibid, 150.

of the apartheid colonial system, could only happen effectively if its legal and judicial culture depart from conservative inclinations and adopt a socially attuned and reformative approach.[4]

Klare further contended that transformative constitutions allow courts to engage in 'transformative adjudication', which entails a politically informed method of constitutional interpretation as opposed to the traditional legalistic approach devoid of socio-political considerations.[5] According to Klare, 'transformative adjudication' thus involves judges instigating policy and social reform through their role of adjudication.[6] To that end, a liberal judiciary with broad powers is central to transformative constitutionalism as it is able to enforce the transformative intents of the constitution.[7]

Klare's views reflected his philosophical background in Critical Legal Studies (CLS) school of thought where law is viewed as a mechanism intended 'to be transformative' in its application.[8] It means engaging with law in a way that reflects 'everyday political and moral argument, struggles and experiences'.[9] For CLS, law is ultimately political,[10] and since 'law is politics,' it logically follows that politics must inform the interpretation and application of law.[11]

This conception of law resonates largely with legal realism, of which CLS is an offshoot.[12] American realist and former Chief Justice of the United States Supreme Court, Oliver Wendell Holmes Jr, for instance, argued that law is a social phenomenon that comes into existence through social and political experiences.[13] His Honour contended that 'what the courts will do' depends on the 'shared, practical experiences' of the society, and not some abstract ideas devoid of current realities.[14] Holmes Jr CJ urged for a 'more conscious recognition of the legislative function of the courts' and maintained that 'judges should base their judgments upon broader consideration of policy'.[15]

---

[4] Ibid 150.

[5] Ibid 157.

[6] Ibid.

[7] Ibid 160–3.

[8] Jay M. Feinman, 'The failure of legal education and the promise of Critical Legal Studies' (1985) 6 *Cardozo Law Review* 739, 757.

[9] Alan Thomson, 'Foreword: Critical Approaches to Law, Who Needs Legal Theory?' in Ian Grigg-Spall and Paddy Ireland (eds), *The Critical Lawyers' Handbook* (Pluto Press, 1992) 2–3.

[10] Duncan Kenedy, 'Legal Education as Training for Hierachy' in David Kaireys (eds), *The Politics of Law: A Progressive Critique* (Basic Books, 2nd ed, 1992) 47.

[11] John Schlegel, 'Notes towards an Intimate, Opiniated and Affectionate History of Conference on Critical Legal Studies' (1984) 36 *Stanford Law Review* 391, 410–11.

[12] Raymond Wacks, *Understanding Jurisprudence: An Introduction to Leg.*

[13] Oliver Holmes, 'The Path of Law' (1897) 10 *Harvard Law Review* 457; N Duxbury, 'The Birth of Legal Realism and the Myth of Justice Holmes' (1999) 20 *Anglo-American Law Review* 81, 93.

[14] Holmes, Ibid.

[15] Oliver Wendell Holmes, 'Primitive Notions in Modern Law' (1877) 11 *American Law Review* 641, reprinted in Fredrick Roger Kellogg, *The Formative essays of Justice Holmes: The Making of an American Legal Philosophy* (Greenwood Press, 1984) 64, 131–2.

Another aspect of the CLS' conception of law as a transformative mechanism is for constitutions to be used to engineer 'social reconstruction' with the aim of affecting the institutional structures of society.[16] This submission considers a constitution as a symbol of power and autonomy against sources of institutional and ideological domination. Being transformative, therefore, means intending to change 'from a particular context' and the constitution becomes a 'vehicle of transformation' that enables 'change out of that context'.[17]

These conceptions provide at least three important insights that distinguish transformative constitutions from other forms of democratic constitutions. First, transformative constitutions stem from a clear intention to depart from the past as well as present practices deemed obstructive and inadequate in addressing the circumstances of a society.[18] Second, transformative constitutions are inspired by, and responsive to, some historical injustices.[19] Third, transformative constitutionalism can only be realised through a process of meaningful enactment, interpretation and enforcement of the constitution, with the judiciary mandated with substantive powers to be at the forefront.[20]

As the rest of the later part of this chapter will demonstrate, these elements are firmly reflected in the Papua New Guinea Constitution, making it a transformative constitution. The body of literature that has developed on transformative constitutionalism since Klare's proposition is significant. However, this book does not intend to delve into it as the main purpose of this discuss is to identify the critical features of transformative constitutionalism. These features can sufficiently be established from the above foundational analysis and the ensuing brief discussions on the examples of transformative constitutions.

2.2 *Models of Transformative Constitution*

The South African, Kenyan and Indian constitutions are frequently cited as examples of transformative constitutions. Since Klare's thesis, the post-apartheid South African Constitution of 1998 has especially gained recognition as a prominent model of global transformative constitutionalism. Jurists and scholars have extensively analysed its foundational principles in their efforts to characterise other constitutions accurately.[21]

---

[16] Robert Unger, 'The Critical Legal Studies Movement' (1983) 96 *Harvard Law Review* 563, 586.

[17] Feinman, above n 8; Klare, above n 2, 150.

[18] Klare, above n 2, 168.

[19] Ibid 169, 172.

[20] Ibid 152.

[21] Oscar Vilhena, Upendra Baxi and Frans Viljoen (eds), *Transformative constitutionalism: Comparing the apex courts of Brazil, India and South Africa* (Pretoria University Law Press, 2013).

South Africa

In 2004, the South African Constitutional Court rejected submissions for a narrow interpretation of the Constitution, asserting that 'ours is a transformative constitution'.[22] The Court further emphasised this stance in *City of Johannesburg v Rand Properties (Pty) Ltd* (2006), stating that '[o]ur Constitution encompasses a transformative provision [and] as such, the State cannot be a passive bystander in shaping the society in which individuals can fully enjoy their rights'.[23]

For the Court, this means actively pursuing the transformative goals embedded in the Constitution, including enforcing the Bills of Rights and holding accountable institutions obstructive to the fuller realisation of the Constitution's intent.[24] The position of the Constitutional Court demonstrated that the notion of transformative constitutionalism, whilst relatively recent in constitutional theory, is a viable and legitimate framework for understanding the nature of a constitution.

An important aspect of the Court's pursuit is its theory of constitutional interpretation, which it holds to be purposive, broad and liberal.[25] Chief Justice Pius Langa, for instance, argued that critical to the transformative role of the courts is not to solely rely on the 'say-so of parliament or technical readings of the legislation' but by turning to 'ideas and values' beyond the legislative framework.[26] The Court reinforced this view in *Rates Action Group v City of Cape Town* (2004), where it distinguished itself from the strict legalistic approach of Justice Scalia of the United States Supreme Court, stating that 'whatever the position may be in the USA or other countries, that is not the purpose of our Constitution'.[27]

Langa CJ further contended that '[t]he core idea of transformative constitutionalism [is] that *we* must change…to heal the wounds of the past and to guide us to a better future'.[28] The conception of 'we' involves understanding that transformative constitutions give unique functions to the judiciary to be actively involved in advancing the 'change' envisaged by the Constitution through judicial means.[29] The courts, therefore, have a mandate to be equal partners in the development of the society. The case of South Africa thus demonstrates that the significant hallmark of a transformative constitution is a judiciary with liberal and expansive powers and a constitution firmly intended to usher change from a determine colonial past to a

---

[22] *Rates Action Group v City of Cape Town* [2004] 12 BCLR 1328, [100] (Constitutional Court).

[23] *City of Johannesburg v Rand Properties (Pty) Ltd* [2006] 6 BCLR 728 (W), [51]–[52].

[24] *Minister of Health v Treatment Action Campaign* (No 2) [2002] ZACC 15 (Constitutional Court).

[25] *S v Makwanyane* 1995 (6) BCLR 665, [302]–[04] (Constitutional Court).

[26] *City of Johannesburg v Rand Properties (Pty) Ltd* [2006] 6 BCLR 728 (W) [51]–[52]; *S v Makwanyane* 1995 (6) BCLR 665, [302]–[04] (Constitutional Court); Pius Langa, 'Transformative Constitutionalism,' (2006) 3 *Stellenbosch Law Review* 351, 352.

[27] *Rates Action Group v City of Cape Town* [2004] 12 BCLR 1328, [100] (Constitutional Court).

[28] Langa, above n 26.

[29] Charles M. Fombad, 'Constitutional Adjudication and Constitutional Justices in Africa's Uncertain Transition' in Charles M. Fombad (eds), *Constitutional Adjudication in Africa* (Oxford University Press, 2017) 351, 358.

future it envisaged. It will be demonstrated later in this chapter and in Chap. 5 how these features are firmly evident in the Papua New Guinea Constitution.

Kenya

Transformative constitutionalism has also been argued to correctly describe constitutions of other African states, notably Kenya.[30] Chief Justice Willy Mutunga of the Kenyan Supreme Court described the 2010 Kenyan Constitution as a 'transformative constitution that replaced both the 1969 Constitution and the past Colonial Constitution in 1963'.[31] His Honour emphasised that the Constitution 'was the culmination of almost five decades of struggles that sought to fundamentally transform the backward economic, social, political, and cultural developments in the country'.[32]

Mutunga's optimism, like that of his South African colleagues, was not to suggest that Kenya would be transformed into a stable, robust and progressive society by enacting the Constitution. Instead, the Chief Justice pointed to the provisions in the Constitution as providing an important basis for the country's socio-political reform, and where the role of the judiciary is elevated from its traditional confines.[33]

As in South Africa, the Kenyan Constitution promotes a theory of interpretation that is broad, purposive and liberal. Its provisions not only afford wide discretion to the courts, but also appear to invite them to shape society.[34] The reformist functions of the courts thus form an important part of the 'constitutional superstructure' central to Kenya's transformative constitutionalism.[35] Matunga CJ distinguishes it from the colonial constitution:

> The very idea of a transformative constitution is that the constitutional superstructure is embedded on a theory that the constitution will be an instrument for the transformation of society rather than a historical, economic and socio-political pact to preserve the status quo as the earlier constitutions did.[36]

According to Professor Yash Ghai, Kenya's new constitutional order thus promoted the expansive role of the courts.[37] Ghai defined transformative constitutionalism in the context of Kenya as

---

[30] Chief Justice Willy Mutunga, 'Theory of Interpreting Kenya's Transformative Constitution', (Speech delivered at the Inaugural Distinguished Lecture Series on the 2010 Constitution of Kenya and its Interpretation: Reflections from the Supreme Court Decisions, University of Fort Hare, 16 October 2014) 1; Yash Ghai, 'Katiba Corner: Interpreting Kenya's Transformative Constitution', *The Star* (online), 14 June 2014.

[31] Chief Justice Mutunga, Ibid.

[32] Ibid.

[33] *The Constitution of Kenya* (revised edition) 2010 (Kenya) s 21.

[34] For instance, see ss 20 (3)(4), 259–(1)(b).

[35] Chief Justice Willy Mutunga, 'Transforming Judiciaries in Africa: Lessons from the Kenyan Experience' (Speech delivered at the Nigerian Bar Association International Conference, Abuja, Nigeria, 23 August 2015) 6.

[36] Ibid.

[37] Ghai, above n 30.

> value laden, going beyond the state, with emphasis on social and sometimes economic change…requiring state organs, particularly the judiciary, to use the constitution as a framework for policies and acts for broader shaping of state and society.

While Ghai's assessment relates to the Kenyan Constitution, it reinforces the earlier observation of the judiciary being central to any transformative constitution. Like the case of South Africa, Ghai suggests the role of the judges as reconfigured beyond the narrow function of only adjudicating legal disputes to acting as agents of social change. As it will become clearer in latter chapters, this is a central theme of this book in the case of Papua New Guinea.

In further relevance to this book, Ghai was a primary adviser to the Papua New Guinea Constitutional Planning Committee (CPC) leading up to the country's Independence.[38] He was influential in the formative ideas underlying the Papua New Guinea Constitution and contributed to the development of many of the post-colonial constitutions in Africa, Asia and the South Pacific.[39] His comments on the Kenyan Constitution came almost forty years after the enactment of the Papua New Guinea Constitution. Papua New Guinea's Constitution is, in many respects, similar to Kenya's Constitution.[40] The features defining Kenya as a transformative constitution are not only similar to Papua New Guinea, but as will be discussed later in this chapter, Ghai's view is important to the task of articulating the proper character of the Papua New Guinea Constitution.

India

The third example of a constitution considered to be 'transformative' is India. India has long seen the advocacy for reformist courts to confront the inherent societal injustices arising from colonialism as well as its systems of status, caste and class.[41]

Describing India's Constitution as a 'transformative constitution', Professor Upendra Baxi argues that it creates a legitimate expectation for India's courts to depart from 'judicial bystanderism' to judicial consciousness whereby courts are informed by extra-legal considerations when exercising their judicial functions.[42] Kalpana Kannabiran takes this to mean that the Indian Constitution 'provides the framework for the judiciary to shape the destiny of our country through judicial creativity'.[43]

---

[38] CPC Report 1974, Chapter 1[7].

[39] Peter Larmour, 'Westminster constitutions in the South Pacific: A "policy transfer" approach' (2002) 10(1) *Asian Journal of Political Science* 39, 44; Brij V. Lal, *In the Eye of the Storm: Jai Ram Reddy and the Politics of Post-Colonial Fiji* (ANU EPress, 2010) 483.

[40] When studied closely, key provisions on decentralisation, provincial governments, judicial power and human rights protections are quite similar.

[41] Upendra Baxi, 'Preliminary notes on transformative constitutionalism' in Oscar Vilhena, Upendra Baxi and Frans Viljoen (eds), *Transformative constitutionalism: Comparing the apex courts of Brazil, India and South Africa* (Pretoria University Law Press, 2013) 40.

[42] Alisha Dhingra, 'Indian Constitutionalism: A Case of Transformative Constitutionalism' (2014) 2 *Asian Journal of Multidisciplinary Studies* 135, 138, 168.

[43] Kalpana Kannabiran, *Tools of Justice: Non-Discrimination and the Indian Constitution* (Routledge, 2012) 444–5.

Similar to South Africa and Kenya, India's transformative agenda is evidenced by an elaborate Bill of Rights entrenched in its Constitution which sets out fundamental rights and provides broad enforcement avenues, including allowance for courts to act on their own volition where necessary in cases of human rights breaches.[44] Recent decisions of the Supreme Court of India suggest that the transformative cornerstone of its Constitution remains intact.

For instance, in the case of *National Legal Services Authority v Union of India* (2014), the Supreme Court declared transgender as a 'third gender' and ordered the government to treat transgender people as minorities with privileges. The privileges acknowledged included providing for reservations in employment and education, and access to adequate health facilities to assist with their medical procedures.[45] The Court went on to observe that since the Indian Constitution is 'a living organism', it must be interpreted in a way that responds to a 'social reality that is constantly changing' or at times, adopt an interpretation that 'precedes societal change and is even intended to stimulate it'.[46]

The direction of India's transformative constitutionalism is clearly enunciated in *Supreme Court Advocates-on-Record Association v Union of India* (1993) where the Supreme Court held that

> [t]he Constitution has not only to be read in the light of contemporary circumstances and values, it has to be read in such a way that the circumstances and values of the present generation are given expression in its provisions.[47]

It firmly resonates with the case of South Africa and Kenya that a transformative constitution promotes a method of judicial interpretation. In this approach, the courts are actively informed by and respond to evolving socio-political conditions of the society.

Canada

The above examples illustrate the evolution of transformative constitutionalism within the Global South, demonstrating that a transformative judiciary can engineer social reform. The centrality of the judiciary in transformative constitutionalism has led some to suggest that Canada also has a 'transformative constitution'.[48] Justice Robert Sharp of the Canadian Supreme Court, for instance, contended that the Human Rights Charter embedded in the Canadian Constitution has empowered Canada to have a transformative constitution.[49] His Honour argued that the Charter has enabled

---

[44] *The Constitution of India* 1950 (India) Parts III, IVA, s 32.

[45] *National Legal Services Authority v Union of India (2014)* No 400 of 2012, 45, 81, 108, 113, 116–17.

[46] *National Legal Services Authority v Union of India (2014)* No 400 of 2012, 119.

[47] (1993) 4 SCC 441 [324].

[48] Justice Robert J. Sharp, 'Interpreting and Shaping a Transformative Constitution: The Canadian Experience' (Paper presented at The International Conference on Interpretation and Shaping of Transformative Constitutions Conference Paper, Nairobi, 9–10 June 2014) 1.

[49] Ibid; Anne F. Bayefsky, 'The Judicial Functions under the Canadian Charter of Rights and Freedoms' (1987) 32 *McGill Law Journal* 792, 810.

the Court to shift from its traditional role as a bystander to being an active partner in protecting human rights.[50]

The Court has generally responded positively to this mandate,[51] insisting that it must depart from 'narrow and technical interpretation' to avoid 'stunt[ing] the growth of law and hence the community it serves'.[52] In *Re Southam Inc. and the Queen,* the Court alluded to its role as a nurturer of a 'living tree' being the Constitution.[53] Chief Justice Antonio Lamer thus admitted that the Canadian Supreme Court has departed from its 'old approach' of strict legalism to a new 'job description'.[54] His Honour stated that 'with the Charter, we are commanded to sometimes judge the laws [which] is a very different activity…asking us to make what is essentially what used to be a political call'.[55] His Honour further described it as 'nothing less than a revolution…'[56] and noted that some judges found it 'somewhat of a shock to see their job description changed so fundamentally'.[57]

The Canadian case supports the assertions in the above examples that a key aspect of transformative constitutions is a clear reconfiguration of the role of the judges from the restrictive traditional function to more liberal and expansive role. However, the extent of this expectation in Canada is limited.[58] While the Charter was a response to Canada's history of anti-Semitism, segregation and deprivation of civil liberties of minorities, including its indigenous population,[59] the Court's liberal powers are constrained and inadequate compared to South Africa, Kenya and India.

Summary

The development of the concept of transformative constitutionalism, from its theoretical genesis to its adoption in post-colonial constitutions of South Africa, Kenya, India, and to an extent, Canada, revealed three key identifying features that could be argued as denoting a transformative constitution. First, a transformative constitution entails a commitment to change from an adverse past. Second, this commitment is entrenched in the constitution in the form of enforceable rights and obligations. Third and most importantly, the judiciary is endowed with a liberal and expansive set of

---

[50] Sharp, above n 48.

[51] See for instance, *R v Big M Drug Mart Ltd* [1985] 1 SCR 295, 352; *R v Oakes* [1986] 1 SCR 103; Sauve v Canada (Chief Electoral Officer) [2002] 3 SCR 519, para 20; *Law Society of Upper Canada v Skapinker* [1984] 1 SCR 357; *Hunter v Southam Inc* [1984] 2 SCR. 145, 649.

[52] *Law Society of Upper Canada v Skapinker* [1984] 1 SCR 357, 366.

[53] *Re Southam Inc. and the Queen* (1983) 3 CCC (3d) 515, 524; *Edwards v. Attorney General of Canada* [1930] AC 124 [136] (Lord Sankey).

[54] *Globe and Mail* Newspaper (1992) cited in Fredrick Lee Morton (eds), *Law, Politics and the Judicial Process in Canada* (University of Calgary Press, 3rd ed, 2002) 128.

[55] Ibid.

[56] Ibid.

[57] CBC News Canada, 'Former Supreme Court chief justice Antonio Lamer dies', *CBS News* (online), 25 November 2007.

[58] Emmett Macfarlane, *Governing from the Bench: The Supreme Court of Canada and the Judicial Role* (UBC Press, 2013) 48.

[59] Canadian Human Rights Commission, *Evolution of Human Rights in Canada* (2012) 7 .

powers to interpret and enforce the constitution. The following discussion applies these features to the case of Papua New Guinea to argue that, like the other countries surveyed, Papua New Guinea has a transformative constitution.

3 A Transformative Constitution for Papua New Guinea

3.1 Commitment to Change

A commitment to change, as the first key feature of a transformative constitution evident from the above discussions, was clearly demonstrated in the case of Papua New Guinea when the country embarked on establishing a 'home-grown' Constitution. As discussed in Chap. 2, the country's exhaustive and unique constitution-making processes were intended to change the adverse ideologies, institutions, and practices of colonialism as well as address the contemporary challenges predicted to affect Papua New Guinea.

The commitment to change is dynamic, beginning from a determined past to an indeterminate future.[60] It means transformative constitutions engage with a constantly evolving society where organs of government, especially the judiciary, are charged to actively respond to guiding the society.

It resonates with what Professor Walter Murphy observed as the ultimate goal of post-colonial constitutions: '[t]he goal of a constitutional text must…not [be] simply to structure a government, but to construct a political system, one that can guide the formation of a larger constitution, a way of life'.[61] A constitution that intends to construct a 'way of life' seeks to configure, though not uniformly, most aspects of people's lives.

The unique approaches Papua New Guinea took to drafting its Constitution, discussed in Chap. 2, were clearly intended to configure a 'way of life,' or as the Constitutional Planning Committee (CPC) puts it, to configure the 'philosophy of life we wish to live by'.[62] Its 'home-grown' constitutional project refused to both conserve a colonial system or to simply consolidate a pact that fosters existing systems and ideas of government. The CPC viewed the road to self-government as 'a chance to define' a Papua New Guinean 'philosophy of life' and its social and economic goals.[63] It argued that 'if the Constitution is to be truly the fundamental charter of our society and the basis of legitimate authority, it should be an instrument which helps

---

[60] Dikgang Moseneke, 'The Fourth Bram Fischer Memorial Lecture: Transformative Adjudication,' (2002) 18 *South African Journal on Human Rights* 309, 315.

[61] Ibid.

[62] CPC Report 1974, Chapter 2 [12].

[63] Ibid [2].

to achieve these goals and not one which obstructs'.[64] As a result, the CPC sought through the Constitution 'to make substantial changes in all of our institutions'.[65]

These intentions for change clearly demonstrated that the commitment for change in Papua New Guinea is not merely aspirational. Like other transformative constitutions discussed above, the Papua New Guinea Constitution has a transformative outlook with a firm commitment to change, possibly even more radically than some of the other countries. It thus satisfies the first key feature of a transformative constitution.

3.2 Entrenched Rights and Obligations

The second feature of a transformative constitution evident from the above discussions is that the commitment for change is translated into a set of identifiable and claimable rights and obligations. All the countries discussed evidence this in the form of a bill of rights.[66] While this does not necessarily mean that any constitution with a bill of rights is a transformative constitution, this feature, when combined with the others, identifies Papua New Guinea as having a transformative constitution.

The constitutional guarantee of human rights provides an important first step in recognising the commitment for societal change.[67] It gives certainty for litigants in seeking enforcement and provides a legitimate platform for organs of government to take affirmative action consistent with a constitution's transformative intent. The kind of rights entrenched, whether civil, political, socio-economic or cultural, allows the courts to intervene, in a positive rather than negative way, into social policy to a much greater extent than simply protecting institutions of government and democracy.

The extensive rights provisions of the countries considered in the case studies identified above are similar to the case of Papua New Guinea. The human rights embedded in the Constitution, primarily in response to the injustices of colonialism as discussed in Chaps. 2 and 3, reflect the intention for change, covering a spectrum of civil, political, socio-economic and cultural rights as well as fundamental rights. The Constitution liberally provides for a range of international conventions and institutions such as the 'Universal Declaration of Human Rights', the 'European Convention for the Protection of Human Rights and Fundamental Freedom', the

---

[64] Ibid [12].

[65] Ibid [5].

[66] *Constitution of India 1949* (India) articles 12–49; *Constitution of Kenya 2010* (Kenya) articles 19–51; *The Constitution of the Republic of Namibia 1990* (Namibia) articles 5–25; *Canadian Bill of Rights 1960* (Canada) article 1; Alisha Dhingra, 'Indian Constitutionalism: A Case of Transformative Constitutionalism' 2014 (2) Issue 7 *Asian Journal of Multidisciplinary Studies* 135, 136; For an argument on American's 14th Amendment as a 'transformative constitution', see Bruce Ackerman, *We the People: Foundations* (Harvard University Press, 1993) 284 and Daniel H. Hoffman, *Our Elusive Constitution: Silences, Paradoxes, Priorities* (Suny Press, 1997) 21.

[67] *Soobramoney v Minister of Helath, KwaZulu-Natal* (1998) 1 SA 765 (Constitutional Court) [8].

'International Court of Justice,' and any other sources or material to be used to interpret, and where applicable, extend the protection of rights.[68]

The enforcement mechanisms for the protection of human rights are substantive and well entrenched as will be discussed in Chap. 5. They include allowance for a range of bodies to seek enforcement of human rights, including those that are not affected by a breach as well as allowing judges to act on their own volition.[69] This demonstrates a serious commitment to rights protection and towards a changed future.

3.3 A Liberal Judiciary

The third feature of a transformative constitution, evident from the models discussed above, is a judiciary with liberal and expansive powers. Rights and obligations alone cannot bring about the desired change. State mechanisms, especially the judiciary, must be constitutionally empowered to ensure that the intention for change entrenched in a constitution is meaningfully realised.

The ultimate hallmark of transformative constitutions is therefore liberal judiciaries with a mandate to enforce and construct change. Ghai makes this point in his definition of transformative constitutions that it 'require[s] state organs, particularly the judiciary, to use the Constitution as a framework for policies and acts for broader shaping of state and society'.[70]

The role of liberal judiciaries in transformative constitutions could be argued as twofold—to supervise the organs of government in their responses to the demands of the transformative constitution and to apply broad and expansive interpretations of existing rights and obligations, sometimes leading to the creation of new rights and obligations. Chief Justice Mutunga of the Kenyan Supreme Court alluded to this when officiating the commencement of Kenya's new Constitution: 'if revolution is to take place it will be in part on the basis of the implementation of this transformative constitution'.[71] The notion of revolution refers to change in the socio-economic, political and legal landscape of the society.[72] However, that revolution is not self-executing. It needs to be actively implemented and enforced. The judiciary is expected to be at the forefront of that role.

In line with this understanding, transformative constitutions expand the traditional judicial review and ensure that policy implementation agencies are held rigorously accountable. As exemplified by the South African Constitutional Court in *City of Johannesburg v Rand Properties (Pty) Ltd*,

---

[68] *Papua New Guinea Constitution* 1975, s 39.

[69] *Papua New Guinea Constitution* 1975, section 57.

[70] Ghai, above n 30.

[71] Chief Justice Mutunga, above n 30.

[72] Langa, above n 26.

> our Constitution encompasses a transformative provision. As such, the State cannot be a passive bystander in shaping the society in which individuals can fully enjoy their rights.[73]

Transformative constitutions allow scope for and provide a mandate to the judiciary to engage with the broader social philosophies for change and the extra-legal considerations that permeate legal issues. Legal interpretation techniques are, therefore, not only a tool for discovering the meaning of the law but also, an instrument for socio-economic and political reform when combined with its transformative character.

Chapter 5 will demonstrate in more detail that Papua New Guinea has a similar liberal judiciary with expansive powers that are constitutionally entrenched. Papua New Guinea thus satisfies the third and final feature of transformative constitutionalism.

4 Considering the Alternatives: An Aspirational or Programmatic Constitution?

The proposition for Papua New Guinea to be considered as having a transformative constitution contrast with the two alternative descriptions often used to describe the Papua New Guinea Constitution—aspirational and programmatic.[74] The meaning these descriptions convey is contrary to the transformative nature of the Constitution. They are derived from the hegemonic Anglo-Australian legal culture that cautions against constitutions having transformative trajectories.[75] The teachings of legal positivism or black-letter law, which have permeated the legal system and continue to dominate Papua New Guinea's legal environment, subscribe to these descriptions. It is therefore critical to assess these descriptions.

---

[73] *City of Johannesburg v Rand Properties (Pty) Ltd* 2006 6 BCLR 728 (W) [51]–[52].

[74] Yash P. Ghai (eds), *Law, Government, and Politics in the Pacific Island States* (Institute of Pacific Studies, 1988) 239; Rhuks Ako, *Environmental Justice in Developing Countries: Perspectives from Africa and Asia-Pacific* (Routledge, 2013) 77; Flint, David, 'Evisceration of reserve powers causes chaos on PNG' on *Online Opinion: Australia's e-journal on social and political debate* (20 December 2011); Eric Kwa, *Constitutional Law of Papua New Guinea* (UPNG Press, 2001) 2; Melanesian Institute for Pastoral & Socio-Economic Service, *Catalyst* (Goroka, 2001) 218.

[75] *Peter v South Pacific Brewery* [1976] PNGLR 537, 555; Peter Bayne, 'Judicial method and the interpretation of Papua New Guinea's Constitution' (1980) 11 *Federal Law Review* 121, 163–66.

4.1 An Aspirational Constitution

Professor Robin West describes an aspirational constitution as one that entrenches 'progressive egalitarian aspirations' or an 'ambitious political viewpoint'.[76] West discusses how these 'aspirations' would inform policy-making and court decisions but concedes that courts do not have a mandate in pursuing these ambitions.[77] Deduced from West's thesis is the point that 'aspirational' constitutions simply serve a political purpose as yardsticks for policy-making or are laden with aspirations to transform the society but lacking any meaningful enforcement capacity.

The Papua New Guinea Constitution may have reflected some of the aspirational qualities, such as the political statements in the National Goals and Directive Principles (NGDPs) and the Basic Social Obligations (BSOs), and the detailed nature of the Constitution, which is considered an attempt to micro-manage the country through the Constitution.[78] It has allowed some to assess that Papua New Guinea has an 'aspirational' Constitution.[79] The unenforceable nature of the NGDPs and the BSOs, along with the detailed nature of the Constitution, have been taken to fortify this view.[80] However, this assessment importantly overlooks the broad enforcement powers of courts in Papua New Guinea and their demonstrable centrality to the Constitution. It assumes that judges in Papua New Guinea, schooled in legal positivism and common law precedents, would not embrace a new job description that constitutes enforcing the aspirations.[81] The notion that Papua New Guinea has an 'aspirational' constitution thus appear to result from an entrenched and formalistic assumption that courts cannot exercise their liberal powers to further the objects of the Constitution. Chapter 5 will demonstrate that is not the case.

The concept of aspirational constitutionalism, which centers on unenforceable idealistic constitutional frameworks, does not accurately represent the Papua New Guinea Constitution. Its use in describing the Papua New Guinea Constitution is misconceived and reflective of legalistic tendencies.

---

[76] Robin West, 'The Aspirational Constitution' (1993–1994) 88 *North Western University Law Review* 241, 252–3.

[77] Ibid.

[78] Yash Ghai, 'Establishing a Liberal Political Order through a Constitution: The Papua New Guinea Experience' (2002) 28 *Development and Change* 303, 312; John Goldring, *The Constitution of Papua New Guinea* (Law Book Company, 1978) 47.

[79] Ibid.

[80] Ghai, above n 78.

[81] Interview with Justice J1 (Supreme Court and National Court) (PhD Research, Port Moresby, 28 November 2017).

4.2 A Programmatic Constitution

The notion of programmatic constitutionalism evolved in the late 1960s as a conceptual framework to describe post-colonial constitutions that have a liberal outlook and appear to set out a 'program' for the development of the country.[82] That 'program' is often regarded as visionary and ambitious, seeking to set goals and stimulate development 'directed at the future'.[83]

Some commentators have accepted these views as accurate descriptions of the Papua New Guinea Constitution.[84] For instance, Eric Kwa argues that Papua New Guinea has a 'programmatic constitution… because it prescribes the programs for Papua New Guinea in great detail'.[85] Kwa went on to envisage the judiciary as having a limiting role within the ambit of the doctrine of separation of powers.[86] Ghai asserts that the Papua New Guinea Constitution provides 'programmatic provisions' that 'deliberately looks to the future, not the present' and expresses 'principles or policies which may not be appropriate or timely (even impossible) to implement'.[87]

The notion of programmatic constitution closely describes the structure of the Papua New Guinea Constitution. The National Goals and Directives Principles and the Basic Social Obligations in the Constitution provide in detail the socio-political and economic vision of the country and the need for the government to give effect in terms of policy and implementation. Similar visions in the Indian Constitution have led some to refer to it as an 'over-programmatic constitution'.[88]

However, absent from these commentaries is the importance of the judiciary and the extent of its powers in bringing into fruition the 'programs' in the Constitution. On their own, constitutional 'programs' and structures, however noble, serve a largely political purpose and give citizens mere hope. The true measure of the Constitution resides in the enforcement mechanisms and the powers afforded to them, especially the courts, to hold parties accountable to its terms. That is to say, 'programs' that may appear to espouse principles or policies in the Constitution are largely decorative unless the courts have the power to take a special interest in their enforcement.

The argument for programmatic constitutionalism in Papua New Guinea largely overlooks this key element. It fails to account for the courts' role, which gives the Constitution its real and distinctive value. Programmatic constitutionalism is thus

---

[82] Henc van Maarseveen and Ger van der Tang, *Written Constitutions: A Computerized Comparative Study* (Brill Nijhoff, 1978) 256.

[83] Ibid.

[84] Eric Kwa, *Constitutional Law of Papua New Guinea* (UPNG Press, 2001) 2; Melanesian Institute for Pastoral & Socio-Economic Service, *Catalyst* (Goroka, 2001) 218; Yash P. Ghai (eds), *Law, Government, and Politics in the Pacific Island States* (Institute of Pacific Studies, 1988) 239.

[85] Kwa, Ibid.

[86] Ibid 107-8.

[87] Ghai, above n 78.

[88] Samirendra N. Ray, *Modern Comparative Politics: Approaches, Methods and Issues* (PHI Learning, 1998) 115.

an inadequate conceptual framework to explain the transformative functions of the courts argued to be present under the 'home-grown' Constitution.

More than twenty years after describing the Papua New Guinea Constitution as 'programmatic', Ghai described the 2010 Kenyan Constitution as a 'transformative constitution'.[89] Ghai's view is important because of his influence as a drafter of the Papua New Guinea Constitution and as an influential post-colonial constitutional scholar. The key difference in Ghai's view of Kenya is that the Kenyan Constitution expects the 'judiciary to use the constitution as a framework for policies and acts for broader shaping of state and society'.[90] As Chap. 5 will demonstrate, the role of the judiciary under the Kenyan Constitution is similar to Papua New Guinea.

The differences in Ghai's conclusions could be that his earlier label on the Papua New Guinea Constitution were influenced by the prevailing ideas at the time of courts having a limited role. Alternatively, Ghai may have assumed that a programmatic constitution can be transformative and, hence, he used the two conceptions interchangeably.

Ghai has acknowledged that 'there have been truly remarkable changes in the ways constitutions are perceived, prepared, and used since I first became interested in the subject nearly five decades ago'.[91] Ghai further conceded the different waves of constitutionalism since the 1950s and how the characterisations afforded to them have changed to better reflect the intents and contexts of constitutions premises.[92]

It could be inferred from this reflection that entrenched conceptions about the character of certain constitutions have evolved from the early post-colonial periods. Ghai, like many of his colleagues, challenged by the dominant colonial model of constitution and Western legal thinking at the time, may have doubted the early indigenous-led decolonial innovation in constitution-making. It is only in hindsight that he was able to describe a constitution properly as a transformative constitution in the case of Kenya. Papua New Guinea's Constitution, in hindsight, warrants similar reassessment as a transformative, and not an aspirational or programmatic, Constitution.

5 Conclusion

This chapter has discussed the notion of transformative constitutionalism and argues that its characteristics firmly resonate with the Papua New Guinea Constitution. It established three defining elements argued to be present in the case of Papua New Guinea—a clear intention to achieve 'change', a set of entrenched rights and

89 Yash Ghai, 'Katiba Corner: Interpreting Kenya's Transformative Constitution', The Star (online), 14 June 2014.

90 Ibid.

91 Yash Ghai, 'A Journey around Constitutions: Reflections on Contemporary Constitutions' (2005) 122 *African Law Journal* 804, 808.

92 Ibid.

obligations that reflect the intention for 'change,' and a liberal judiciary with wide powers to enforce the intended 'change'. It rebutted other contrary assertions of the Constitution, namely aspirational and programmatic, as inaccurate.

Characterising the Papua New Guinea Constitution as transformative does not mean that the society will be suddenly transformed, nor does it judge the workability or otherwise of the transformative goals embedded in the Constitution. The aim is to discover the correct nature of the Constitution so that it informs actors engaging with the Constitution, and assist in creating an environment in which the 'home-grown' constitutional designs, especially the expansive role of the judiciary, are better understood and implemented.

While the case of Papua New Guinea may not be like the scale and expectations afforded in other countries with transformative constitutions, it, nevertheless needs to advance in its own context. The Constitution is 'no longer tied down with that colonial legacy' [93] to be concerned of a re-assessment of its character and the constitutional culture, perceptions, and institutions under which it operates. Recharacterising it as a transformative Constitution affirms that it is not a document containing aspirations of a bygone era, but rather a living document capable of interceding in all facets of everyday social and political life in Papua New Guinea.

Ascribing the Papua New Guinea Constitution as transformative is, therefore, not merely a descriptive or semantic exercise; it is a fundamental undertaking in constitutional thought. As the CPC aptly puts it, '[o]ur Constitution should look towards the future and act as an accelerator in the process of development, not as a brake'.[94] This chapter invites a re-envisioning of the Constitution to achieve such transformative intents. The later parts of the book expand on this to discuss the need for a broader constitutional reimagining in Papua New Guinea.

[93] *Special reference by Allan Marat & Special reference by the National Parliament* [2012] PGSC 20, [364].

[94] CPC Report 1974, Chapter 2 [2].

Chapter 5
A Liberal Interventionist Judiciary for Papua New Guinea

Abstract This chapter argues there are twelve textual indicators, as interpreted by the courts, that demonstrates the liberal and interventionist character of the Papua New Guinea judiciary is firmly entrenched within the country's Constitution. It contends that these textual indicators provide the constitutional mandate for the judges to have a role beyond legal to social and political realms. The ensuing expectation is for judges to depart from legalistic approaches and attempts to undermine or doubt the judicial powers, and instead, embrace their new job description as active agents of social and political reform in Papua New Guinea.

Keywords Liberal judiciary · Judiciary of Papua New Guinea · Judicial powers · Judicial interventionism · Decolonial constitution · Constitutional drafters

1 Introduction

One of the most distinctive outcomes of the 'home-grown' constitution-making process that epitomises the intentions for creating structures suitable to the circumstances of the Papua New Guinea society was the nature and character of the judicial arm of the government. The powers given to the judiciary are wide-ranging, large and liberal—powers unparalleled to other judiciaries in the Pacific region, including Australia and New Zealand, and many across the Commonwealth. When implemented meaningfully, these powers are intended to define the transformative outlook of the Papua New Guinea Constitution.

This chapter identifies twelve textual indicators in the Constitution that firmly establish Papua New Guinea as having a liberal judiciary with a transformative role in the society. The textual indicators, as interpreted by the courts, affirms not only the intention to depart from the legalistic approaches and sensibilities of the Anglo-Australian judicial culture, but also the broader role judges are expected to play in the development of the Papua New Guinea society.

B. Kama, *Rethinking Judicial Power in Papua New Guinea*,
https://doi.org/10.1007/978-981-97-2946-3_5

The chapter begins with a brief discussion of what it means to have a liberal judiciary and proceeds to assessing the drafting intentions of the Constitutional Planning Committee (CPC). It concludes with an analysis of the various constitutional provisions as interpreted by the courts that demonstrate how the desire for a liberal judiciary is firmly entrenched within the 'home-grown' constitutional architecture.

2 Judicial Behaviour in a Liberal Judiciary

The phrase 'liberal judiciary' refers to a judiciary characterised by its judges exercising their functions in a way that embodies progressiveness, responsivness and reform-orientation.[1] An exercise of their power in this manner can be through either an express or an implied mandate under a constitution. As judges primarily deal with law, the expected 'reformist' behaviour of judges is dependent on a judge's understanding of what law is and how it should be applied. There are two broad understandings of law—classical and liberal—that influence how judges should approach the task of judicial interpretation.[2]

2.1 Judicial Approach Under the Classical Understanding of Law

The classical understanding of law is that a sovereign body, in this case, parliament, makes the law and its validity is not subject to a judge's reason, morality or notion of justice but is entirely for the parliament to decide.[3] According to this view, judges should only interpret and apply the law within the ordinary meaning of the text of the law.[4] It expects of judges to abide strictly by the legislative intentions of the parliament when exercising their adjudicative and interpretative functions.[5]

Proponents of this understanding of law argue that a state's parliament is the only authority charged with law-making. They view parliament as a superior body among the three arms of government and reason that since laws are commands, commands can only come from a superior and 'the inferior is bound to obey'.[6] The doctrine of parliamentary supremacy objects to judicial review of parliament's actions as well

---

[1] Paul Moke, *Earl Warren and the Struggle for Justice* (Lexington Books, 2015) 13.

[2] Roscoe Pound, 'Theories of Law' (1912) 2 *Yale Law Journal* 114, 115.

[3] Hans Kelsen, *Pure Theory of Law* (University of California Press, 1967) 18–19.

[4] Ibid.

[5] John Locke, *Two Treatise of Government* (1690) II, xi [136]; Woinarski J (ed), *Jesting Pilate and Other Papers and Addresses* (Law Book Co, 1965) 247.

[6] John Austin, *The Province of Jurisprudence Determined: And, The Uses of the Study of Jurisprudence* 1861 (Hackett Publishing, Reprinted 1998) 21, 142, 234–5.

as judicial decisions that amount to making laws or initiating reforms.[7] However, proponents of the classical understanding of law acknowledge that in 'hard cases', judges can exercise some discretion in their interpretative role.[8] Nevertheless, they insist that this discretion is only to the extent that it is consistent with the legislative intent and free from moral or philosophical considerations.

2.2 *Judicial Approach Under the Liberal Understanding of Law*

On the other hand, the liberal understanding of law argues that law is a system of principles that reflect the ethical and moral ideals of the community. It contends that the basis of law's authority is reason and conformity to ideals of what is right.[9] This implies that in order to reach a just outcome, the court's construction of the law must take into account the extra-legal considerations that permeate the intent and provisions of the legislation.[10] The task of judging is therefore not merely to discern the will of the parliament, but rather an independent critical exercise aimed at uncovering the principles of justice inherent in the various interpretative options available to judges.

This liberal conception of law results in two types of approaches that define a judciary—one where the judges 'read into' the constitution to affirm their liberal character and the other where the judges have a direct mandate from the constitution to be liberal, progressive and reformist. The former is discretionary on the judge whereas the latter is mandatory and a cornerstone of the judicial oath. The Papua New Guinea judiciary is intended to adopt the latter approach, as the rest of this chapter will demonstrate.

2.3 *Influence of the Common Law Principle of* Stare Decisis

The common law principle of *stare decisis* or precedent also affects the classical and liberal understandings of law. The principle permits judges of superior courts to develop legal principles or *ratio decidendi,* through their interpretation of the relevant

[7] Tom Ginsburg, *Judicial Review in New Democracies: Constitutional Courts in Asian Cases* (Cambridge University Press, 2003) 3; Thomas Jefferson's letter to William Jarvis (1820) cited in William J. Quirk and R. Randell Bridwell, *Judicial Dictatorship* (Transaction Publishers, 1995) 3. Jefferson contended that 'it is a very dangerous doctrine to consider the judges as the ultimate arbiters of all constitutional questions'.

[8] H.L.A Hart, *The Concept of Law* (Oxford University Press, 2nd ed, 1994) 124–25.

[9] Ronald Dworkin, *Law's Empire* (Harvard University Press, 1986) 263, 409; Julius Stone, *Precedent and Law: Dynamics of Common Law Growth* (Butterworths, 1985) 271.

[10] Duncan Kenedy, 'Legal Education as Training for Hierarchy' in David Kaireys (ed), *The Politics of Law: A Progressive Critique* (Basic Books, 1992) 47.

laws and the facts, which then becomes binding on courts dealing with like cases. The principle of precedent does not involve active lawmaking,[11] but adhering to the *ratio decidendi* of precedents is in fact following a set of judge-made laws.[12] Law is therefore not purely self-executing as the classical understanding of law asserts.

Additionally, the principle of *stare decisis* acts as a limitation on the law-making ability of the judges because it expects judges to follow precedents. Judges may distinguish the precedents and develop the law 'as the necessities of the time may require, and as the dictates of justice may demand'.[13] However, reform-oriented adjudicative approaches are unsustainable in an assertive political and legal environment, especially where there is no formal constitutional mandate for the judiciary to be liberal or adopt such approaches. As demonstrated in the case of Australia, reform-oriented adjudication that is not expressly supported by the constitution is entirely dependent on the composition of the superior court judges and their ideological persuasions.[14] Adding to these limitations, judges who are not constitutionally mandated to exercise liberal powers are mindful of their lack of political and constitutional legitimacy.[15]

This is not the case for Papua New Guinea. As will be demonstrated later in this chapter, the constitutional framework of Papua New Guinea promotes law-making as a shared responsibility between the parliament and the superior courts beyond the narrow limitations of the common law tradition of judicial law-making.

2.4 Methodology of a Liberal Judiciary

The liberal understanding of law generally meant that in liberal judiciaries, the role of the courts is to be conscious agents that use law to shape the broader socio-economic and political development of the society.[16] The courts' interpretative functions, for instance, are purposive, broad and value-laden with the intention of not only interpreting posited laws, but to address the legislature's inertia to respond to societal changes. This means the consensus among the judges, as Chief Justice Langa of South Africa puts it, must be that 'it is no longer sufficient for [them] to rely on the say-so of parliament or technical readings of the legislation as providing justifications for their decision'.[17]

---

[11] William B. Hornblower, 'A Century of "Judge-Made" Law' (1907) 7(7) *Columbia Law Review*, 453, 458.

[12] Anthony Mason, 'The Judge as Law-maker' (1996) *James Cook University Law Review* 1, 2.

[13] Hornblower, above n 11.

[14] Rosalind Dixon and Sean Lau, 'The Gleeson Court and the Howard era: A tale of two conservatives (and isms)' in Rosalind Dixon and George Williams (eds), *The High Court, the Constitution and Australian Politics* (Cambridge University Press, 2015) 297.

[15] Chief Justice Murray Gleeson, 'The Role of a Judge in a Representative Democracy' (Speech delivered at the Judiciary of the Commonwealth of the Bahamas, Nassau, 4 January 2008) 2.

[16] Aharon Barak, *Purposive Interpretation in Law* (Princeton University Press, 2005) 41.

[17] Pius Langa, 'Transformative Constitutionalism' (2006) 3 *Stellenbosch Law Review* 351, 352.

Not all judiciaries can claim to have a liberal character. Some constitutions encourage broad function, while others admonish any judicial latitude.[18] The latter regard liberal judges unfavourably as 'activists'[19] reigning in 'judicial dictatorship'[20] or in extreme cases accused of 'treason' against the constitution.[21] This is often seen in Australia where attempts at judicial liberalism continues to be challenged.

On the other hand, judiciaries with a liberal mandate are typically encouraged to strengthen their society's commitment to socioeconomic development, human rights and constitutionalism.[22] They act as accountability institutions amid institutional weaknesses and democratic decline. As Chief Justice Lamer of Canada stated, a liberal judicial regime changes the 'job description' of judges from being 'trained and expected just to apply, and if necessary, to interpret laws, [to making] what is essentially what used to be a political call'.[23]

3 A Liberal Judiciary in the 'Home-Grown' Constitution

The nature of the Papua New Guinea judiciary can be gleaned at the preliminary when considering how the judges have alluded to their 'job description' under the Papua New Guinea Constitution. A year after Independence in 1976, Deputy Chief Justice Prentice remarked that

> the Supreme Court of Papua New Guinea should be prepared and is empowered to, not only eliminate a phrase from an Act.., but also to add a phrase or change a phrase with the intent of construing (translating) an Act so that it is valid and still expressing the clear Parliamentary intent,…though Constitutional experts of other lands might consider this process to be [judicial legislating].[24]

His Honour went on to conclude that the judges have been invested with 'a collation of tremendous and humbling powers' and 'frightening responsibilities' 'to select, discard, interpret, modify and apply the law.'[25]

In 1980, Justice Wilson, in a judgement in which he rejected the 'literal rule of statutory interpretation', stated that 'I am conscious of the special responsibility

---

[18] Michael Kirby, 'Judicial Activism: authority, principle and policy in the judicial method', *Sydney Morning Herald* (online), 20 November 2003; John Gava, 'The Rise of the Hero Judge' (2001) 24(3) *University of New South Wales Law Journal* 747, 748–10.

[19] Kirby, Ibid.

[20] Quirk and Bridwell, above n 7.

[21] Campbell, Tom, 'Judicial Activism—Justice or Treason?' (2003) 10 *Otago Law Review* 307, 311–3.

[22] Rachel E. Bowen, *The Achilles Heel of Democracy* (Cambridge University Press, 2017) 108.

[23] Chief Justice Lamer, Canadian Supreme Court in *Globe and Mail*, 06 April 1992, cited in Fredrick Lee Morton (ed), *Law, Politics and the Judicial Process in Canada* (University of Calgary Press, 2002) 128.

[24] *Rakatani Peter v South Pacific Brewery Ltd* [1976] PNGLR 537 (unnumbered judgement).

[25] Ibid.

which is imposed on the Supreme Court to assist in the development of our indigenous jurisprudence adapted to the changing circumstances of Papua New Guinea.'[26]

In more recent years, judges have been more pronounced with their peculiar role under the Constitution as they grappled with assertive executive governments and issues of good governance, as explored in the later parts of this book. Justice Cannings, one of the leading judges in advancing the liberal role of the judges under the Constitution whose jurisprudence is examined further in the book, remarked in 2013 that

> Judges in Papua New Guinea are given a breathtaking array of powers, functions, duties and responsibilities not clothed upon Judges in many other jurisdictions, including those in the Commonwealth. The *Constitution* provides insight, inspiration and instructions as to how these daunting tasks are to be achieved.[27]

The 'breathtaking array of powers, functions, duties and responsibilities' Justice Cannings referred to needs to be understood more deeply to ascertain their drafting impetuses and how they are embedded in the Constitution, to firmly establish the character of the Papua New Guinea judiciary.

3.1 *Intentions of the Constitutional Planning Committee*

Based on their exhaustive consultation, the drafters of the Papua New Guinea Constitution, the Constitutional Planning Committee (CPC), proposed a different model of judiciary that should separate 'our judicial system and that of Australia' so that it could 'reflect, to a much greater degree...our own values and circumstances'.[28] They advocated that there be a 'cutting [of] the legal ties between our judicial system and that of Australia'[29]—a 'cutting' that not only represented structural, but also institutional and ideological autonomy. The CPC notably objected to the prevailing legalistic jurisprudence of the colonial courts that followed the lead of the Australian High Court:

> The courts tend to be formalistic and legalistic. While it is true that the Constitution is law, it is a special kind of law. All too often, the courts approach the Constitution as if it were like ordinary law. They adopt a literal approach and sacrifice the spirit for the letter of the Constitution. By failing to recognise the dynamic character of a Constitution, the courts have often introduced unnecessary rigidities.[30]

Chief Minister and Chairman of the CPC Michael Somare was explicit in calling for 'a system of laws appropriate to a self-governing, independent nation...[and that]

---

[26] *Request by Principal Legal Adviser on a Point of Law arising in a case where a Person tried upon Indictment has been Acquitted* [1980] PNGLR 326.

[27] *Central Provincial Government v National Capital District Commission* [2013] PGNC 91, [56]. *Bernard v Duban* [2016] PGNC 121, [14].

[28] CPC Report 1974, Chapter 8 [12].

[29] Ibid.

[30] Ibid [144].

it must respond to our own needs and values.'[31] He unequivocally stated that '[we do not want to create an imitation of the Australian, English, or American legal system.'[32]

The CPC envisaged a judiciary that must be 'tuned to the wishes of that society' and one that would apply 'judicial ingenuity to do justice'.[33] While they acknowledged the 'cardinal principle that the courts should be independent', they also argued that 'like other government institutions', courts 'do not exist in a vacuum' and need to 'be politically conscious'.[34]

It was an extraordinary approach for a new country that had been under Australia's conservative judicial regime for over seventy years, which, for the most part, had been administered with strict legalism.[35] While renowned legalist Chief Justice Dixon of Australia reassured at the time that in the 'Australian High Court [we] have had as yet no deliberate innovators bent on express change of acknowledged doctrine',[36] the CPC were determined to chart a different course for the Papua New Guinea Supreme Court. The CPC stated:

> Our recommendations on the judiciary stressed the need for the laws...to be applied in a manner that takes adequate account of conditions in our country...*We cannot afford to have our courts take a narrowly legalistic approach if the law is to be justly applied.*[37]

The CPC's intentions were for judges to be socially conscientious adjudicators with a broad and reformist function for the Papua New Guinea society. Uncritical adherence to legalism was therefore rejected as a source of injustice and an ideological instrument of the colonial legal order.

3.2 Establishment of a Liberal Judiciary in the Constitution

The intentions of the drafters of the Constitution, acquired through the exhaustive consultation with the people, translated into the texts of the Constitution. Upon studying the Constitution, there are twelve textual indicators as interpreted by the courts that demonstrates Papua New Guinea has a liberal judiciary.

---

[31] Cited in Abdul Paliwala and David Weisbrot, 'Changing society through law: an introduction,' in David Weisbrot, Abdul Paliwala and Akilagpa Sawyerr (ed), *Law and Social Change in Papua New Guinea (1982)* Butterworths, 4.

[32] Ibid.

[33] CPC Report 1974, Chapter 8 [6]–[9].

[34] Ibid [4]-[5].

[35] Tony Blackshield, 'Strict Logic and High Technique' (2003) *Australian Book Review* 8, 9; Leslie Zines, 'The Australian Constitution 1951–1976' (1976) 7 *Federal Law Review* 89, 90.

[36] Blackshield, Ibid.

[37] CPC Report 1974, Chapter 8 [9] [88] (emphasis added).

Mandate to apply liberal standard for judicial interpretation

The first textual indicator is the express mandate for judges to apply a broad and liberal standard of constitutional and legislative interpretation. Schedule 1.5(2) of the Constitution states that '[a]ll provisions of, and all words, expressions and propositions in, a Constitutional Law shall be given their fair and liberal meaning'.[38] As 'Constitutional Law' includes the Papua New Guinea Constitution and more than twenty Organic Laws,[39] the body of law subject to this standard of constitutional interpretation is very broad. Section 109(4) provides a similar standard of interpretation for ordinary legislation:

> Each law made by the Parliament shall receive such *fair, large and liberal construction and interpretation* as will best ensure the attainment of the *object of the law according to its true intent, meaning and spirit*..." (emphasis added)

The Supreme Court has consistently interpreted these provisions to mean that the standard of constitutional and legislative interpretation is broad and expansive. For instance, the Court held in *Special Reference by Morobe Provincial Government* (2002) that

> [g]oing by this expressed dictation in the Constitution, it is now an accepted principle of both constitutional and other statutory interpretation, that the provisions of the Constitution and all Acts of Parliament must be given their fair and liberal meaning.[40]

One of the earlier judges that laid the foundations profoundly for the liberal judicial interpretation was Justice Wilson who, in his interpretation of the constitutional provisions in 1980, remarked that

> special responsibility is imposed on the Supreme Court to assist in the development of our indigenous jurisprudence adapted to the changing circumstances of Papua New Guinea [and that] there is no place in a developing country where the courts, as well as the Law Reform Commission, are given special responsibilities in the process of development, for the narrow interpretation of statutes without adequate regard to the social purpose of particular legislation...[41]

Justice Wilson further urged against 'a tendency to over-emphasize the literal meaning of a provision at the expense of the meaning to be derived from other possible contexts' and held that '[t]he letter of the law should not be allowed to prevail over the spirit of the law in a case of statutory interpretation.' His Honour went on to conclude that '[t]here is, therefore, no place for a literalist approach to statutory interpretation in the law of Papua New Guinea.'[42]

---

[38] Schedule 1.5(2).

[39] Schedule 1.2.

[40] *Special Reference Pursuant to Constitution Section 19; Special Reference by Morobe Provincial Government* [2002] PGSC 9 (Salika and Kandakasi JJ).

[41] *Request by Principal Legal Adviser on a Point of Law arising in a case where a Person tried upon Indictment has been Acquitted* [1980] PNGLR 326 (unnumbered judgement).

[42] Ibid.

Emphasis is often made in politically sensitive constitutional cases against attempts to limit the Court's liberal interpretative approaches. For instance, in the 2011 landmark case of *East Sepik Provincial Executive* (ESP Case) where the country had a constitutional crisis with 'two' prime ministers (discussed in Chap. 6), Chief Justice Injia maintained that Papua New Guinea's standard of constitutional interpretation is 'broad and expansive over the strict, technical and legalistic approach'.[43] In *Haiveta v Wingti* (No 3) (1994) where the executive interfered with the constitutional processes involved in the election of a prime minister, Chief Justice Amet reminded the Supreme Court 'to adopt a broad goal-oriented and purposive approach' in their interpretation of the constitutional provisions in question.[44]

The Supreme Court was more assertive in *Re Organic Law on Integrity of Political Parties and Candidates* (2010) (OLLIPPAC Case), another landmark and politically sensitive case concerning the constitutionality of a law that regulates the integrity of political parties.[45] As will be discussed further in Chap. 6, the government argued that the law was intended to ensure political stability.[46] However, the Court applied a broad reading of the law and its policy implications to conclude that it was an attempt to restrict the MPs' freedom of political speech and association as well as a recipe for executive tyranny.[47] The full bench of the Supreme Court backed their broad findings on the basis that

> [t]he Constitution mandates this Court to construe the Constitution in a fair and liberal manner, to think expansively and to be dynamic and where necessary, to use judicial ingenuity. The body of law developed in this way would then form a part of the homegrown jurisprudence.[48]

The government pleaded for judicial restraint based on the Anglo-Australian legalistic judicial approach.[49] However, the Court was adamant that it would not consider

> any doctrine of constitutional interpretation founded on some foreign political theories and ideologies... [or that the constitutional] provisions, should be measured against to test their validity.[50]

[43] *In re Reference to Constitution section 19(1) by East Sepik Provincial Executive* [2011] PGSC 41 [9] (Injia CJ); Rowan Callick, 'Papua New Guinea in crisis with two PMs, two police chiefs', *The Australian* (online), 14 December 2011.

[44] *Haiveta v Wingti* (No 3) 1994 PNGLR 197, 207 (Amet CJ).

[45] *Special Reference By Fly River Provincial Executive Council; Re Organic Law on Integrity of Political Parties and Candidates* [2010] PGSC 3, [104].

[46] Political instability has long been a major concern for Papua New Guinea and one of the causes is the ease in which Members of Parliament (MPs) shift allegiances between different political parties. As a response, the government undertook legislative reform to discipline MPs and their political parties engaged in such practices.

[47] *Special Reference By Fly River Provincial Executive Council; Re Organic Law on Integrity of Political Parties and Candidates* [2010] PGSC 3, [130], [165], [182], [256].

[48] Ibid [104].

[49] Ibid [90]–[91].

[50] Ibid [109]. The Supreme Court went on to state that 'interpretation and materials developed or used elsewhere as aids, should be discouraged' (at [100]–[102]).

It held that 'the correct approach to interpreting the Constitution is to adopt the approach that the Constitution itself provides'.[51]

In *Ex parte Sasakila* (1976), a year after Papua New Guinea's Independence, Justice Kearney, an Australian colonial jurist, reasoned that the liberal interpretative method meant judges should not be 'totally divorced from considering socio-political considerations which permeate the Constitution'.[52]

In the *ESP Case* (2011), the Supreme Court declared that it cannot 'turn a blind eye and come to the view that it should not enter the arena of politics'.[53] In *Reference by the Ombudsman Commission of Papua New Guinea* (2010), the Court further held that the liberal standard of interpretation meant it 'must not shy away' from considering the underlying socio-economic and political issues.[54]

These provisions as interpreted by the Supreme Court demonstrate the liberal character of the judiciary in the following ways. First, the broad directive for constitutional interpretation, together with the Court's intention 'to think expansively and to be dynamic… [and] to use judicial ingenuity',[55] clearly provides an extensive scope for reform-oriented adjudication capable of effecting the transformative intents of the Constitution. Second, reference to the importance of considering socio-political conditions indicates flexibility in the interpretative methods—to evolve and respond to the changing conditions of Papua New Guinea society.[56] This is reinforced by Schedule 1.4, which aptly notes that 'Constitutional Law speaks from time to time' (discussed as another textual indicator below). Third, in accepting that the Supreme Court cannot 'turn a blind eye and come to the view that it should not enter the arena of politics', the judges affirmed a key aspect of their liberal and transformative character—they have an active political and social accountability function beyond the traditional black-letter law approaches.

This constitutional mandate for liberal interpretation is unparalleled in judiciaries in the Pacific, including Australia and New Zealand and most of the Commonwealth, and demonstrates a clear separation from colonial judicial practices.

Mandate to use aids to interpretation

The second textual indicator of a liberal judiciary entrenched in the Constitution is the direction in section 24, to use a set of materials as 'aids to interpretation' when interpreting the Constitutional Laws. The materials include the official records of debates in the pre-Independence House of Assembly and in the National Constituent

---

[51] Ibid [100].

[52] *The State v The Independent Tribunal; Ex parte Sasakila* (1976) PNGLR 491, 506–7 (Kearney J).

[53] *In re Reference to Constitution Section 19(1) by East Sepik Provincial Executive* [2011] PGSC 41 [10], [397]–[98].

[54] *Reference by the Ombudsman Commission of Papua New Guinea* [2010] PGSC 10, [30] (Injia CJ); The Court went on to note that 'the Parliament can always by subsequent legislative act, correct it if [it] feels the Court has usurped its function'.

[55] *Special Reference By Fly River Provincial Executive Council; Re Organic Law on Integrity of Political Parties and Candidates* [2010] PGSC 3, [104].

[56] *Namah v Pato* [2014] PGSC 1 [38]–[39].

Assembly, and the politically infused Constitutional Planning Committee Report predominantly featured in this book. It also include submissions from the different political factions.[57] These set of materials are very broad and can be contrasted to Australia, for instance, where until the *Cole v Whitfield* decision in 1988, the Australian High Court excluded the Convention debates that recorded proposals for the draft Australian Constitution as a source for constitutional interpretation.[58]

Section 24 firmly augments the liberal standard of interpretation discussed above. For instance, in the *OLIPPAC Case*, the Court, after refusing 'to adopt legal doctrines of constitutional interpretation developed elsewhere', went on to declare that '[o]ur Constitution is homegrown or autochthonous and it provides the principles and materials as aids to interpretation, which this Court should adopt and apply'.[59] Schedule 1.3(1) of the Constitution extended the 'aid to interpretation' to include the Preamble of the Constitution 'in cases of doubt'.[60]

A pertinent question in dealing with section 24 is when to invoke these 'aids to interpretation', which are extrinsic material. The common law position on extrinsic material is to only invoke them when 'the ordinary and grammatical meaning of the words of the provision, having regard to their context and legislative purpose,' cannot be clearly ascertained.[61] For instance, in *Cole v Whitfield*, the need to refer to the records of constitutional debates in Australia arose only after the Australian High Court found that there was clear and prolonged uncertainty in the interpretation of the constitutional provision in question.[62]

However, the Supreme Court of Papua New Guinea rejected this limitation.[63] For instance, Chief Justice Amet, held that 'all aids to interpretation' are to be used concurrently with the Constitution 'in every question relating to the interpretation or application of any provision of a constitutional law…and not only when there is some deemed ambiguity or uncertainty'.[64] It followed from the Supreme Court's decision barely a year after Independence that 'in carrying out its [interpretative] functions, the words actually used in the Act do not have to be strictly adhered to but are to be construed with the assistance of the materials referred to in s 24'.[65]

---

[57] *Constitutional Documents (Manner of Proof) Act 1976* (PNG). A. J. Regan and E. P. Wolfers, 'Aids to Interpretation of the *Constitution*—Some Preliminary Thoughts' (1986) 14 *Melanesian Law Journal* 153.

[58] *State of Tasmania v Commonwealth of Australia and State of Victoria* (1904) 1 CLR 329, 333 (Griffith CJ); The High Court reversed this position in *Cole v Whitfield* (1988) 165 CLR 360, 385.

[59] *Special Reference By Fly River Provincial Executive Council; Re Organic Law on Integrity of Political Parties and Candidates* [2010] PGSC 3, [100].

[60] *Supreme Court Reference by the Western Highlands Provincial Executive* [1995] PGSC 6; *Peter v South Pacific Brewery Ltd* [1976] PGLawRp 674.

[61] *Australian Education Union v Department of Education and Children's Services* (2012) 248 CLR 1 13; *Acts Interpretation Act 1901*(Cth) s 15AB.

[62] *Cole v Whitfield* (1988) 165 CLR 360, 384.

[63] *Supreme Court Reference by the Western Highlands Provincial Executive* [1995] PGSC 6 (unnumbered judgment).

[64] Ibid (Amet CJ).

[65] *State v Independent Tribunal, Ex parte Sasakila* [1976] PGSC 27, [61] (Kearney J).

This approach resonates with the direction of the CPC and the weight it wanted the courts to place on its socio-political vision. For instance, the CPC argued that the National Goals and Directive Principles (NGDPs) and the Basic Social Obligations (BSOs), which are statements of policy, and embedded in the CPC Report, 'should not be regarded by any court…as being of less weight than other directly justiciable provisions'.[66]

This is fortified by sections 25 and 63 of the Constitution, which state that, although the NGDPs and the BSOs are non-justiciable, 'it is the duty of all governmental bodies to apply and give effect to them as far as lies within their respective powers'.[67] The Supreme Court has interpreted the NGDPs and BSOs as applicable not only 'to all governmental bodies exercising executive power, but also to courts when interpreting and applying constitutional laws and ordinary legislation'.[68]

In *Namah v O'Neill* (2015), the Court expanded the 'aids to interpretation' to include affidavits from some of the early former prime ministers and surviving members of the CPC to assist with ascertaining the intents and purposes of certain constitutional provisions.[69]

The following could be said regarding this provision on the 'aids to interpretation' and how it demonstrates a liberal judiciary. First, the direction to use extrinsic materials concurrently in judicial interpretation is unconventional considering the general understanding in common law, which typically refers to extrinsic materials only in cases of uncertainty. It extends the broad interpretative tools identified in the preceding discussion.

It further reinforces the autonomy of the Papua New Guinea judiciary and the unique designs of the 'home-grown' Constitution to the task of judicial interpretation in which its judges are expected not to readily relying on common law precedents without fully examining its own constitutional materials.[70]

Second, the highly political nature of some of the extrinsic materials listed firmly reinforces the ability of the judiciary to give effect to the transformative intentions of the Papua New Guinea Constitution—intentions that goes beyond the narrow questions of law to the socio-economic and political spheres. As Anthony Regan and Professor Edward Wolfers observed, the broad nature of the aids to interpretation was intended to ensure 'that judicial interpretation [is] flexible and responsive to the surrounding society in other ways'.[71]

Third, the use of affidavits from people involved in the drafting of the Constitution and founding politicians as 'aids to interpretation' in the case of *Namah v O'Neill*

---

[66] CPC Report 1974, Chapter 2 [153](3)(2).

[67] See *Ref By Simbu Provincial Executive* [1987] PGSC 17 (Barnett J) (unnumbered judgment).

[68] *Ref By Simbu Provincial Executive* [1987] PGLawRp 151 (unnumbered judgment).

[69] *Namah v O'Neill* [2015] PGSC 77, [23]–[26].

[70] Bernard Narokobi, 'History and Movement in Law Reform in Papua New Guinea' in David Weisbrot, Abdul Paliwala and Akilagpa Sawyerr, *Law and Social Change in Papua New Guinea* (Butterworths, 1982) 22.

[71] Regan and Wolfers, above n 57, 168

(2015) firmly demonstrates the liberal nature of the 'aid to interpretation' methodology and the significance of judicial discretion to expand the 'aids', augmenting with the liberal interpretative approach discussed above.[72]

An expansive judicial review mechanism

The third textual indicator suggesting a liberal judiciary in Papua New Guinea is the wide judicial review mechanism under sections 18 and 19. Remarking on its significance, Chief Justice Salamo Injia observed that '[t]he Supreme Court, as the apex Court, is given special and exclusive powers to guard the *Constitution* against abuse [and] sections 18 and 19 of the *Constitution* are the pinnacle of that power'.[73]

Section 18(1) sets out the original jurisdiction of the Supreme Court over 'any question relating to the interpretation or application of any provision of a Constitutional Law'.[74] As 'Constitutional Law' includes the Papua New Guinea Constitution and more than twenty Organic Laws,[75] the body of law subject to this standard of constitutional interpretation is very broad. Section 18(2) provides for lower courts to refer any constitutional issues arising from their proceedings to the Supreme Court 'unless the question is trivial, vexatious or irrelevant'.[76]

Section 19, on the other hand, is a 'special reference' provision that 'exhaustively' provides for over three hundred governmental bodies to have 'automatic standing' to seek judicial review 'on any question relating to the interpretation or application of any provision of a constitutional law, including any question as to the validity of a law or a proposed law'.[77]

Review under section 18

The pertinent issue concerning judicial review under section 18 of the original jurisdiction is *locus standi* or 'standing'. Standing under section 18(2), where a constitutional issue is referred from the lower courts, is restricted to parties in the original proceedings. However, section 18(1) has been interpreted as providing the Court with discretion to accept a direct application from the public on any constitutional issue.[78] For instance, in the landmark case of *Namah v Pato* (2014), Opposition

[72] *Namah v O'Neill* [2015] PGSC 77, [23]–[26].

[73] *In re Constitution Section 19(1)—Special reference by Allan Marat* [2012] PGSC 20, [48].

[74] S 18(1). A Constitutional Law constitutes the Constitution, constitutional amendments and any Organic Law (Schedule 1.2). An Organic Law is deemed as a constitutional law because it is enacted as an extension of the Constitution on a subject matter the Constitution inadequately deals with but gives direction or intends that the subject be dealt with through an Organic Law (S 12). The requirements for the enactment and amendment of Organic Laws are therefore more stringent than ordinary legislation (Ss 13, 14 & 17).

[75] Schedule 1.2.

[76] For instance, see *Somare, Re* [1981] PGSC 23; *Re Tribunal established under the Organic Law on the Duties and Responsibilities of Leadership S27 and Leo Robert Morgan* [1978] PNGLR 460.

[77] See *In the Matter of Section 18(1) of the Constitution and in the Matter of Jim Kas, Governor of Madang Province* [2001] PGSC 15 (Kapi DCJ, Sheehan and Salika JJ).

[78] *Namah v Pato* [2014] PGSC 1 (Salika DCJ, Sakora, Kandakasi, Cannings, Poole JJ).

Leader Belden Namah applied to the Court's original jurisdiction to seek a declaration that a constitutional amendment passed by the parliament, regarding the bilateral arrangement between the governments of Papua New Guinea and Australia to detain asylum seekers on Manus Island, was unconstitutional.[79] The initial issue was whether the Opposition Leader had standing. However, the application also raised a broader question as to whether the Opposition Leader, having been unable to defeat a constitutional amendment in parliament, could resort to the Court and invoke the Court's original jurisdiction.

The Court responded by laying out four very broad tests for standing on public interest matters. According to the Court, the application must concern:[80]

(a) a citizen who has a genuine concern for the subject matter of the application;
(b) wishes to raise significant constitutional issues;
(c) not a mere busybody and has no improper motive;
(d) though there are other ways of having the constitutional issues determined by the Courts, this does not mean that one should be refused standing.

This broad approach follows a long line of authorities that consistently held that any citizen has standing to bring an action of 'serious constitutional matters'.[81]

In *Ila Geno* (2014),[82] the Supreme Court extended these tests to include any retired senior public servant who has had a distinguished career in public service and has demonstrated a 'genuine concern' for the wellbeing of the Constitution.[83] In that case, Ila Geno, a retired Chief Ombudsman, was granted standing to challenge constitutional amendments that sought to reform the parliamentary 'vote of no-confidence' mechanism. His 'genuine concern' was further affirmed by the fact that he approached five constitutional institutions that have automatic standing to pursue the case, but they were unwilling.[84]

The judicial approach in *Ila Geno* can be contrasted with the common law position on standing to seek declaratory or injunctive relief in public interest litigation. Standing in common law can only be attained with the consent of the Attorney-General or in instances where a private right is affected or where 'a person suffers

---

[79] The constitutional amendment provided an exception under the freedom from arbitrary detention provision, permitting detention of persons under a bilateral agreement (S 42(1)(ga)). The amendment provides that a 'foreign national' can be deprived of his personal liberty 'under arrangements made by Papua New Guinea with another country or with an international organisation that the (Foreign) Minister responsible for immigration matters, in his absolute discretion, approves'.

[80] *Namah v Pato* [2014] PGSC 1, [24] (Salika DCJ, Sakora, Kandakasi, Cannings, Poole JJ); *Somare, Re* [1981] PGSC 23 (Kidu CJ & Kapi J) (unnumbered judgment).

[81] *Southern Highlands Provincial Government v Somare, Chairman of the National Executive Council* [2007] PGSC 2, [13], [149] (Kapi CJ & Sakora J); *Somare, Re* [1981] PGSC 23 (Kidu CJ & Kapi J) (unnumbered judgment).

[82] *In re Application by Ila Geno* [2014] PGSC 2, [27].

[83] Ibid [10].

[84] Ibid [39–40].

special damage peculiar to himself'.[85] For instance, Australia developed the latter limb with the 'special interest' test, which limits persons seeking judicial review to show a greater degree of loss, or that the person suffers more adversely compared to the other members of the public.[86] In contrast, the Papua New Guinea Supreme Court formulated its test for 'sufficient interest' broadly to mean 'a citizen who has a genuine concern for the subject matter of the application'.[87]

This highly liberal approach began in the landmark case of *Re Petition of MT Somare* (1981),[88] notably at the same time as the *ACF* and *Onus* cases where the Australian High Court laid out the restrictive standard for Australia.[89] The issue in *Somare* was whether or not an Opposition Leader should have standing to seek judicial review of two decisions of the Parliament—one approving the commitment of troops to Vanuatu for peacekeeping purposes and the other enacting the *Defence Force (Presence Abroad) Act 1980* to effect the Parliament's decision.[90] Chief Justice Kidu, in the majority, held that 'in cases where the constitutionality or otherwise of an Act of the National Parliament arises, *locus standi* should not be restricted to any particular group'.[91]

A key policy concern with regards to restricting standing in Australia and England is to not 'open the floodgates' to cases that could interrupt government and executive function.[92] However, Justice Kapi, with whom the majority agreed, pointedly refused such policy concerns:

> I observe that in other countries this policy consideration often restricts the scope of locus standi. With respect, this is no question of policy. Under our Constitution the legislative power belongs to the people. *I do not think it is proper for this Court to deny a citizen right to locus standi by a policy consideration. After all, the judicial power belongs to the people. It is the people's court and let them come by the hundreds if they have the right to come.*[93] (emphasis added)

---

[85] *Boyce v Paddington Borough Council* [1903] 1 Ch 109, 114; *Gouriet v Union of Post Office Workers* [I9781 AC 435, 513; *Australian Conservation Foundation Inc. v Commonwealth* (1980) 146 CLR 493, 526-7.

[86] *Onus v Alcoa of Australia Ltd* (1981) 149 CLR 27, 35 (Gibbs CJ); *Byron Environment Centre Inc V Arakwal People* (1997) 78 FCR 1, 33; For examples of legislation adopting this approach, see *Administrative Decision Judicial Review* 1977 (Cth) s 3(4); *Judicial Review Act 1991* (Qld) s 43. There is still a conflicting view at the High Court with some judges suggesting a broader test to include any person, unless the right or interest of the plaintiff is insufficient to support a justiciable controversy: *Bateman's Bay Local Aboriginal Land Council v Aboriginal Community Benefit Fund Pty Ltd* (1998) 194 CLR 247; *Alphapharm Pty Ltd v SmithKline Beecham (Australia) Pty Ltd* (1994) 49 FCR 250.

[87] *Namah v Pato* [2014] PGSC 1, [24].

[88] *Re Petition of MT Somare* [1981] PNGLR 265 (unnumbered judgment).

[89] *Australian Conservation Foundation Inc. v Commonwealth* (1980) 146 CLR 493, 526–7; *Onus v Alcoa of Australia Ltd* (1981) 149 CLR 27, 35.

[90] *Re Petition of MT Somare* [1981] PNGLR 265 (Kidu CJ).

[91] Ibid.

[92] Ibid [143] (Miles J).

[93] Ibid (Kapi J) (unnumbered judgment) (emphasis added); Accepted in *Namah v Pato* [2014] PGSC 1, [15]; *Ombudsman Commission v National Parliament* [2003] PGSC 19 (unnumbered judgment).

The Court's interpretation on 'standing' under section 18(1) firmly demonstrates its liberal character in two ways. First, by liberally allowing people to bring constitutional issues for interpretation, it creates a dynamic judicial environment that the Court can use to implement the transformative intents of the Constitution. Second, a liberal approach to standing allows the people to participate in the judiciary's accountability role against the other two arms of government—the executive and the legislature. The liberal standing thus demonstrates a responsive judiciary attuned to the circumstances of the Papua New Guinea society and its increasing need for constitutional governance.[94]

Review under section 19

Section 19 of the Papua New Guinea Constitution is a special provision that grants automatic standing to over three hundred public institutions to bring constitutional questions to the Supreme Court 'relating to the interpretation or application of any provision of a Constitutional Law, including any question as to the validity of a law or proposed law'.[95] Two important elements in the provision are worth considering.

First, as Australian jurist Deputy Chief Justice Kearney observed, it allows an 'exhaustive' list of governmental bodies with 'automatic standing to attack the validity of law'.[96] This list includes the Governor-General (acting with, and in accordance with, the advice of the National Executive Council), the Speaker of Parliament, the Ombudsman Commission, the Law Reform Commission, the Public Solicitor, the Public Prosecutor, as well as the twenty-one provincial governments, and the three hundred and nineteen local level government councils.[97] Some of the statutory bodies, especially the Ombudsman Commission, have actively used this provision to become effective guardians of the Constitution.[98]

Those that are not on the list in section 19 can seek standing under section 18, as discussed above. The combined effect of sections 18 and 19 means a remarkably broad and unprecedented judicial review mechanism. It provides a wide range of persons and institutions, a mechanism to directly challenge constitutional amendments and legislation. The Supreme Court attested that the mechanism is 'more liberal than that of any other democracy'.[99] It is a firm indication of a liberal judiciary with the capacity to not only scrutinise the parliament but also to effect the

[94] The broad rules on locus standi are accepted as part of the underlying law of Papua New Guinea, see *Re Petition of MT Somare* [1981] PNGLR 265; *Southern Highlands Provincial Government v Somare, Chairman of the National Executive Council* [2007] PGSC 2; SC854 (1 March 2007), [13], [15]; *Namah v Pato* [2014] PGSC 1, [23] (Salika DCJ, Sakora, Kandakasi, Cannings, Poole JJ).

[95] Ss 19(1)(2)(3), 156 ('law officers'); *Re Petition of MT Somare* [1981] PNGLR 265 (Kearney DCJ) (unnumbered judgment).

[96] *Re Petition of MT Somare* [1981] PNGLR 265 (Kearney DCJ) (unnumbered judgment).

[97] S 19(3); See *Re Ombudsman Commission Investigations of the Public Solicitor* [1978] PGSC 7.

[98] See cases such as *Re Constitutional (Amendment) Law 2008, Reference by the Ombudsman Commission of Papua New Guinea* [2013] PGSC 67; *Reference by the Ombudsman Commission of Papua New Guinea* [2010] PGSC 10.

[99] *Somare, Re* [1981] PNGLR 265, 275–6.

transformative intentions of the Constitution through direct engagement with the grievances of the people and the state institutions.

The second important aspect of section 19 is that the listed statutory bodies can apply for the Supreme Court's opinion on 'any question as to the validity of a law or proposed law'.[100] Section 19(5) defines 'proposed law' to mean 'a law that has been formally placed before the relevant law-making body'. This means the Court can undertake an anticipatory review of a law that is still in the legislative process, either in its Bill stage or awaiting certification.[101] As the Supreme Court puts it, the authorities under section 19, therefore, 'need not wait until an actual dispute arises between parties…[or] even wait until the proposed law comes into force before seeking the court's opinion'.[102] The Court upheld this position in 2013, that in essence, 'there is no distinction between a law passed by Parliament and a proposed law'.[103]

The Supreme Court further clarified that the provision provides a 'very special' function and 'enlarge[s]' the Court's judicial review jurisdiction beyond the traditional limits.[104] Justice Bernard Sakora, a senior member of the Supreme Court, justified that since people are the source of all governmental and judicial powers, judicial review should not only be exercised according to the traditional prescription but must be taken to give the Court overall 'supervisory and controlling powers over the exercise of both legislative and executive powers'.[105]

The Court's interpretation of these provisions affirms its liberal character in two distinct ways. First, its ability to police the legislative work of the parliament is a firm indication of a liberal judiciary capable of enforcing the transformative intents of the Constitution unrestrained by the traditional conceptions of parliamentary superiority.

---

[100] S 19(1).

[101] *Somare, Re* [1981] [1981] PNGLR 265 (Miles J). A later decision held that the 'proposed law' period meant a month was given from when it is gazetted to when it is introduced in Parliament. After that, the Court should not interfere until the law is passed, see *Reference by the Ombudsman Commission; Re Section 19 of the Constitution* [2010] PGSC 43, [34]–[36] (Injia CJ, Kirriwom and Gavara-Nanu JJ). However, this view was later overturned in *In Re Constitutional (Amendment) Law 2008, Reference by the Ombudsman Commission of Papua New Guinea* [2013] PGSC 67, [21] (Injia CJ, Salika DCJ, Sakora, Kirriwom, & Gavara-Nanu JJ) with support from *SCR No.1A of 1981: Re Motor Traffic Act* [1982] PNGLR 122. The Court held that 'proposed law…include a law already passed but not yet come into force or a law that is still in the Bill stage…a draft law that is awaiting or has gone through the required number of readings by the Parliament or a law that was passed by the Parliament except it is still awaiting certification'.

[102] *Somare, Re* [1981] PGSC 23 (Miles J) (unnumbered judgment).

[103] *In re Constitutional (Amendment) Law 2008, Reference by the Ombudsman Commission of Papua New Guinea* [2013] PGSC 67, [21] (Injia CJ, Salika DCJ, Sakora, Kirriwom, & Gavara-Nanu JJ).

[104] Ibid.

[105] *Southern Highlands Provincial Government v Somare, Chairman of the National Executive Council* [2007] PGSC 2, [20] (Sakora J); *Somare, Re* [1981] PGSC 23 (Kidu CJ). Equating the People and the government as in a beneficiary-trustee relationship, his Honour held: 'As a beneficiary in trust is entitled to invoke the powers of the courts to ensure that the trustees act in their interest so should the People whose legislative power the Parliament exercises, complain to this Court if they think the Legislature acts contrary to the *Constitution* through which their power has been given to it'.

Second, the provisions empower the Court to hold accountable public bodies that are 'sleeping at the wheel' in their duties by ensuring that private individuals can intervene.[106] This leads to a robust constitutional accountability system and demonstrates a judiciary capable of instigating change in Papua New Guinea society.[107]

Broad judicial review standards for human rights protection

The fourth textual indicator suggesting Papua New Guinea has a liberal judiciary is the direction under section 38(1), which mandates that when conducting judicial review, the courts must determine whether a law is 'reasonably justifiable in a democratic society having a proper respect for the rights and dignity of mankind'.[108] The Papua New Guinea Constitution provides an exhaustive list of sources the superior courts may consider when making this determination.[109] This includes considering the NGDPs and the BSOs, as well as the Charter of the United Nations, 'recommendations of the United Nations concerning human rights and fundamental freedoms' and 'any other international conventions, agreements or declarations concerning human rights and fundamental freedoms'.[110] The list also includes

> judgments, reports and opinions of the International Court of Justice, the European Commission of Human Rights, the European Court of Human Rights and other international courts and tribunals dealing with human rights and fundamental freedoms; declarations by the International Commission of Jurists and other similar organizations; [and] any other material that the court considers relevant.[111]

These provisions support the liberal character of the judiciary in two ways. First, the requirement—'reasonably justifiable in a democratic society having a proper respect for the rights and dignity of mankind'—is a very broad criterion. It deals not only with legal but also contested political and social concepts, requiring the courts to exercise considerable discretion and value judgment. The courts have observed in numerous cases that this requirement must be satisfied both in the formality of making the law and in the substantive content of the law.[112]

As to the former, the Supreme Court in *Matter of Bill Skate MP* (2001) held that a law affecting human rights 'must strictly comply with the formal requirements [by]...clearly set[ting] out the particular public purposes for which the law is made, the freedom or rights regulated, and the reasons why it is necessary for the law to regulate or restrict that right'.[113] The Court was adamant that it is not sufficient to

---

[106] *In re Application by Ila Geno* [2014] PGSC 2, [40].

[107] Ibid.

[108] S 38(1)(b).

[109] S 39(3). This includes 'determining whether or not any law, matter or thing is reasonably justified in a democratic society'.

[110] S 39(3)(a, b, c, d).

[111] S 39(3)(e, j).

[112] *Special reference by Allan Marat & Special reference by the National Parliament* [2012] PGSC 20, [120] – [9]; *In the Matter of Section 18(1) of the Constitution and in the Matter of Bill Skate MP* [2001] PGSC 6; *The State v NTN Pty Ltd and NBN Ltd* [1992] PGSC 11 (Kapi DCJ & Amet J).

[113] *In the Matter of Section 18(1) of the Constitution and in the Matter of Bill Skate MP* [2001] PGSC 6 (Injia J) (Amet CJ and Sawong J made similar comments) (unnumbered judgment).

'merely set out the qualified right affected by the law and simply say the new law is to regulate that right and declare that the law is reasonably justifiable in a democratic society'.[114]

An objective test is then applied to decide whether the formality requirements have been satisfied and the onus is on the parliament to show that they have.[115] This requirement ensures, firstly, that members of parliament are well informed of the proposed law before legislating; secondly, it ensures that the community is fully aware of the implications of the proposed law; and thirdly, that it holds an assertive executive accountable.

The second way in which section 38 demonstrates a liberal judiciary is the plethora of international human rights instruments and mechanisms the Court is charged to consider when reviewing the law. These instruments not only offer a high standard of rights protection, but also provide an exhaustive range of sources for constitutional interpretation, in addition to the 'aids to interpretation' discussed earlier.[116] While it may be a response to colonial experiences and the need for protection against human rights violations discussed in Chap. 2, these broad sources of human rights equip the Court with the potential to be reformist and interventionist in their adjudication.

The effect of these provisions was demonstrated in the landmark *Manus Island* case in 2016, where the Supreme Court ruled against the Australian-sponsored asylum seeker detention as unconstitutional.[117] The Court was asked to determine whether persons forcefully brought into Papua New Guinea and held against their will as a result of an administrative arrangement between Papua New Guinea and Australia breached section 42 of the Constitution which guarantees liberty of all persons. To implement the bilateral arrangement between the two countries and to circumvent the constitutional guarantee, the Papua New Guinea government successfully introduced an amendment to the Constitution as an exception to the human rights guarantee. The amendment provided for a person's liberty to be deprived 'for the purposes of holding a foreign national under arrangements made by Papua New Guinea with another country…'.[118]

The Supreme Court overturned the amendment, noting that the 'forceful transfer and continued detention…by the PNG and Australian governments' was 'unconstitutional and illegal'.[119] Australia was not a party in the legal proceedings. However, the Court found that

> [i]t was the joint efforts of the Australian and PNG governments that has seen the asylum seekers brought into PNG and…this (sic) arrangements were outside the Constitutional and legal framework in PNG.[120]

---

[114] Ibid.

[115] Ibid; *The State v NTN Pty Ltd* [1992] PNGLR 1 (Kapi DCJ).

[116] *Namah v Pato* [2016] PGSC 13, [47]–[50], [64].

[117] Ibid.

[118] Section 42 (1)(ga).

[119] *Namah v Pato* [2016] PGSC 13, [37].

[120] Ibid.

The Court invoked international human rights instruments in its decision and this contrast with the decision of the Australian High Court a few months earlier concerning Australia's involvement at the Nauru detention centre where the High Court did not refer to international human rights instruments and ruled that Australia's actions in Nauru were consistent with its Constitution.[121] The Supreme Court's ability to widely engage with international human rights instruments and going beyond the confines of the litigating parties to rule against Australia as being equally culpable clearly demonstrated its liberal and expansive character.

Powers to act on own volition to enforce human rights

The fifth textual indicator suggesting a liberal judiciary is the power of the Supreme Court and the National Court under section 57 to act *sua moto* or on their 'own initiative' to enforce human rights. According to Deputy Chief Justice Kandakasi, the jurisprudence on section 57 has resulted in a change to traditional judicial role in which judges

> depart from the court's regular mode of operation. Instead of the courts taking a more passive role they have become more active...They have stepped out of the normal or traditional adversarial role to more inquisitorial roles.[122]

The section 57 regime essentially allows the courts to police the human rights provisions. For instance, in *Re section 57 of the Constitution of Papua New Guinea* (2006),[123] Justice Cannings acted on his own initiative to order the closure of a police lock-up cell in Bougainville on the basis that the condition of the facility was inhumane and unliveable.[124] His Honour also ordered the Police Commissioner 'to clean and renovate the lock-up to make it a suitable facility' and directed all relevant government officials to make 'meaningful consultation' to address the issue and to report on the progress.[125]

Justice Cannings is an Australian jurist and former academic. He was a senior counsel of the Papua New Guinea Ombudsman Commission before his judicial appointment. Appointed President of the Human Rights Track in the superior courts, Justice Cannings has been a staunch enforcer of section 57. In a 2017 landmark case at the National Court, his Honour conducted an inquiry, on his own volition, into potential human rights breaches of prisoners on death row. The inquiry was initiated due to the failure of the executive government to staff the Advisory Committee

---

[121] *Plaintiff M68/2015 v Minister for Immigration and Border Protection* (2016) HCA 1, [24]–[37], [45] (French CJ, Kiefel and Nettle JJ), [176]–[185] (Gageler J) and [259] (Keane J)..

[122] Morua v China Harbour Engineering Co (PNG) Ltd [2020] PGNC 16, [47].

[123] *Re Section 57 of the Constitution of Papua New Guinea, Enforcement of Basic and Human Rights* [2006] PGNC 201; See also, *In the matter of enforcement of Basic Rights under the Constitution re conditions of detention at Bialla Police Lock-up* (2006) N3022; *Lack of Correctional Service (CS) Facilities in Enga Province, In re* [2010] PGNC 251.

[124] *Re Section 57 of the Constitution of Papua New Guinea, Enforcement of Basic and Human Rights* [2006] PGNC 201.

[125] Ibid [2], [5]–[7].

to deliberate on their applications for pardon.[126] His Honour issued an injunction against any execution and ordered the executive government to staff the Advisory Committee.[127]

Another initiative taken in 2014 implicated Australia.[128] His Honour undertook a human rights inquiry, on his own volition, following public 'reports of alleged human rights violations and complaints about the conditions of detention' at the Manus Island asylum detention centre.[129] The Supreme Court later overturned His Honour's' initiative in an appeal by the government.[130] However, his Honour's action would inspire Opposition Leader Belden Namah to take up the case, eventually leading to the Supreme Court's decision two years later to nullify the detention centre arrangement.[131]

In another landmark case in 2021, Justice Cannings summoned government officials in Madang, including the Governor for Madang Peter Yama and the local Member of Parliament for Madang District Bryan Kramer, to inquire on the deteriorating conditions of the public road system in Madang town.[132] Kramer was also the Minister for Justice in the national government. Justice Cannings reasoned that the neglect of government authorities to fix the deteriorating road conditions amounted to potential human rights breaches and risk of imminent breaches.[133] These cases are in addition to other instances where the courts have used section 57 against state agencies such as the police and the correctional services, ordering them to carry out investigations or attend to human rights breaches.[134]

Section 57 is thus a dynamic provision that firmly provides the judges with a direct oversight function over the executive as well as members of the legislature. It is a unique provision when compared to constitutions globally. Similar provisions are not found in the costitutions of any other Pacific Island countries, including Australia.

Section 57 decisively indicates the judiciary has a reformist and interventionist role in Papua New Guinea society. This is evident in Justice Cannings' judgment:

---

[126] *Re Enforcement of Basic Rights under Section 57 of the Independent State of Papua New Guinea* [2017] PGNC 266.

[127] Ibid [5].

[128] *Re Enforcement of Basic Rights under Sect. 57, Constitution of the Independent State of Papua New Guinea* [2014] PGNC 222.

[129] Ibid [2], [28]–[30].

[130] *Independent State of Papua New Guinea v Transferees* [2015] PGSC 45; *Re Enforcement of Basic Rights under Section 57, Constitution of the Independent State of Papua New Guinea* [2014] PGNC 222, [2], [28]–[30]. (Allegedly with pressure from Australia).

[131] *Namah v Pato* [2016] PGSC 13.

[132] *In Re Effect of Dilapidated Road Conditions on Enforcement of Human Rights in Madang Town* [2021] PGNC 8.

[133] Ibid [9].

[134] *Enforcement of Basic Rights, In re Section 57 Constitution of the Independent State of Papua New Guinea* [2014] PGNC 36; *In re Enforcement of Basic Rights under the Constitution of Papua New Guinea, Section 57* [2014] PGNC 18; *In re Conditions of Detention at Kimbe Police Lock-up* [2006] PGNC 183; *In re Lack of Correctional Service (CS) Facilities in Enga Province* [2010] PGNC 251.

> *Judges in this country do not have the luxury of just being able to sit in court and wait for parties to come to them to resolve their disputes.* The duty of a Judge in PNG is to enforce the human rights, as prescribed by the *Constitution*, and to do so on application or on his or her own initiative, as the circumstances require it.[135] (emphasis added)

While section 57 is indicative of the ingenuity of the drafters in designing the 'home-grown' Constitution, the voluntary oversight function of the judge reflects the role of judicial officers in the colonial courts. Section 23 of the *Native Administration Regulation 1924* (Cth) allowed a colonial judge to, 'of his own accord, summon and try any native whom he has good ground for suspecting has committed an offence, notwithstanding that no complaint has been made by anyone against such native.' It provided that the judge 'shall have the same powers and shall proceed in the same way as if a complaint in respect of such offence had been made.'

However, the intent of the provision under the colonial order was discriminatory and paternalistic. According to the Australian colonial Chief Justice Beaumont Phillips of the Territory of New Guinea Supreme Court, the provision was aimed at arming the colonial judicial officers to deal only with locals, especially those in official positions who 'tend to regard power as a licence…[to be applied in] an arbitrary, even an oppressive way'.[136] The Constitutional Planning Committee broadened the scope of section 57 as part of an extensive accountability system against the abuse of power by all persons.

Other unique aspects of section 57

There are four further aspects of section 57 that reinforces the liberal and interventionist role of the judiciary. First, it allows standing, apart from an aggrieved person,[137] to 'any person who has an interest in the maintenance of the principles of Rule of Law'.[138] This has been interpreted broadly to include other state agencies and incorporated civil societies and community advocacy groups.[139] It corresponds with the liberal approach to *locus standi* in constitutional interpretation matters discussed earlier.

Second, the power of the judges to act on their own initiative is broadened in section 57(5) to include intervening in 'cases of actual or imminent infringement'.

---

[135] *Re Section 57 of the Constitution of Papua New Guinea, Enforcement of Basic and Human Rights* [2006] PGNC 201, [7] (emphasis added).

[136] Letter from Sir Beamount Phillips to Colonel Hubert Murray, 11 October 1946, [15], available online at http://asiapacific.anu.edu.au/pambu/catalogue/index.php/%3bpmUploadsPlugin/view?f=r/pacific-manuscripts-bureau/8/1/81937/PMB_1168_Reel_6sm_item_78.pdf.

[137] *In re Anderson Agiru; Enforcement pursuant to Constitution Section 57* [2002] PNGLR 587; *In re Application for Enforcement of Human Rights under Section 57 of the Constitution, by Jacob Eddie* [2014] PGNC 133.

[138] S 57(2).

[139] *In the Matter of an Application under Section 57 of the Constitution; Application by Individual and Community Rights Advocacy Forum Inc (ICRAF); In re Miriam Willingal* [1997] PGNC 7. The Court granted standing to a 'community interest group' that was legally incorporated with clear objectives to advocate for human rights to apply for enforcement against human rights breaches.

This allows the Court to make anticipatory or pre-emptory orders against potential breaches.[140]

Third, subsection 6 provides that '[t]he jurisdiction and powers of the courts…are in addition to, and not in derogation of, their jurisdiction and powers under any other provision of this Constitution'. The Supreme Court has interpreted this to mean that the orders made under section 57 can be wide-ranging, including compensation and directives for criminal prosecution and for government to undertake certain policy decisions.[141]

Fourth, section 57(3) gives the National Court legislative review powers, directing it to 'make all such orders and declarations as are necessary [including] an order or declaration in relation to a statute at any time after it is made (whether or not it is in force)'.[142] The Supreme Court has taken this direction to mean that an action under section 57 allows the National Court to have 'concurrent powers with the Supreme Court and these powers include declaring a statute to be unconstitutional'.[143] It contrast section 18(2) discussed earlier where the National Court, as a lower court, is restricted to only refer constitutional issues to the Supreme Court.[144]

These additional aspects of section 57 firmly indicate the human rights policing function afforded on the judiciary under the 'home-grown' Constitution is extensive and unprecedented. Although unorthodox to traditional judicial function, it was designed to consolidate constitutional accountability, including enabling judges to respond to development and governance issues. Deputy Chief Justice Kandakasi commented on the usefulness of section 57 in these terms:

> The imperative has been to connect with the immediacy of the events. The courts have been able to project themselves into the "moment of action, to act at the coal face, where the rubber meets the road" so to speak. These kinds of interventions have been very public with much public endorsement.[145]

Section 57 firmly demonstrates the importance the Constitution places on addressing the lack of human rights protection in the colonial era as well as the people's intent

---

[140] *In re Section 57 of the Constitution of Papua New Guinea, Enforcement of Basic and Human Rights* [2006] PGNC 201, [2].

[141] *SCR No 1 of 1977; Re Rights of Person Arrested or Detained* [1977] PGSC 15 (Frost CJ).

[142] S 57(3). The section further states:

> A court that has jurisdiction under Subsection (1) may make all such orders and declarations as are necessary or appropriate for the purposes of this section, and may make an order or declaration in relation to a statute at any time after it is made (whether or not it is in force).

[143] *Dibusa Mining Pty Ltd v Wapula Akipe, Simon Kambe, and Anton Pakena* [1991] PNGLR 265 (Kidu CJ, Woods, Hinchliffe, Sheehan JJ).

[144] That said, the National Court has the discretion to refer the question to the Supreme Court if it considers it necessary under Section 18(2). See *Ikowari v Minister for Foreign Affairs* [2018] PGNC 236, [38]; *Dibusa Mining Pty Ltd v Wapula Akipe, Simon Kambe, and Anton Pakena* [1991] PNGLR 265.

[145] *Morua v China Harbour Engineering Co (PNG) Ltd* [2020] PGNC 16, [47].

for the judiciary to be empowered to play an active and transformative role in Papua New Guinea society.

Inherent power to do justice

The sixth textual indicator is in section 155 of the Constitution. It sets out the structure of the national judicial system and grants two respective powers to the superior courts.[146] First, that the Supreme Court 'has an inherent power to review all judicial acts of the National Court'.[147] Second, that both courts 'have an inherent power to make…orders in the nature of prerogative writs and such other orders as are necessary to do justice in the circumstances of a particular case'.[148] These provisions have raised significant questions on what constitutes 'inherent powers', when can the courts invoke their 'inherent power' and what are the limits.

A landmark case that deals with these issues is *Aihi v The State* (1981).[149] The applicant failed to file an appeal to the Supreme Court within the statutory requirement of 40 days against her criminal conviction at the National Court and applied to file the appeal more than 12 months later. Her appeal was on two grounds. First, that the Supreme Court has 'inherent power to review all judicial acts of the National Court' and second, that the Court has an inherent power 'to do justice in the circumstances of a particular case'. With the latter, she argued that since her constitutional right to appeal was not exhausted, the Court should do justice by granting her appeal.[150]

However, the Court dismissed this latter argument on the basis that her constitutional right was subject to the statutory time limit and was therefore exhausted upon her failure to comply.[151] As to the former, a majority of the Supreme Court held that the 'inherent power to review all judicial acts of the National Court' is entirely discretionary on the Supreme Court and cannot be subjected to any statutory

---

[146] S 155. The National Judicial System

> (2) The Supreme Court
>
> > (a) is the final court of appeal; and
> >
> > (b) has an inherent power to review all judicial acts of the National Court; and
> >
> > (c) has such other jurisdiction and powers as are conferred on it by this Constitution or any other law.
>
> (4) Both the Supreme Court and the National Court have an inherent power to make, in such circumstances as seem to them proper, orders in the nature of prerogative writs and such other orders as are necessary to do justice in the circumstances of a particular case.

[147] S 155(2)(b).

[148] S 155(4).

[149] (No 1) [1981] PGSC 9.

[150] Ibid (unnumbered judgment); S 37(15) provides the constitutional right to appeal.

[151] (No 1) [1981] PGSC 9 (Kidu CJ, Kearney DCJ, Granville, Andrew and Kapi JJ) (unnumbered judgment).

limitation.[152] As a result, the Court granted the appeal despite the application being more than 11 months after the expiration of the statutory appeal period.

Justice Granville, an Australian judge in dissent, considered that the Court's decision was a radical attempt 'to amend the legislative provision—to usurp the function of the legislature—to legislate'.[153] His Honour refused 'the proposition that the Supreme Court has an unfettered discretion to review' and adopted the Anglo-Australian common law position on judicial restraint.[154] However, Chief Justice Buri Kidu rejected Justice Granville's approach as an attempt to curb legitimate judicial power:

> We cannot cut down the powers of this Court if the Constitution has invested it with extra jurisdiction or power. If this Court has been granted inherent powers by the people through the Constitution, we must be bold in stating the fact.[155] (emphasis added)

Chief Justice Kidu, who was the first national Chief Justice, was adamant that the 'home-grown' endeavours of constitution-making and the sovereign power of the people, which underpinned judicial power in Papua New Guinea, were not curtailed by common law:

> *The inherent power of the Supreme Court to review all judicial acts of the National Court emanates from the people through the Constitution.* Whatever the nature or extent of this power might be, it does not derive from any statute or the common law or any prerogative powers of persons or bodies outside Papua New Guinea. *The common law should not and cannot be used to cut down powers given to the Supreme Court by the Constitution.*[156] (emphasis added)

The Supreme Court, in later years, followed similar line of thinking. For instance, in *Application by John Mua Nilkare* (1997) which concerned a judicial review proceeding arising from a Leadership Tribunal, the Court held that its 'inherent powers' under section 155(4) allows it 'to make any orders' considered necessary even beyond those prescribed by the common law and the legislature.[157]

In *Application by John Mua Nilkare*, the Leadership Tribunal found the applicant, a local MP representing Gumine District, guilty of misconduct in office. He appealed to the National Court for a judicial review of the Tribunal's decision. However, while the appeal was pending in the National Court, the appellant applied to the Supreme

---

152 Ibid.

153 Ibid (Granville J).

154 Ibid (Granville J): 'As I have already said, in my view the principles upon which the Supreme Court was intended to exercise its power to review are to be found in the adopted common law, and those do not avail the applicant. Cited Lord Mansfield in *R v Wilkes* [1917] 1 KB 176...'discretion, when applied to a Court of Justice, means sound discretion guided by law. It must be governed by rule, not by humour: it must not be arbitrary, vague, and fanciful; but legal and regular'.

155 Ibid (Kidu CJ).

156 Ibid.

157 *Application by John Mua Nilkare, Review Pursuant to S155(4) of the Constitution* [1997] PGSC 20, [[7]–[8] (Held) (Amet CJ and Los J). The Court held that its power to review is 'not limited to the traditional judicial review basis for grant of review, such as excess of jurisdiction, error in exercise of discretion or unreasonableness in the common law *Wednesbury* sense'.

Court for it to assume jurisdiction pursuant to section 155(4). The Court, based on its broad interpretation of section 155(4), accepted the application, removed the case from the National Court and not only reviewed the Tribunal's decision, but also decided on the penalty instead of remitting the matter back to the Tribunal for a decision on the penalty as prescribed under the *National Court Rules 1983*.[158]

Deputy Chief Justice Kapi in dissent considered that 'to interpret section 155(4) in this manner is...a piece of judicial legislation'.[159] His Honour insisted that the Supreme Court's 'inherent power to do justice' is only 'justice according to law'[160] and the 'law' limits any judicial innovation outside its prescription. His Honour argued that judicial conduct must be 'in light of the doctrine of separation of powers' which mandates keeping the 'law making powers of the National Parliament separate from the functions of the judiciary'.[161] However, Chief Justice Amet, as part of a joint majority judgment, responded in another profoundly liberal direction:

> We believe the power to fashion a remedial order 'to do justice in the circumstances of a case' gives *wide discretion to this court*. It means, in our view, *this court is invested with unfettered discretion to fashion orders that will 'do justice' that is that which is just and fair*.[162] (emphasis added)

Amet CJ went on to reject the notion of 'justice according to law' as 'a narrow interpretation' and instead, held that justice should be according to 'fairness', 'equity' and 'moral principles'.[163] These are fairly broad standards consistent with the liberal character of the judicial power. Australian jurist Justice Bredmeyer had earlier supported this liberal direction of section 155 a few years after Independence, and against the imposing narrow and legalistic influence of Anglo-Australian common law:

> *[T]he Supreme Court and the National Court should not hesitate to use s 155(4) to make new law on occasions* and on other occasions *to declare parts of the English common law and equity inapplicable and inappropriate to the circumstances of Papua New Guinea*.[164] (emphasis added)

The fact that an Australian jurist advocated for the Court's innovative function, particularly its ability to 'make new law', less than a decade after Independence speaks firmly to the liberal nature of the judiciary and the necessity of departing from judicial attitudes drawn from elsewhere that are doubtful or suppressive of the judiciary's transformative role. Both the judgments of Chief Justices Kidu and Amet clearly rejected the common law limitations and fears of judicial discretion and

---

[158] Section 9(4).

[159] *Application by John Mua Nilkare, Review Pursuant to S155(4) of the Constitution* [1997] PGSC 20 (Kapi DCJ) (unnumbered judgment).

[160] *Application by John Mua Nilkare, Review Pursuant to S155(4) of the Constitution* [1997] PGSC 20 (Kapi DCJ) (unnumbered judgment).

[161] Ibid.

[162] Ibid (Amet CJ, Los J) (emphasis added).

[163] Ibid.

[164] *Kupil v The State; Kensi v The State* [1983] PNGLR 350 (Bredmeyer J) (unnumbered judgment) (emphasis added).

promoted section 155 as a dynamic provision capable of effecting a transformative constitution.[165] The reference by Chief Justice Kidu to the people as the source of the judicial powers, which will be examined in detail later in the book, further reinforces the importance of judges not succumbing to the forces and legalistic doctrines that attempt to delegitimise or undermine the liberal powers conferred by the people on the Papua New Guinea judiciary.[166]

The Court has, in recent years, put in place procedural rules to prevent potential abuses of section 155 by applicants bypassing proceedings in the lower courts and directly accessing the Supreme Court and at the back of competing precedents on its scope.[167] However, some judges are cautious that such constraints may lead the Court to 'forever barricad[e] itself with procedural rules' and to adopt narrow interpretations that 'curb or limit a right of recourse to the Supreme Court'.[168]

The consensus thus remains that the Court has a wide discretion for applications seeking orders under section 155. This firmly reflects the liberal character of the judiciary and the dynamic role of the Supreme Court to actively shape notions of justice in Papua New Guinea.

Power to impose sanctions on constitutional breaches

The seventh textual indicator suggesting Papua New Guinea has a liberal judiciary with a transformative function is section 23. This provision grants broad powers to the National Court to prohibit an act or to impose a duty on a person or agency in cases where their actions have breached or are likely to breach their prescribed constitutional duties and prohibitions.[169] The wide scope of remedial powers under

---

[165] *Special Reference By Fly River Provincial Executive Council; Re Organic Law on Integrity of Political Parties and Candidates* [2010] PGSC 3, [109].

[166] Jeffrey D. Pinsler, 'The Inherent Powers of the Court' (1997) *Singapore Journal of Legal Studies* 1, 4–9.

[167] *In re Anderson Giru; Review Pursuant to Sections 155(2) and 155(4) of the Constitution* [2002] PNGLR 27 (Kapi DCJ) (unnumbered judgment).

[168] Ibid (Los J).

[169] S 23. Sanctions.

> (1) Where any provision of a Constitutional Law prohibits or restricts an act, or imposes a duty, then unless a Constitutional Law or an Act of the Parliament provides for the enforcement of that provision the National Court may–
>
> > (a) impose a sentence of imprisonment for a period not exceeding 10 years or a fine not exceeding K10 000.00; or
> >
> > (b) in the absence of any other equally effective remedy under the laws of Papua New Guinea, order the making of compensation by a person (including a governmental body) who is in default, or both, for a breach of the prohibition, restriction or duty, and may make such further order in the circumstances as it thinks proper.
>
> (2) Where a provision of a Constitutional Law prohibits or restricts an act or imposes a duty, the National Court may, if it thinks it proper to do so, make any order that it thinks proper for preventing or remedying a breach of the prohibition, restriction or duty, and Subsection (1) applies to a failure to comply with the order as if it were a breach of a provision of this Constitution.

section 23, including anticipatory orders, complements those prescribed in other parts of the Constitution previously discussed.

In *Re Calling of the Parliament* (1999),[170] the Supreme Court, upon a constitutional reference from the Ombudsman Commission, determined that section 23 gives the National Court power to order the parliament to resume parliamentary sitting if it fails to convene for the required number of days.[171] The Court characterised the sanctions under section 23 as 'very severe' and emphasised that the 'National Court is given very wide powers to' issue other appropriate orders.[172]

A landmark use of section 23 was in 2016 where the National Court directed the Speaker of Parliament to reconvene parliament to address a vote of no-confidence motion against Prime Minister Peter O'Neill.[173] The Speaker, who is an appointee of the government, had postponed the sitting as a political maneuver to avoid the vote of no-confidence. The Court, in an unreported judgement, criticised the Speaker's actions as 'an affront to the rule of law'.[174] Chapter 8 will delve into the signficance of judicial accountability regarding the Speaker's power.

The authority of the National Court to compel the National Parliament to resume its sitting is a significant judicial power as it strikes at the heart of the operations of the other two arms of government and notions of parliamentary sovereignty. It underscores the transformative nature of the Papua New Guinea Constitution that allows the National Court, a lower court, to scrutinise the internal affairs of the highest legislative body, the Parliament.

In *Petrus v Telikom PNG Ltd* (2008), the National Court utilised section 23 to rule that a government-owned telecommunication company had mistreated a group of casual employees who had worked for four years without receiving allowances and benefits typically provided to permanent employees.[175] While the claim for damages was not sufficiently established under the existing employment law or the human rights framework, the Court exercised its discretion under section 23 to award damages.[176]

Granting the superior courts the authority to directly oversee the actions of the legislature and executive and take corrective measures in such instances demonstrates the presence of a liberal judiciary with interventionist powers.

---

(3) Where the National Court considers it proper to do so, it may include in an order under Subsection (2) an anticipatory order under Subsection (1).

[170] *SC Reference No 3 of 1999; Re Calling of the Parliament* [1999] PNGLR 285, [7]–[10] (Held).

[171] Ibid.

[172] Ibid (Kapi DCJ) (unnumbered judgment).

[173] Eric Tlozek, 'PNG court orders the recall of Parliament to hear no-confidence motion in Prime Minister', *ABC News* (online), 12 July 2016.

[174] Ibid.

[175] *Petrus v Telikom PNG Ltd* [2008] PGNC 85, [30].

[176] Ibid.

Power to 'fill the gap' in the implementation of rights and duties

The eighth textual indicator suggesting a liberal judiciary was envisaged under the Papua New Guinea Constitution is section 22. This provision grants the National Court the discretion to establish procedures, policies, and machineries to enforce the rights and duties of individuals and authorities outlined in the Constitution in cases where such things are unavailable or are inadequate in the Constitution or in statutes.[177] Essentially, it empowers the Court to address any deficiencies in the constitutional framework to implement rights and perform duties, including shortcomings in the functioning and administration of the parliament and the executive branch.[178]

A notable case on section 22 is *Moresby Northeast Parliamentary Election Petition* (1977), where the National Court held that if parliament fails to amend election laws that are found to be unconstitutional, the Court may intervene to develop the necessary election procedures and machineries to facilitate the right of citizens to run for Parliament.[179] However, the Court cautioned that this power should only be invoked when other avenues are unavailable, highlighting that the Court possesses a constitutional tool to regulate and intervene directly in public policy issues, including compelling a hesitant executive or inactive legislature to take action.[180]

The provision affords the judiciary the ability to engineer reform and proactively address institutional deficiences. When combined with the human rights oversight mechanisms discussed earlier, section 22 can be utilised to directly monitor governmental inaction in cases where there is a constitutional obligation, thereby upholding the country's commitment to democracy and preserving the integrity of constitutional institutions.

Mandate to develop the Underlying Law

The ninth textual indicator suggesting Papua New Guinea has a liberal judiciary is the mandate to develop an indigenous jurisprudence or body of law known as the 'Underlying Law'.[181] According to the Joe Lynch, a draftsman of the Papua New

---

[177] S 22. Enforcement of the Constitution

The provisions of this Constitution that recognize rights of individuals (including corporations and associations) as well as those that confer powers or impose duties on public authorities, shall not be left without effect because of the lack of supporting, machinery or procedural laws, but the lack shall, as far as practicable, be supplied by the National Court in the light of the National Goals and Directive Principles, and by way of analogy from other laws, general principles of justice and generally-accepted doctrine.

[178] *Re Rights of Person Arrested or Detained [1977] PGSC 15 (Frost CJ); In re Reference to Constitution Section 19(1) by East Sepik Provincial Executive [2011] PGSC 41, [397].*

[179] *Moresby Northeast Parliamentary Election Petition; Lowa v Damena* [1977] PGSC 11 (unnumbered judgment).

[180] *In the Matter of Enforcement of Basic Rights under the Constitution Section 57* [2006] PGNC 29 (Cannings J). In justifying its use, the Court noted that 'the rights and duties conferred by the Constitution are not meant to be illusory, ephemeral or just feel-good principles, but real, tangible, powerful and enforceable obligations capable of immediate effect through court orders and declarations'.

[181] Schedule 2.3.4. JUDICIAL DEVELOPMENT OF THE UNDERLYING LAW.

Guinea Constitution, the underlying law 'means the same in essence as the common law (including the rules of equity)' as it is to be 'enunciated and developed by the courts'.[182]

The constitutional mandate specifically directs judges, when developing this law, to take into account customs and traditional norms as well as relevant common law principles that were in force before Papua New Guinea's Independence.[183] Parliament reinforced its importance by enacting the *Underlying Law Act 2000* (PNG) (the Act) to properly administer its development 'as a coherent system in a manner that is appropriate to the circumstances of the country'.[184]

The Act ranks traditional customs of Papua New Guinea as superior to common law and mandates that judges develop the worthy customs and traditional values into a coherent body of law that is 'specifically designed for Papua New Guinea' and 'adapted to [its] changing circumstances'.[185] In *Magiten v Beggie* (No.2) (2005), the National Court held that 'custom, if it is enforceable, is a superior law to common law [and] the superiority of custom over common law has since been reinforced by the *Underlying Law Act*'.[186]

This mandate to actively develop a body of law extends the liberal role of the judiciary from not only the application and enforcement of the Papua New Guinea Constitution, but also to the development of substantive law. It is an extension, in some respects, of the duty of the superior courts to 'fill a gap' under section 22 discussed earlier. Instead of readily resorting to Anglo-Australian common law, the courts are directed to look to local customs and traditional values, including 'Papua New Guinean procedures and forms of organization,' to formulate legal principles appropriate to its society.[187]

As Justice Sakora observed, this directive to develop the Underlying Law means the Constitution 'goes beyond just vesting the traditional law-finding and law-application functions of the superior courts; [vested] are also law-making powers'.[188] According to Justice Cannings, the mandate to develop the Underlying Law means 'the duty statement of a Papua New Guinea Judge is imposing [as] it includes the

---

In all cases, it is the duty of the National Judicial System, and especially of the Supreme Court and the National Court, to ensure that, with due regard to the need for consistency, the underlying law develops as a coherent system in a manner that is appropriate to the circumstances of the country from time to time, except insofar as it would not be proper to do so by judicial act.

Sections 20, 21, 60; *Underlying Law Act 2000* (PNG) s 5.

182 Joe Lynch, 'The Adoption of an Underlying Law by the Constitution of Papua New Guinea' (1976) 4(1) *Melanesian Law Journal* 37, 38.

183 *Underlying Law Act 2000* (PNG) s 3.

184 *Underlying Law Act 2000* (PNG) s 6; *Magiten v Beggie* (No.2) [2005] PNGLR 647 (Cannings J).

185 *Underlying Law Act 2000* (PNG) ss 5, 21, 60.

186 *Magiten v Beggie* (No.2) [2005] PNGLR 647 (unnumbered judgment).

187 Section 60.

188 *Southern Highlands Provincial Government v Somare, Chairman of the National Executive Council* [2007] PGSC 2, [119] (Sakora J); Bernard Sakora, 'Judicial Law-making' in Peter Sack (ed), *Pacific Constitutions,* (Australian National University, 1982) 257–70.

power and duty to check, examine, critically analyse, develop and that means change, if necessary, the underlying law. If that is judicial legislation, so be it.'[189]

The condition for the formulation of the 'underlying law' is that it can only be formulated in a case where, considering its circumstances, no legislation, customary law or common law is adequately applicable or 'appropriate to the circumstances of Papua New Guinea'.[190] Given judges have the discretion to decide if one of these sources of laws are applicable, they have the latitude to exercise their mandate to develop the Underlying Law. It is a clear invitation and permission for judicial law making. Leaving open for the judges to develop a law based on the 'circumstances of the country' also invites judges to take a socio-economic, cultural and political analysis of the country's affairs.

The importance of the duty to develop the Underlying Law is further reinforced by a tripartite reporting system in the Constitution on the progress of its development. First, the judiciary is obliged to provide an annual 'report on the work of the National Judicial System' to the Parliament and part of that is to 'report on the development of the underlying law'.[191] Second, while the Chief Justice is mainly responsible for compiling the annual report, the Constitution also allows individual judges to provide reports 'on the state, suitability and development of the underlying law, with any recommendations as to improvement that they think it proper to make'.[192] Third, the Constitution also provides for the Constitutional and Law Reform Commission 'to investigate and report to the Parliament and to the National Executive on the development…of the underlying law'.[193]

This elaborate tripartite reporting mechanism demonstrates the importance of the task of developing the Underlying Law and distinguishes it from the way common law is developed. The reporting system is intended to promote accountability among the institutions and to encourage judges to invest in developing an organic body of law instead of opting for ready-made but inappropriate legal principles from other jurisdictions. The reporting mechanism further promotes dialogue between the arms of government and ensures that statutory reforms and enactments directly reflect 'home-grown' judicial developments, echoing the transformative intents of the Papua New Guinea Constitution.

While this overview sets out the constitutional framework of the underlying law, it should be noted that this is often not fully utilised. Some reasons for that failing include lack of interest from Parliament and reluctance and judicial timidity from judges to depart from legal positivism to adopting a direct role of law-making.[194]

---

[189] *Sukuramu v New Britain Palm Oil Ltd* [2007] PGNC 21, [88].

[190] Schedules 2.1.1, 2.3.3; *Underlying Law Act 2000* (PNG) ss 4, 7; *Namah v Pato* [2014] PGSC 1, [23]; *Somare, Re* [1981] PGSC 23.

[191] S 187(1).

[192] S 187(2), schedule 2.3.5.

[193] Schedule 2.6.14.

[194] Bernard Narokobi, 'History and Movement in Law Reform in Papua New Guinea' in David Weisbrot, Abdul Paliwala and Akilagpa Sawyerr, *Law and Social Change in Papua New Guinea* (Butterworths, 1982) 22; David Gonol, 'Enforcement of the Underlying Law: Customary Law Perspective'

Commenting on this judicial attitude in the context of Papua New Guinea, Professor Jean Zorn stated:

> If the courts are to accomplish their task of discovering and developing the underlying law of Papua New Guinea, *the judges need to adopt a jurisprudential philosophy and method that contradicts positivism*, one that gives judges broader scope for the exercise of their discretion and that recognises custom as a source of law.[195] (emphasis added)

The mandate to develop the underlying law as a direct law-making power of judges remains highly necessary and unprecedented. It firmly reinforces the CPC's view of judges as 'leaders', who, with a better understanding of the complex legal issues the people face, have a shared responsibility with Parliament to construct appropriate rules that respond to and govern the Papua New Guinea society.

Power to petition support facilities for constitutional institutions

The tenth textual indicator suggesting Papua New Guinea has a liberal judiciary is section 225. It imposes a duty on all government agencies and service providers to provide adequate facilities to assist the functions of 'all constitutional institutions [and] offices of all constitutional office-holders'.[196] A 'constitutional institution' is broadly defined as any office or institution established or provided for by the Constitution, except the offices of the Governor-General, the Ministers and the National Executive Council'.[197] 'Constitutional office-holders' refer to judges, the Public Prosecutor and the Public Solicitor, the Ombudsman Commissioners, the Electoral Commissioner, the Clerk of Parliament and the Auditor-General amongst others.[198]

The National Court has used its general enforcement powers under section 23, either on its own initiative or from an application, to enforce the duty under section 225 against statutory bodies and service providers that either interfere with or fail to provide adequate services to the constitutional agencies. This include corporatised public enterprises.[199]

(Paper presented at the National Conference on the Judicial Development of the Underlying Law, Port Moresby, November 27–28, 2017).

[195] Jean Zorn, 'Common Law Jurisprudence and Customary Law' in R.W. James and I. Fraser, *Legal Issues in a Developing Society* (University of Papua New Guinea, 1990) 104–5.

[196] S 225. Provision of Facilities, etc.

> Without limiting the generality of any other provision of this Constitution, it is the duty of the National Government and of all other governmental bodies, and of all public office-holders and institutions, to ensure, as far as is within their respective legal powers, that all arrangements are made, staff and facilities provided and steps taken to enable and facilitate, as far as may reasonably be, the proper and convenient performance of the functions of all constitutional institutions and of the offices of all constitutional office-holders.

[197] S 221.

[198] S 221.

[199] *PNG Power Ltd v Augerea* [2013] PGSC 53; SC1245 (70) (Kandakasi, Manuhu, Kawi JJ).

A notable invocation of section 225 was in the case of *Re Constitution section 225* (2011)[200] where the National Court, in response to a lack of building infrastructure to house the court hearing, ordered the government officials on its own volition 'to collaborate and…provide adequate facilities for the proper and convenient performance…of the National Court'.[201] The Court reprimanded the government's inefficiency, citing it as causing a 'constitutional mockery'.[202]

In the case of *Operation of National Court in The Eastern Highlands and Simbu Provinces* (1990),[203] the Court, again acting on its own volition, rejected an administrative fiat by the Ministry of Finance to reduce the budgetary allocation for the judiciary as contrary to section 225. The Court held that the fiat would negatively impact the functioning of the judiciary.[204] The Court acknowledged that while it 'does not mean that the courts or other constitutional offices must be given everything they ask for in the [budget] estimates, [especially in] times of financial difficulty', it defended its action against what it considered as an unjustifiable decision that could jeopardise the legitimate operations of a constitutional agency.[205]

In the case of *Lack of Water Supply to Mount Hagen National Court* (2011), Justice Makail of the National Court acted on his own volition to summon the Branch Manager of the Papua New Guinea Water Board, a state-owned entity, for failing 'to provide water supply to the Mt Hagen National Court premises'.[206] Justice Makail held that the absence of water supply is 'a hindrance to the dispensation of justice', constituting a breach of section 225.[207]

In *PNG Power Ltd v Augerea* (2013), the Supreme Court Registrar initiated proceedings against the national electricity company, which was predominantly state-owned, due to power outages during court sessions. The Supreme Court determined that despite the company's corporatisation, it still represented a state entity and was required to 'maintain power supply to the National Court premises at all time…[even] in the event of a planned or unplanned power outage'.[208]

In *National Court Circuit* (1989), the Department of Justice failed to cover the accommodation costs for lawyers from the Public Prosecutor's office. The National Court, acting on its own volition, directed the Department to make the

---

200 *In re Constitution Section 225; Re National Court circuit to Bali and Vitu Island* [2011] PGNC 266.

201 Ibid (Held (4)) (Kawi J).

202 Ibid [10].

203 *Operation of National Court in The Eastern Highlands and Simbu Provinces; Re Constitution S23(2), Constitution S225* [1990] PNGLR 82 (Brunton J) (unnumbered judgment).

204 Ibid.

205 Ibid.

206 *In Re Lack of Water Supply to Mount Hagen National Court* [2011] PGNC 319, [5], [11], [12]. The official was reminded that the Court 'deserves the highest respect from the National Government, governmental bodies and public institutions'.

207 Ibid.

208 *PNG Power Ltd v Augerea* [2013] PGSC 53, [3], [70]; Charles Moi, 'PNG Power in contempt', *The National* (online), 09 August 2013.

payment, citing that the failure to support the Public Prosecutor's office hindered its constitutional obligation to administer justice.[209]

These cases exemplify the protective nature of section 225 which shields constitutional institutions from neglect or abuse by government and private agencies. Section 225 is another of the provisions where the drafters of the Constitution demonstrated ingenuity in mitigating possible interference and adverse action against the operations of constitutional institutions.

The provision not only grants constitutional institutions an automatic access to redress but extends the voluntary enforcement powers of the superior courts. The latter means the superior courts are able to intervene proactively when constitutional institutions or officeholders face obstacles in seeking redress, such as administrative hurdles, political pressures, or adverse policy decisions.

This provision thus expands the judiciary's role beyond traditional legal matters to include oversight of public policy and commercial decisions, reflecting a liberal judiciary with interventionist powers to safeguard the effective implementation of the transformative Constitution.

Semi-enforceability of the NGDPs and BSOs

The eleventh textual indicator suggesting Papua New Guinea has a liberal judiciary is the semi-enforceability of the National Goals and Directive Principles (NGDPs) and the Basic Social Obligations (BSOs). The NGDPs and the BSOs are purely socio-political statements that outline the vision for the country's development.

The Papua New Guinea Constitution explicitly states that the NGDPs and BSOs are non-justiciable.[210] However, it mandates that 'nevertheless, it is the duty of all governmental bodies to apply and give effect to them as far as lies within their respective powers'.[211] The Supreme Court has interpreted this to mean that the NGDPs and BSOs are 'elevated to a more important position,' requiring different arms of government to consider them when making decisions.[212]

In addition to the NGDPs and the BSOs being included as 'aids to interpretation' in the Constitution,[213] and in contrast to its 'non-justiciability' status for courts, the Constitution permits the Ombudsman Commission to enforce or consider the NGDPs and the BSOs as a basis for its investigations.[214]

An example of a notable case in which the superior courts dealt with the enforceability of the NGDPs and BSOs was the case of *Medaing v Ramu Nico Management* (MCC) Ltd (2011), where the National Court ruled that while a proposed mining system may have been compliant with the *Environment Act 2000* (PNG), it was

---

[209] *National Court Circuit, Southern Highlands Province, Re* [1989] PGNC 70.

[210] Ss 25, 63.

[211] Ss 25(2), 63(2).

[212] *Ref By Simbu Provincial Executive* [1987] PGLawRp 151 (unnumbered judgment).

[213] S 24.

[214] S 219; For a discussion on the enforceability of the NGDPs, see Vergil Narokobi, *The implementation of Papua New Guinea's national goals and directive principles and basic social obligations* (PhD Thesis, Victoria University of Wellington, 2016) 67–70.

nevertheless contrary to the NGDPs related to the protection of 'natural resources and environment'.[215] The case was later appealed and a majority of a three-member bench Supreme Court overturned the decision. However, the National Court's ruling illustrates the potential for courts to make greater use of the NGDPs as a basis for judicial review or a determinative factor in judicial construction.[216]

The importance of the NGDPs and the BSOs to judicial construction was further affirmed in the case of *Bernard v Duban* [2016] PGNC 121, which dealt with the issue of obtaining consent from landowners of a petroleum resource site. Justice Kandakasi (as he then was), remarked:

> [I]t is important that the question of what is the relevant legal framework for petroleum related development in the country must start with the country's *Constitution*...The founding fathers of the *Constitution* considered it important that the country's development and future should be guide by a set of national goals and directive principles.[217]

His Honour went on to observe that

> [t]hese goals and directive principles are of course non justiciable. Nevertheless, they are serious and important principles. They are to guide government, policy and all other decision makers, including the Courts for the betterment and the future of our peoples, their cultures, traditions, societies and environments as against the pressures development and a modern PNG can impose upon our people.[218]

The treatment of the NGDPs and BSOs by the judiciary has demonstrated that while there may not yet be explicit judicial endorsement, there is firm indication of indirect justiciability through the broad interpretative and enforcement tools available to the courts. The courts' ability to engage with the socio-economic and political statements in the NGDPs and BSOs demonstrates the intent of the constitutional drafters for judges to be attuned to the wishes of the people espoused in these statements and the larger transformative intents of the Constitution.

'Constitutional Laws speak from time to time'

The twelfth and final textual indicator suggesting Papua New Guinea has a liberal judiciary is Schedule 1.4, which states that the 'Constitutional Laws speak from time to time'. The Supreme Court construed the provision to mean that '[t]he Constitution is a living document, dynamic in character and it speaks from time to time'.[219]

The notion that 'law speaks from time to time' denotes a dynamic approach to interpretation in which contemporary conditions shape the meaning and understanding of the law or in other words, the law speaks to 'modern needs'.[220] This means the language of the statute remains but the interpretation of its meaning is changed

---

[215] *Medaing v Ramu Nico Management* (MCC) Ltd [2011] PGNC 95 [141].

[216] *Medaing v Ramu Nico Management (MCC) Ltd* [2011] PGSC 40.

[217] *Bernard v Duban* [2016] PGNC 121, [22].

[218] Ibid.

[219] *Reference by the Ombudsman Commission re the Organic Law on Provincial Governments and Local-Level Governments (Amendment No 10) Law 2006* (2010) SC1058, [28].

[220] Aharon Barak, *Purposive Interpretation in Law* (Princeton University Press, 2005) 41.

'to adapt the law to contemporary conditions'.[221] It requires proactively formulating appropriate rules and dealing with issues where the legislature fail to keep up with the changing conditions of the society. As Sir Richard Scott VC from the House of Lords puts it, 'an "always speaking" construction...takes account of development which has taken place since the provision [in question] was enacted...'.[222]

Taken together with the highly liberal interpretative approaches and tools discussed earlier, the role of the Papua New Guinea judiciary in legal interpretation goes beyond the traditional expectations and black-letter law approaches. The courts are empowered to adjudicate with the intent of actively responding to and influencing larger socio-economic and political charge, in tune with the changing circumstances of Papua New Guinean society.[223]

4 Conclusion

The twelve textual indicators in the Constitution, as interpreted by the courts, firmly indicate that the 'home-grown' Constitution entrenched a liberal judiciary. Many of the provisions are extraordinary and unique when measured against comparative jurisdictions globally. The Constitution elevate the role of the judiciary to ensure it actively polices, reforms, and guards the democratic and constitutional realms of the country.

The powers established for the judiciary are revolutionary, considering the country was under Australia's conservative judicial system for over seventy-five years. The above discussion consolidates the argument in Chap. 4 that Papua New Guinea has a transformative constitution in which the judiciary is intended to have a broader social interventionist and reformative function capable of shaping the development of the country.

Soon after independence, Australian jurist Deputy Chief Justice Prentice, alarmed by the wide powers of the judiciary, described it as 'frightening'.[224] However, the Constitutional Panning Committee, from their exhaustive consultation, found the liberal character of the judiciary as appropriate to the circumstances of the country. Justice Sakora relevantly affirmed:

> It can be seen that the judiciary in PNG, unlike its counterpart in other countries, has an explicit and far-reaching law-making responsibility to discharge. Our judges have to do

---

[221] Ibid.

[222] *Victor Chandler International v Customs and Excise Commissioners and another* [2000] 2 All ER 315, 322–3.

[223] J. Raz, 'On the Authority and Interpretation of Constitution: Some Preliminaries' in L. Alexander, *Constitutionalism: Philosophical Foundations* (Cambridge University Press, 1998) 152, 177.

[224] *Peter v South Pacific Brewery* [1976] PNGLR 537, 555.

> more than just perform their traditional functions of applying the law. They are in a unique position to participate fully in the overall development of the country.[225]

The liberal powers of the judiciary are not to be feared. They do not imply a license for judicial governance. Instead, they affirm the judiciary's shared responsibility as an agent of societal development and as an implementer of the Constitution's transformative intentions. By virtue of their judicial oath, judges have a duty to exercise their expansive powers granted by the people, vigilantly protecting them against subversive entities, ideologies and influences. In upholding this duty, the judiciary must anticipate that, on occasion, it will encounter tensions, especially with the other branches of government, as the next chapter will demonstrate.

[225] Bernard Sakora, 'Judicial Law-Making under the Papua New Guinea Constitution' in Peter Sack (ed), *Pacific Constitutions* (Australian National University, 1982) 263.

Chapter 6
Case Studies: Tensions and Constitutional Crises

Abstract This chapter discusses two key cases studies of disputes between the executive and the judiciary, wherein the former rejected the liberal and interventionist role of the judiciary: *Rooney* case in 1979 and the *East Sepik Province* case (Somare-O'Neill) in 2011. The resulting tension between the executive and the judiciary led to constitutional crises, including mass resignation of judges in the case of *Rooney* and charge of sedition against judges in the *East Sepik Province* case. The chapter analyses how, despite the liberal role of the judiciary being firmly entrenched in the Constitution, misunderstandings continue. It demonstrates that these misunderstandings are rooted in outdated doctrinal arguments regarding the supremacy of parliament and a narrow interpretation of the doctrine of separation of powers, wherein the judiciary is expected to have a subservient role. It argues that such assertions have no place under the 'home-grown' Constitution and suggest a need to reassess these doctrinal foundations.

Keywords Judiciary and the executive · Constitutional crisis · Judicial power · Interventionist judiciary · Doctrine of separation of powers · Activism

1 Introduction

The implementation of the liberal powers of the judiciary has sometimes led to tensions with the other two arms of government, the legislature, and the executive. More often, the root cause has been a lack of understanding of the liberal powers of the judiciary under the 'home-grown' Constitution. The two most significant cases illustrating this tension, resulting in constitutional crises, are the *Rooney* case in 1987 and the *East Sepik Province case* (Somare-O'Neill) case in 2011. This chapter discusses how these, and other cases, demonstrate different understandings of the role of the judiciary perpetuated by a certain conception of the separation of powers doctrine in Papua New Guinea.

B. Kama, *Rethinking Judicial Power in Papua New Guinea*,
https://doi.org/10.1007/978-981-97-2946-3_6

2 Judicial Review and Constitutional Tensions

Judicial review has become a cornerstone of almost all democracies, including Papua New Guinea, since the pioneering decision of the United States Supreme Court in *Marbury v Madison* (1803). The Court established that all actions of the executive and legislative arms of government are subject to the American Constitution, with the judiciary having the sole prerogative to make judgments on their constitutionality.[1] Papua New Guinea proceeded on the basis that judicial review is fundamental to its constitutional system. The scope of judicial review was highlighted in Chap. 5.

Despite the entrenched nature of judicial review, disagreements have arisen regarding its scope and the role of the judiciary in enforcing the constitutional system against the other branches of government. The resulting tensions are somewhat expected. Both the drafters of the Constitution and the Supreme Court have acknowledged that the judicial review 'role would involve the courts in PNG in political controversy and sometimes in confrontation with the executive and other branches of government.'[2] However, the extent of and the basis for these tensions have revealed a deep misunderstanding about the role of the judiciary under the 'home-grown' Constitution. This chapter analyses two significant cases of constitutional crisis to demonstrate the tensions and the underlying doctrinal disputes on the doctrine of separation of powers.

2.1 Constitutional Crisis of 1979: Rooney Case *(No. 2) (1979)*

The first major case of judicial review that demonstrated the differing conceptions about the role of the judiciary and the doctrine of separation of powers in Papua New Guinea was the *Rooney Case* in 1979.[3] Both the judges of the Supreme Court and legal scholars described it at that time as the country's first 'constitutional crisis'.[4] Justice Kearney of the Papua New Guinea Supreme Court characterised it as 'our *Marbury v Madison* [moment, albeit] a little more quickly than did the Americans,' in reference to the fact that the case occurred only four years after Papua New Guinea's Independence.[5]

[1] 5 US (1 Cranch) 137 (1803); See for instance, Mark V. Tushnet, *Arguing Marbury V. Madison* (Stanford University Press, 2005) 40.

[2] CPC Report 1974, Chapter 8 [144]; Enforcement Pursuant to Constitution section 57, Application by Gabriel Dusava [1998] PGSC 59, per Sakora J.

[3] *The Public Prosecutor v Nahau Rooney* (No. 2) (1979) PGSC 23 (11 September 1979) (unnumbered judgment).

[4] Ibid (Wilson and Grenville-Smith JJ); David Weisbrot, 'Papua New Guinea: Judges and Politicians' (Part 1) (1979) 4 *Legal Service Bulletin* 240.

[5] *The Public Prosecutor v Nahau Rooney* (No. 2) (1979) PGSC 23 (Kearney J) (unnumbered judgment).

Facts and Issues

The case concerned the revocation of the work visa of an American academic, Dr Ralph Premdas, on 07 June 1979, on the basis that he breached his visa conditions.[6] Premdas applied to the National Court and was granted an injunction against a deportation notice. Premdas argued that the deportation notice breached principles of natural justice and other constitutional rights—arguments of a constitutional nature, and subsequently referred to the Supreme Court for deliberation.

On 13 July 1979, while the Supreme Court review was pending, the Minister for Justice, Nahau Rooney, wrote to Chief Justice William Prentice and expressed her disappointment in the judicial intervention. Prentice CJ was one of the Australian colonial judges who continued after Independence. Minister Rooney argued that 'it is up to the Elected Government and *no one else* to decide what criteria are used to deport foreigners'.[7]

Minister Rooney further argued that the Court's decision demonstrated its failure to understand the 'principle of being a Papua New Guinean, [stating that it] transcends any semantic or legalistic argument.' She asserted that 'the court has jeopardized its independence and neutrality by intervening in a matter which is obviously the sole prerogative of the Government'.[8] The Minister urged 'the judiciary to make a greater effort to use their discretion effectively to develop the National legal system in the context of a proud and growing National consciousness' (sic).[9]

Chief Justice Prentice replied in a letter to the Minister two days later, on 13 July 1979, that he was 'shocked [of] what appear[ed] to be the grave improprieties of [the Minister's] letter'.[10] His Honour clarified that the 'judges of the National and Supreme Court will not accept directions from or pressure by the Minister for Justice or anyone else,' and that they 'will not be deterred from carrying out to the best of [their] abilities the role given [to them] by the Constitution'.[11]

Minister Rooney responded four days later, on 17 July 1979, contending that she was merely 'raising some grey areas in which there is a potential area of conflict between the executive and the judiciary'.[12] She noted that her 'chief concern [was] the integrity of the Government and [that] the citizen's trust in their elected Government should always be maintained'. The Minister cautioned that 'the Government has the power and authority to act immediately and decisively against any foreigner who

[6] *Premdas v The State* [1979] PGSC 20 (1 September 1979). Premdas' engagements were considered by the government to be 'disruptive and detrimental to the good government of [the] country' (unnumbered judgment).

[7] *The Public Prosecutor v Nahau Rooney* (No. 2) (1979) PGSC 23 (Raine DCJ reproduced the letter dated 11 July 1979).

[8] Ibid.

[9] Ibid (Raine DCJ). The copies of the letter were found to be circulated 'very, very widely' including to the Prime Minister, the Opposition Leader, fellow ministers and to all the judges of the National and Supreme Courts.

[10] Ibid.

[11] Ibid.

[12] Ibid.

may threathen (sic) the security or be seen to undermine the sovereignity (sic) of the Nation'.[13] The Supreme Court perceived the latter statement as a tacit warning to the judges of the National and Supreme Courts, as all of them were foreigners.[14]

In a separate letter to the Opposition Leader, the Minister demonstrated the underlying differences in the understanding of the role of the judiciary and its origins with a prediction of future tensions:

> My letter to the Chief Justice which has also been circulated to all members of the judiciary and to all Ministers *is concerned with the fundamental issue of the separation of powers between the judiciary and the legislature. It must be remembered that the power of the judiciary has been given to them by the elected legislature. This issue effects (sic) any Government now and in the future.*[15] (emphasis added)

The Minister concluded that 'the foreign judges on the bench are only interested in administration of foreign laws, and not the feelings and aspirations of the Nation's political leaders'.[16]

Contempt Charges and the Court Decision

The Office of the Public Prosecutor intervened and instituted contempt of court proceedings against Minister Rooney on charges of scandalising the courts and for interfering with the course of justice. The case provided an opportunity for the Full Court of the Supreme Court, comprised of all foreign judges, to respond. The decision was handed down on 11 September 1979, five days before the country's fourth anniversary of Independence.

Deputy Chief Justice Raine remarked that 'the Executive, through the Minister for Justice [appeared as the] ultimate, or near ultimate repository of power [while] the judiciary was plainly told to "toe the line"'.[17] Justice Saldanha rebuked that the Constitution 'is not to be brushed aside lightly at the capricious whim of a wayward Minister'.[18] Justice Wilson described the Minister's actions as indicative of a 'totalitarian approach' and that the 'Executive arm of the National Government as above the law'.[19]

Justice Greville Smith considered that the Minister's letters amounted to 'a splenetic political attack upon the judges which exceeded all bounds of moderation and reason, and was clearly calculated to undermine confidence in the courts'.[20] Only Justice Kearney dissented on the seriousness of the charge on the premises that 'the novelty of the case [and] the fact of recent Independence' warranted special

---

[13] Ibid.

[14] Ibid (Saldanha and Kearney JJ).

[15] *The Public Prosecutor v Nahau Rooney* (No. 2) (1979) PGSC 23 (emphasis added).

[16] Interview on *National Broadcasting Corporation Radio*, 20 July 1979, cited in Ibid (Raine DCJ and Saldanha, Kearney, Wilson JJ).

[17] *The Public Prosecutor v Nahau Rooney* (No. 2) (1979) PGSC 23 (Raine DCJ).

[18] Ibid (Saldanha J).

[19] Ibid (Wilson J). His Honour rejected the shallow content of the Minister's apologies as amounting to 'no apologies at all'.

[20] Ibid (Greville Smith J).

consideration.[21] The majority judges sentenced Minister Rooney to eight months imprisonment.[22]

However, the prison sentence was short-lived as Prime Minister Michael Somare intervened to release Minister Rooney after a day in prison. Somare appointed himself as the acting Minister for Justice and used his discretion in that capacity under section 615 of the *Criminal Code Act 1974* (PNG) to release the Minister on license. In response, three of the five sitting judges of the Court together with the Chief Justice resigned. Earlier in the proceedings, the trial judge also resigned, thus five judges out of the eight foreign judges on the National and Supreme Courts resigned. This escalation made the *Rooney Case* the country's first constitutional crisis.

Implications on the Understandings of Judicial Power

The *Rooney* case demonstrates that the Executive did not expect an assertive form of judicial review in the context of Papua New Guinea. The Minister's differing view of the judicial role was evident in the argument that the injunction was contrary to 'the principle of being a Papua New Guinean [that] transcends any semantic or legalistic argument'.[23]

The 'principle of being a Papua New Guinean' includes respecting the decisions of those in leadership positions, including tribal leaders, often without much questioning of the merits of the decisions.[24] This 'principle' coincided with the colonial perception of parliamentary supremacy that the political leaders inherited, which elevates the parliament and consequently the ruling government above the judiciary. It was reinforced by the Minister's admission that her primary concern was 'with the fundamental issue of the separation of powers between the judiciary and the legislature' and that the judges ought to 'remember that the power of the judiciary has been given to them by the elected legislature'.[25]

This statement implies that the people, through the parliament, established the Constitution and, by doing so, created and gave to the judiciary its powers. It thus assumes that the judiciary is subservient to the legislature.[26] However, as it will become clear later in this chapter, this democratic legitimacy argument does not apply to the context of Papua New Guinea in which the people are the repository of all powers.

---

[21] Ibid (Kearney J). However, his Honour held that 'these scandalizing statements were not made by just anybody [but by] a Minister for Justice, in relation to courts, [hence] [t]he comments must be strongly disapproved'.

[22] Ibid (Wilson J).

[23] The *Public Prosecutor v Nahau Rooney* (No. 2) (1979) PGSC 23 (11 September 1979) (Letter reproduced in the judgment).

[24] Paul Sillitoe, *An Introduction to the Anthropology of Melanesia: Culture and Tradition* (Cambridge University Press, 1998) 99–100.

[25] The *Public Prosecutor v Nahau Rooney* (No. 2) (1979) PGSC 23 (11 September 1979) (Letter reproduced in the judgment).

[26] A. V. Dicey, *Introduction to the Study of the Law of the Constitution* (First published 1885, Palgrave MacMillian, 10th ed, 1959) 39–40.

The case thus demonstrated a struggle in the formative years of Papua New Guinea between an executive government, whose understandings of judicial power was influenced by the traditional leadership model and the autocratic practices and ideas that underpinned colonialism, and a judiciary intended to function differently as co-equals in a newly established constitutional system. The intervention of the Prime Minister and the resulting mass resignation of the Supreme Court judges ultimately reinforced this struggle between the two arms of government. This contestation continued in contemporary Papua New Guinea, most significantly demonstrated in the 2011–2012 constitutional crisis.

2.2 Constitutional Crisis of 2011–2012: ESP *(2011) and* Marat *(2012)*

The second major incident of tension arising from the exercise of judicial review powers, and in which the differing conceptions of the role of the judiciary and the doctrine of separation of powers were demonstrated, took place between 2011 and 2012. It gave rise to two Supreme Court references—*Reference to Constitution section 19(1) by East Sepik Provincial Executive* (2011)[27] (herein referred to as the 'ESP Case') and in *References by Allan Marat and the National Parliament* (2012)[28] (herein referred to as the 'Marat Case').

2.2.1 ESP Case 2011

The issue in the ESP Case was whether Prime Minister Michael Somare, who was in Singapore for five months seeking treatment for a heart condition, should be disqualified as the Prime Minister because of physical and mental incapacity. Section 142 of the Constitution provides that a Prime Minister can be dismissed from office where he or she is deemed to be 'unfit by reason of physical or mental incapacity to carry out the duties' of a Prime Minister.[29] The five months absence was beyond the statutory limit of three months leave allowed for illness.[30]

The procedure for the removal of the Prime Minister under section 142 starts with the appointment of two doctors by the Papua New Guinea Medical Board upon request from the Governor-General.[31] The doctors then share their findings on the

[27] *Reference to Constitution Section 19(1) by East Sepik Provincial Executive* [2011] PGSC 41 (12 December 2011).

[28] Reference by Allan Marat & Reference by the National Parliament [2012] PGSC 20 (21 May 2012).

[29] S 142(5)(c); Prime Minister and National Executive Council Act 2002 (PNG) s 6(10).

[30] *Prime Minister and National Executive Council Act 2002* (PNG) s 5.

[31] S 142(5); *Reference to Constitution Section 19(1) by East Sepik Provincial Executive* [2011] PGSC 41, [79].

health of the Prime Minister with the Governor-General, who will then present a report to the Parliament.[32] Parliament then decides whether a new Prime Minister should be elected and proceeds with an election in Parliament.

Under the Constitution, the Governor-General is strictly instructed, in the performance of his or her duties, to 'act only with, and in accordance with, the advice of the National Executive Council (Cabinet)'.[33] There are no reserve powers afforded to the Governor-General as in the case of Australia despite the understanding that reserve powers are an 'indispensable feature of British notions of responsible government'.[34] The Papua New Guinea Governor-General is therefore described as 'toothless…mere rubber stamp' with 'virtually no freedom of action'.[35] Sir Wiwa Korowi, a former Governor-General, poignantly noted that 'the Governor-General is very simply a constitutional rubber stamp who has no executive powers of veto'.[36]

The very docile nature of the Governor-General under the Constitution meant that the constitutional processes to remove Prime Minister Somare were supposed to be triggered by Somare's own Cabinet. However, that did not happen. Concerned with the delay, members of parliament moved a motion on 2 August 2011 to disqualify Somare, and on the same day, in a vote of 70–24, elected Peter O'Neill as the new Prime Minister. In response, Somare's provincial government, East Sepik Province, invoked its standing under section 19 to challenge the constitutionality of Parliament's action in the Supreme Court.

There were two intervening events that took place before and during the proceedings, which are worth highlighting as they also impacted the Court's judgment and will inform the discussions in later parts of the book. The first concerned the Somare government. Leading up to his removal, there was widespread dissatisfaction at his government for lack of service delivery and accusations of high-level corruption, among other issues. The Ombudsman Commission brought twenty-five charges of 'misconduct in office' against Somare, and public resentment against his government intensified when he strenuously challenged the charges in the courts for two years and refused to resign or step aside as the Prime Minister to allow for an investigation.[37]

The Supreme Court eventually quashed Somare's challenge in 2010, allowing a Leadership Tribunal to be convened in early 2011 to prosecute Somare. The Tribunal comprised three specially hired overseas judges, one each from Australia, New

---

[32] S 142(5)(c).

[33] S 86(2).

[34] George Winterton, 'Reserved Powers in an Australian Republic' (1993) 12 *University of Tasmania Law Review* 249, 252.

[35] *Reference to Constitution Section 19(1) by East Sepik Provincial Executive* [2011] PGSC 41, [517]; Reference by *Allan Marat & Reference by the National Parliament* [2012] PGSC 20, [157]; Imtiaz Omar, 'Parliament, Executive and the Court in PNG' (1996) 70 *Australian Law Journal* 313, 314.

[36] Omar, Ibid.

[37] *Somare v Manek* [2011] PGSC 17, [6]–[12] (Salika DCJ, Kirriwom and Kandakasi, JJ); *Re Reference to Constitution Section 19(1) by East Sepik Provincial Executive* [2011] PGSC 41, [211]–[212].

Zealand, and the United Kingdom.[38] The Tribunal found him guilty of thirteen of the twenty-five charges.[39] However, to the surprise and dissatisfaction of many, including Supreme Court judges,[40] Somare was only suspended for two weeks without pay.[41]

The second set of incidents concerned the O'Neill government. At the initial stages of the hearing into the *ESP Case*, Prime Minister O'Neill publicly questioned the integrity and independence of Chief Justice Sir Salamo Injia, who was an appointee of the Somare government.

On 9 December 2011, three days before the Court gave its decision in the *ESP Case*, O'Neill's cabinet again publicly accused the Chief Justice of colluding with Somare and applied for the Chief Justice to recuse himself.[42] The Court, on which the Chief Justice himself presided, rejected the application.[43] On the same day, Parliament unanimously moved a motion to declare Somare's seat as the member for the East Sepik Provincial seat vacant on the basis that Somare failed to attend the required number of parliamentary sittings in a year.[44] Parliament argued that its decision to remove Somare is 'irrespective of the Court decision that is [forthcoming]' because 'the Courthouse belongs to the lawyers' and the Parliament belongs to leaders concerned with issues of national importance.[45] Parliament's view was clearly indicative of a differing conception of the judiciary as an institution of lesser importance.

Judgment of the Supreme Court

On 12 December 2011, a five member Supreme Court in a split decision of 3–2, with the Chief Justice in the majority, ruled in favour of Somare as the legitimate Prime Minister.[46] The judges reached different conclusions but unanimously agreed that an expansive, fair and liberal standard of constitutional interpretation should be applied.[47] For instance, Injia CJ, who provided the leading judgment for the majority, held that 'a broad and expansive approach is favoured over the strict, technical and

---

38 *Somare v Manek* [2011] PGSC 17, [10]; *In re Michael Somare; Recommendation on penalty* [2011] PGLT 1.

39 *Re Reference to Constitution Section 19(1) by East Sepik Provincial Executive* [2011] PGSC 41, [202]–[212], [334], [592]–[93]; *In re Michael Somare; Recommendation on penalty* [2011] PGLT 1.

40 *Re Reference to Constitution Section 19(1) by East Sepik Provincial Executive* [2011] PGSC 41, [202]–[212], [334], [592]–[93].

41 *In re Michael Somare; Recomendation on penalty* [2011] PGLT 1, [59].

42 'CJ 'secretly' met with Somare', *Post Courier* (online), 9 December 2011.

43 Noted in *Reference by Allan Marat & Reference by the National Parliament* [2012] PGSC 20, [241], Appendix C.

44 Noted in *Reference by Allan Marat & Reference by the National Parliament* [2012] PGSC 20, [256].

45 Noted in *Reference by Allan Marat & Reference by the National Parliament* [2012] PGSC 20, [19] (Injia CJ) (citing parliamentary Hansard).

46 *Re Reference to Constitution Section 19(1) by East Sepik Provincial Executive* (ESP Case) [2011] PGSC 41 (Injia CJ, Kirriwom and Gavana JJ).

47 Ibid [9], [61], [170]–[71], [535], [682]–[83], [779].

legalistic approach' in this matter.[48] A closer examination of the judges' opinions is warranted to understand how this liberal approach shaped their decisions, as well as their conceptions of their power, and how it differs to that held by the O'Neill and Somare governments.

Responding to the O'Neill Government

A primary argument advanced by the O'Neill government was that the Court should not interfere with Parliament's internal matters of removing and electing a new Prime Minister.[49] However, the majority judges found that the proper procedures and processes to replace a Prime Minister were not followed.[50] Injia CJ described the members of Parliament as being 'anxious, frustrated and impatient' and that 'frustration and emotion took the better of members of Parliament'.[51] Justice Kirriwom was more forthright that 'it was indeed an illegal seizure of government by the Opposition…with all attendant features and hallmarks of a *coup d'etat*.'[52]

The majority judges agreed that there were widespread concerns about the Somare government and that the failure by Somare's own Cabinet to trigger the reporting process was unreasonable.[53] However, they insisted that despite these failings, the constitutional and parliamentary processes had to be followed and the Court cannot 'shirk from its duty' to hold O'Neill accountable for acting outside these processes.[54] Justice Kirriwom remarked that 'the *Constitution* was abused and violated or even sabotaged for the sake of elevating him (O'Neill) to the office of Prime Minister' and cautioned that 'condoning the breach' would mean 'setting a bad precedent that can be repeated again in the future'.[55] Justice Gavara-Nanu summed up the majority's devotion to procedures and processes:

> Express constitutional provisions which set out mandatory requirements and processes must be fully complied with and given effect to. Considerations outside of those constitutional requirements must not be allowed to stand in the way of such express mandatory constitutional requirements and processes so as to compromise and to circumvent those mandatory constitutional requirements and processes.[56]

---

[48] Ibid [9]. Claiming to adhere to this standard of constitutional interpretation, his Honour explained: 'I am of course obliged by the *Constitution*…to adopt an expansive approach, and to accord a fair and liberal meaning to the provision in question' [61].

[49] Ibid [73], [727]–[28].

[50] Ibid.

[51] Ibid [87].

[52] Ibid [697] (Kirriwom J). His Honour further held that '[t]ruth and honesty must prevail above subversion and disquiet' and that 'this is a case of an illegal take-over of government in a very clever and carefully crafted motion disguised in terms of the Constitution' [727] (emphasis added).

[53] Ibid [85], [854].

[54] Ibid [87]–[90], [727]–[28]. Kirriwom J pressed that the 'Constitution prevails above everybody and everything else and only those who have met the constitutional requirements must run the country' [728].

[55] Ibid [743]. While acknowledging that Prime Minister O'Neill, since taking office on 02 August 2011, has brought about some important reforms, His Honour insisted that 'the end does not justify the means'.

[56] Ibid [856].

The insistence of the majority on a strict application of the processes and procedures pertaining to the operation of the Parliament suggest, on one hand, a legalistic approach that overlooked the underlying political interests and concerns of self-preservation that appeared to prevent Somare's Cabinet from triggering the procedure to remove its own Prime Minister. On the other hand, the insistence on the strict compliance of internal parliamentary procedures, despite questions of non-justiciability, indicates the judges as undertaking judicial policing of the Parliament.[57] It indicates a differing understanding of their role compared to that held by the O'Neill government.

Responding to the Somare Government

The minority judges—Deputy Chief Justice Salika (as he then was) and Justice Sakora—contrasted with the majority judges by going beyond the legal argument to find that the removal of Prime Minister Somare was justified as his Cabinet deliberately undermined proper constitutional processes for self-serving political interests.

They held that while the O'Neill government may have failed to strictly follow the prescribed processes and procedures in removing an ailing Somare, an expansive, fair and liberal interpretation of the relevant constitutional provisions meant taking into account the underlying political realities.[58] These realities, according to their Honours, strongly suggested that Somare's Cabinet 'deliberately failed' to invoke the reporting procedure to trigger the removal of Somare as part of a political tactic to remain in power.[59]

Deputy Chief Justice Salika found that the 'delay' in triggering the removal processes by Somare's Cabinet was 'very considerable [and] unreasonable' such that the 'Constitutional process to declare a vacancy [under section 142] was frustrated'.[60] His Honour considered it to be 'an abuse and misuse of the people's power' and proceeded to find on these premises that 'some ingenious solutions' were required to remedy in keeping with the 'spirit of the autochthonous nature of the Constitution'.[61]

Holding Somare's own Cabinet responsible for his demise, Salika DCJ emphatically concluded:

> In the light of the inaction by [Somare's] NEC (National Executive Council)...Can the [Somare] Government fairly 'cry' over something they brought on themselves? Have they come to court with clean hands? The answer is 'no' they have not come with clean hands. In colloquial terms, can they 'have their cake and eat it?' Again the answer is 'no'.[62]

[57] Ibid [29], [37]–[9]. Further discussion in Chap. 8.

[58] Ibid [290], [357], [416]–[18], [437], [540]–[42] (Salika DCJ, Sakora J).

[59] Ibid.

[60] Ibid [271], [416], [419], [421].

[61] Ibid [266], [419], [423].

[62] Ibid [267]–[77], [381].

It may appear that in reaching these views, the dissenting judges took the orthodox approach that Parliament found a solution to its own internal issues. However, their views firmly indicate that they, like the majority judges, were also taking a liberal approach by adjudicating on internal parliamentary matters as well as going beyond the legal issues to deal with the underlying politics. Reinforcing the accountability powers of the Supreme Court, Salika DCJ emphasised that '[t]he Courts have power to control Executive acts…[and that] [a]buse of power by the NEC must not be tolerated by the Court.'[63]

In holding that '[t]he Courts have power to control Executive acts', his Honour not only demonstrated that the judicial review powers of the courts are entrenched and extensive, but that they have a superior place such that even if the Executive becomes assertive and manipulative of the Parliament, it cannot evade the Court's supervision. It firmly indicates that a different conception of judicial power, compared to that of the colonial era, exists under the constitutional framework in Papua New Guinea.

This is also demonstrated by the approach of Justice Sakora, who was prepared to assess the whole of Somare's political reign.[64] His Honour proceeded on this premise that Somare's removal did not just happen 'out of the blue' as there were 'tell-tale signs, the writing on the wall' with 'the grievous default of [Somare's] NEC [Cabinet]' giving 'the final impetus'.[65] His Honour described Parliament's action to replace Somare as 'democracy but not as we have been used to'.[66] His Honour went on to describe the conduct of Somare's executive government as playing 'a silly game [of] political cleverness' and that Somare 'does not own the office' of the Prime Minister.[67]

This observation also provided an opportunity for both dissenting judges to comment on Somare's insistence over the years to remain as Prime Minister despite mounting allegations of corruption and multiple charges of misconduct in office discussed earlier. Salika DCJ observed that Somare should have

> by convention resign[ed] for breaking the laws of his country [but] his continued occupation and grip on power diminished the respect for and integrity of the Office of Prime Minister [and sets] a bad precedent.[68]

---

[63] Ibid [372], [419], [597]. His Honour further held that Somare's cabinet 'down played the urgency' and 'failed to attend speedily' to activate the reporting and removal process, hence, it 'was a serious mistake [and] this court cannot ignore that mistake' [404]–[05], [413].

[64] Ibid [540].

[65] Ibid.

[66] Ibid [540]–[41].

[67] Ibid [528], [589]: 'The Office of the Prime Minister does not belong to one man, or one family, or a particular group. It is an important public office such that there must be no time to be playing a waiting game' (Sakora J).

In response to the issue of whether voting should have happened on the 'next sitting day' after vacancy is announced as provided in the Constitution, Sakora J held that a vacancy already existed after three months had passed so parliament acted to fill an existing vacancy that had been there the previous two months. This was distinguished from *Christopher Haiveta v Paias Wingti (No 3)* [1994] PNGLR 197, the leading authority on this provision. In that case, there was a sudden resignation and a move to vote, all which happened on the same day [383]–[88], [394], [554]–[55].

[68] Ibid [210]–[12].

Sakora J went further to comment broadly on the growing trend in the country of public officials resisting and interfering with lawful investigations:

> We do not resign, step aside or step down in PNG, even if only to ensure that whatever suspicions or allegations that may have been levelled against us are properly attended to and investigated by the proper State authorities.[69]

In a further candid assessment, Sakora J referred to Somare's widely regarded honorary titles as the 'Father of the Nation' and 'Grand Chief', and observed that resignation and compliance with investigations would have been 'the proper course of action a "father" or a "chief" would take in order to save his family or his clan/tribe from dysfunctional outcomes'.[70]

While some may view these opinions as extraordinary and beyond the legal realm into the political sphere, they can be argued to align with the judges' transformative role as social interveners. As previously discussed, the 'home-grown' constitutional framework considers judges as 'leaders' in Papua New Guinea society. They, are therefore expected to address broader socio-political issues, contrasting with the traditional role of judges.

Implications on the Understandings of Judicial Power

The judgments of both the majority and dissenting judges suggest elements of orthodox approaches to the judicial role. The former leaned towards a legalistic interpretation of procedures and processes, while the latter allowed Parliament to find solutions to its own internal issues. However, a closer examination indicates that both sides of the Court ultimately adjudicated in a way that directly policed the actions of Parliament and the executive governments of the contesting prime ministers. They adopted an assertive form of judicial review that scrutinised the internal matters of parliament, while openly considering the underlying socio-political conditions and interests.

Their judgments reflect a commitment to apply 'a broad and expansive approach' to constitutional interpretation instead of a 'strict, technical and legalistic' approach.[71] The judges demonstrated a different understanding of judicial power and the doctrine of separation of powers compared to traditional interpretations advanced by opposing parties.

---

[69] Ibid [520]: '...More often than not, because of the chronic inefficiency and ineffectiveness of the regulatory, investigative and prosecutorial agencies of the State, nothing of any real seriousness and consequence ever takes place' (Sakora J).

[70] *Re Reference to Constitution Section 19(1) by East Sepik Provincial Executive* (*ESP Case*) [2011] PGSC 41, [593]. His Honour observed that had Somare defeated the motion against him in parliament, there would have been no constitutional challenge, dismissing the matter as 'just a case of 'bad losers' asking this court to do what the previous regime (Somare) failed to do on the floor of Parliament' [586].

[71] *Re Reference to Constitution Section 19(1) by East Sepik Provincial Executive* (*ESP Case*) [2011] PGSC 41, [9], [61].

2.2.2 Marat Case 2012

The differing understandings of judicial power and the doctrine of separation of powers evident in the *ESP Case* intensified a few months later in the *Marat Case* (2012).[72] The *Marat Case* was filed as a section 19 reference by Attorney-General Dr Allan Marat and Speaker of Parliament Jeffery Nape on behalf of the O'Neill government in response to the decision in the *ESP Case*.

The *Marat Case* primarily addressed two issues. First, it questioned the constitutionality of various legislative actions undertaken by the O'Neill government following the decision in the *ESP Case*. Second, it explored the limits of judicial power under section 19 of the Constitution, which the Court in the *ESP Case* relied on to declare Somare as the Prime Minister. Both issues dealt with the scope of judicial review, albeit in a contrasting manners. The first issue affirmed the Court's exclusive jurisdiction to decide questions of constitutionality, while the second issue intended to limit the Court's judicial review jurisdiction.

The Court found the references to be 'unusual,' as they were filed by the O'Neill government, which, despite ostensibly being in power after rejecting the judgment in the *ESP Case*, sought the Supreme Court to affirm the constitutionality of its actions.[73] The O'Neill government contended that this 'unusual reference' was undertaken 'in the hope of finding a solution to this [constitutional] crisis'.[74] The reference partially responded to the growing unrest in the country concerning the legitimacy of the O'Neill government.[75]

Regarding the second issue on section 19, which allows the Supreme Court to give its 'opinion' on any question relating to the application of a constitutional provision or a law or proposed law, the referrers argued that the provision should be interpreted as only providing the Court power to give a non-binding advisory opinion, not binding declaratory orders.[76] The O'Neill government contended that the decision in the *ESP Case*, declaring Somare as the Prime Minister, meant 'the Court has overstepped its limits under the doctrine of separation of powers and politicized the bench'.[77] They insisted that the Court make amends as its actions 'sparked off a constitutional crisis'.[78] Evident in these claims are the differences in understandings, on the part of the executive government, of judicial power and the doctrine of separation of powers assumed to be applicable in Papua New Guinea.

---

[72] *Reference by Allan Marat & Reference by the National Parliament* [2012] PGSC 20 (21 May 2012).

[73] Ibid [202].

[74] Ibid [203] (Kirriwom J, citing Counsel's submission).

[75] Ibid [30].

[76] Ibid [34].

[77] Ibid [39].

[78] Ibid.

Before examining the Court's response, it is crucial to note three significant intervening events that exacerbated tensions between the judiciary and the executive. First, allegations of judicial impropriety and bias against Chief Justice Injia CJ and later Justice Kirriwom continued when these references were filed. The O'Neill government applied for the two judges to recuse themselves due to perceived bias, but they declined.'

Allegations against Justice Kirriwom further intensified after the *Marat Case* hearing, where his Honour was accused of circulating a memo to all the judges in the country considering the treatment of the Chief Justice. The memo condemned the charges against the Chief Justice as 'politically motivated' and called for judges 'to demonstrate more collegiality in this war' against the Executive.[79] Alluding to Prime Minister O'Neill, the memo stated that '[t]his regime is in a way like a puppet that is dancing to the tune that somebody else is playing, somebody who wants this institution (judiciary) under current CJ dismantled permanently'.

The memo described the charges and suspension of the Chief Justice as not only 'an attack against the Chief Justice [but] an attack on the Third Arm of the Government by the Executive'. The memo urged judges, stating: ' [R]ise up now against [the executive] in the best and long-term interest of the judiciary [as] [w]e owe it to the people of this country, our children, and grandchildren to save it from ruins'.[80]

The second significant intervening event was the passage of the *Judicial Conduct Act 2012* (PNG) (JCA) in March 2012, granting Parliament the authority to determine judicial bias and refer judges to a tribunal.[81] The penalties for judges included imprisonment and loss of retirement benefits.[82]

Critics condemned, the JCA as unconstitutional while the government portrayed it as a measure to address judicial misconduct.[83] On 4 April, while the Court's decision in the *Marat Case* was pending, Injia CJ and Kirriwom J were referred by the Parliament to be tried under the JCA. Prime Minister O'Neill, in response to mounting opposition against the JCA, revealed its objective:

[79] 'Is Papua New Guinea's judiciary no longer independent?' on *PNG Exposed Blog* (13 March 2012). http://pngexposed.wordpress.com/2012/03/13/is-papua-new-guineas-judiciary-no-longer-independent/. A copy of the memo can be viewed from this publicly accessible blog. The memo refers to the crisis between the parliament and the judiciary as a 'war' and denounced the O'Neill government as an 'illegal regime'.

[80] Ibid.

[81] *Judicial Conduct Act* 2012 (PNG) s 5.

[82] *Judicial Conduct (Amendment) Act* 2012 (PNG) s 6.

[83] Grace Tiden, 'Parliament enacts law to defend itself: Brown', *Post Courier* (online), 4 April 2012; Eoin Blackwell, 'PNG govt pushes new legislation on judges', *Sydney Morning Herald* (online), 18 April 2012; James Apa Gumuno, 'Critics label bill as criminal' The National (online), 23 March 2012.

> On the Judicial Bill, what has led to this? Why did Parliament come up with the law? There was gross conflict of interest on the bench. The judiciary is bigger than any Judge. I will repeal that Act. I will repeal that act (sic) only on one condition…CJ and Judge Kirriwom must step down.[84]

Following these developments and on the same day of O'Neill's statement, the Supreme Court, excluding Injia CJ and Kirriwom J, issued a stay order against the JCA, effectively releasing them from parliamentary referral.[85] In separate court proceedings, the Supreme Court, with Injia CJ and Kirriwom J participating, issued permanent injunctions against all charges and suspensions.[86] In response, the O'Neill government amended the JCA, imposing severe penalties of seven years in prison and lose of all retirement benefits for judges defying parliamentary suspension.[87]

The third event occurred before the *Marat Case* verdict when Chief Justice and Justice Kirriwom's refusal to recuse themselves led two judges of the five-member bench, Salika DCJ and Sakora J, to abstain from giving their decision in the Marat Case, citing concerns about the judiciary's integrity.[88] In this unprecedented move, the two judges described the actions of their brother judges as 'dragging [the] Judiciary's integrity into the mud'.[89]

Judgment of the Supreme Court

The Supreme Court issued its judgement in the *Marat Case* on 21 May 2012, nearly five months after the proceedings began in January. It was another momentous decision considering the intervening events. With two judges abstaining, the three judges—Injia CJ, Kirriwom and Gavara-Nanu JJ, all part of the majority decision in the *ESP Case*, again ruled in favour of Somare.

---

[84] Todagia Kelola, 'PM will repeal the 'Bill' if Injia, Kirriwom step down', *Post Courier* (online), 11 April 2012.

[85] *Re Judicial Act 2012; Special Reference by Morobe Provincial Executive* [2012] PGSC 12 (11 April 2012), [25] (Mogish, Manuhu & Sawong JJ). The Court noted that the stay included 'the decision made by the National Parliament to refer the Chief Justice Sir Salamo Injia and Justice Nicholas Kirriwom [as well as] all or any of steps taken including a decision by the National Executive Council in respect of the referral'.

[86] *Reference by Allan Marat & Reference by the National Parliament* [2012] PGSC 20, Appendixes C (Injia CJ); *Injia v Eluh* [2012] PGNC 23, [11] (Manuhu J); Adrian Mathias, 'Sir Salamo's hearing adjourned indefinitely', *The National* (online), 8 May 2012; Eoin Blackwell, 'PNG court drops chief justice case', *Sydney Morning Herald* (online), 13 March 2012.

[87] *Judicial Conduct (Amendment) Act 2012* (PNG) ss 5(2)-(8), 6; 'PNG government introduces amendment to Judicial Conduct Act', *Radio New Zealand* (online) 18 April 2012.

[88] Todagia Kelola, 'Two judges step aside', *Post Courier* (online), 22 May 2012.

[89] Ibid.

They held that since the decision in the *ESP Case* recognised the Somare government as constitutionally legitimate, all legislative and policy actions of the O'Neill government were unlawful.[90] Regarding the Court's authority to issue binding and declaratory orders under section 19, the Court confirmed its mandate to do so.[91]

The judgment not only allowed the judges to address the actions of the O'Neill government but also delved into the conflicting interpretations and understandings of judicial power and the separation of powers doctrine evident in both the ESP and Marat cases. Chief Justice Injia remarked that the O'Neill government's actions represented 'a new and dangerous trend in the development of constitutional law and respect for the integrity and independence of the Courts'.[92] The Chief Justice admonished that the people were witnessing 'a country ruled by the rule of law replaced by a country ruled by men who resort to scare tactics, intimidation, threat of force and force'.[93] Alluding to the actions against him and Kirriwom J and the role of the judiciary generally, the Chief Justice firmly responded:

> [A] fearless National Judicial System, as the custodian of the *Constitution*, is jealously guarding the *Constitution* to ensure that its provisions are not flouted, subverted or destroyed by powerful elements within the society that control the very democratic processes that the *Constitution* itself has availed to them to operate within prescribed limits.[94]

Justice Kirriwom was even more direct in his judgment, asserting that there was a 'unilateral over-throw of the Somare regime by O'Neill/Namah led government' and that they maintained power in defiance of the Constitution.[95]

His Honour concluded by exposing the underlying doctrinal disputes and misunderstandings that permeated both the *ESP* and the *Marat* cases:

> [A] deliberate and calculated breach or violation of the separation of powers principle purposely instigated or caused into motion by members of Parliament, acting on deliberate bad legal advice from those with ulterior motive to create a collision between two arms of government to suit their own selfish ends while hiding behind the pigment of parliamentary supremacy over the judiciary.[96]

Justice Kirriwom pertinently stated further that '[t]he deliberate decision to disobey legitimate court orders was disguised in the separation of powers argument fuelled by misconceived notion that Parliament was supreme'.[97]

---

[90] For instance, see *Reference by Allan Marat & Reference by the National Parliament* [2012] PGSC 20, [172].

[91] Ibid [42], [48]–[69], [164]–[69], [172].

[92] Ibid [81].

[93] Ibid [92].

[94] Ibid [91].

[95] Ibid [307]. Similar to Injia CJ, Kirriwom J refuted the assertion that the Supreme Court created the constitutional crisis: '[It] was not created by the ruling in *SCR 3 of 2011* [ESP Case]. That is what the lawyers and lawyer-cum politicians want the public and the nation to believe. The crisis generated was [due to] the disobedience of the court order' [210], [228].

[96] Ibid [378].

[97] Ibid [379].

These judgements exposed fundamental disagreements over judicial power and the roles of parliamentary and judicial bodies. By affirming the binding nature of advisory opinions under section 19, the Court not only reinforced the judiciary's extensive judicial review role but also prompted a reassessment of the separation of powers doctrine under the Constitution.

Aftermath of the Judgement

The O'Neill government reacted to the Court's decision by accusing the Supreme Court of attempting to 'create a chaotic situation in the country',[98] arresting the Chief Justice on charges of sedition,[99] and enacting a legislation to overturn the Supreme Court ruling.[100]Justice Kirriwom was also charged with sedition in his chamber.[101] His Honour described his arrest as 'a very sad day for Papua New Guinea, for democracy [and] for the Constitution', but remained steadfast, asserting that his arrest 'doesn't mean that we are going to submit that easily…We will stand up and fight for the Constitution in this country'.[102]

The stalemate between the judiciary and the O'Neill government persisted until the formation of a new coalition government a few months later in August 2012, three months after the *Marat* decision. In an unexpected turn, the former bitter rivals, Sir Michael Somare and Peter O'Neill formed the coalition government. They promptly dropped the sedition charges against the judges,[103] apologised to the judges and the public for creating the crisis,[104] and repealed all the contentious laws. In response, the judiciary did not pursue the contempt of court charges against the former members of the Executive.[105]

This mode of resolution meant that Papua New Guinea's most significant constitutional crisis was not resolved through the Supreme Court as the designated forum for constitutional conflicts. Instead, it was resolved through the spirit of 'forgive and forget,' aligned with cultural values of reconciliation and consensus. It reflected the 'home-grown' and indigenous foundations of the Constitution.[106]

There are two contrasting implications of this outcome. On one hand, while the election acted as a 'circuit breaker,' returning power to the people who are the repository of all constitutional powers, it did not address the substantive conceptual issues regarding judiciary's role or the doctrine of separation of powers.

---

98 Liam Fox, 'Fresh uncertainty as PNG parliament recalled', *ABC News* (online), 22 May 2012..

99 Liam Fox, 'PNG chief justice charged with sedition', *ABC News* (online), 24 May 2012.

100 *Supreme Court (Amendment) Act 2012* (PNG).

101 Liam Fox, 'Second PNG judge charged with sedition', *ABC News* (online), 28 May 2012.

102 Liam Fox, 'PNG chief justice charged with sedition', *ABC News* (online), 24 May 2012.

103 Liam Fox, 'Sedition charges dropped against PNG Chief Justice', *ABC News* (online), 30 August 2012.

104 'Namah: Sorry for political impasse', *The National* (online), 24 October 2012.

105 Liam Fox, 'PNG parliament repeals judiciary law', *ABC News* (online), 06 February 2013.

106 'Don Polye's call for Melanesian Way', *Post Courier* (online), 28 May 2012.

On the other hand, the judiciary's willingness to allow external political and cultural agencies to guide the resolution of a serious constitutional conflict, coupled with their decision not to pursue contempt charges against members of the executive, demonstrates the dynamic and adaptable nature of the judiciary. By accepting an alternative way to resolve a constitutional conflict, the judiciary illustrates that applications of judicial power and notions of justice are not to be limited to the narrow dictates of defined institutions or Western developed dispute resolution methodologies.

This liberal character of judicial power further reinforces the Constitution's legal pluralism foundations. It is in harmony with the CPC's direction for judicial powers to be exercised in line with Papua New Guinea's 'own values and circumstances'.[107]

The resolution further underscores that Papua New Guinea's governmental framework is not strictly within the traditional tripartrite structures that advances a restrictive judiciary to the exclusion of informal institutions—an analysis developed further in the next chapter.

2.3 *Competing Understandings of Judicial Power and Parliament*

The cases discussed directly involved members of the executive against the judiciary. However, the substantive arguments concerning parliamentary supremacy and conceptions about the restricted role of the judiciary primarily originate from or are closely linked to parliament. Therefore, it is important to also briefly assess cases where the Supreme Court interpreted and responded particularly to Parliament's conduct and its conceptions of the role of the judiciary and the doctrine of separation of powers.

Some of the areas within the Constitution where the actions of the legislature are subject to judicial review are the constitutional validity of laws and amendments (s 19), as well as the exercise of Parliament's other explicit duties such as the election of the Prime Minister (s 142), the raising of loans (s 209), conducting motions of no confidence (s 145), ensuring compliance with the required number of days Parliament must sit in a year (s 124) and the election of the Governor-General (s 88). There are specific processes and procedures that Parliament must follow in discharging these duties, and they are amenable to judicial review.[108]

---

[107] CPC Report 1974, Chapter 8 [12]; The Constitution provides for the judicial system of Papua New Guinea to include both formal and informal tribunals and conflict resolution forums (ss 155(1)(c), 172; Schedule 1.2).

[108] *Kipalan v National Parliament* [2004] PGSC 42; *Re Calling of the Parliament* [1999] PGSC 55; *In re Re-Election of the Governor General* [2010] SC1085.

In the *Marat Case*, Parliament argued that its stance on parliamentary proceedings being non-justiciable and the Court's opinion being merely advisory was based on a particular interpretation of the doctrine of separation of powers, which advocates for non-interference with the operation of other government branches.[109] Section 134 of the Constitution is the non-justiciability provision, which provides that

> [e]xcept as is specifically provided by a Constitutional Law, the question, whether the procedures prescribed for the Parliament or its committees have been complied with, is non-justiciable.

However, the Court held that non-justiciability should not be taken to 'permit Parliament to commit breaches of constitutional provisions…with impunity [leading to] political instability'.[110] Kirriwom J asserted that 'this court's inherent powers and jurisdiction must not be subdued by section 134 (non-justiciable provision) of the Constitution'.[111] This signals an expansive view of judicial power, contrasting with Parliament's stance.

A similar contention arose in the case of *Re Organic Law on Integrity of Political Parties and Candidates* (2010). Here, a section 19 reference was brought against the government for passing amendments to the Constitution and the *Organic Law on the Integrity of Political Parties and Candidates.*[112] These amendments aimed to discipline Members of Parliament and their political parties for frequently shift allegiances, leading to a high turnover of vote of no confidence motions and causing political instability.[113]

The government argued that these were political matters and only Parliament should address them. It contended that 'the Court should avoid construing [the] provisions [of the amendments] in such a way that interferes with Parliament's law-making powers on matters of political nature'.[114] It warned that judicial interferences in parliamentary enactments amounts to 'legislating by judicial act'.[115] However, the Supreme Court disagreed. In a profoundly liberal response, the Court held that '[o]ur Constitution has unique and dynamic features' in that

> the Constitution, though law, is a document derived from a political process and that many of its components contain political statements…It is therefore difficult for Judges to be totally divorced from considering socio-political considerations which permeate the Constitution.[116]

---

[109] *Reference by Allan Marat & Reference by the National Parliament* [2012] PGSC 20, [44], [455].

[110] Ibid [48].

[111] Ibid [724].

[112] [2010] PGSC 3 (7 July 2010).

[113] Bill Standish; 'The dynamics of Papua New Guinea's democracy: an essay' (2007) 22 *Pacific Economics Bulletin* 135, 145.

[114] *Re Organic Law on Integrity of Political Parties and Candidates* [2010] PGSC 3, [90]–[91].

[115] Ibid [92].

[116] Ibid [102], [105], [107].

The Court maintained that its powers extend to 'deciding politically charged cases,' demonstrating differing conceptions of judicial power and the separation of powers doctrine.[117]

Another example was a 2016 case concerning an application by the Opposition Leader to compel the Speaker to convene the sitting of the Parliament according to the schedules prescribed in the Constitution.[118] The Speaker deferred the sitting to a later date as part of a political tactic to prevent a vote of no confidence against incumbent Prime Minister Peter O'Neill.[119] The Supreme Court, relying on its enforcement powers under sections 22 and 23, 'ordered the recall of the Parliament,' affirming its role in upholding the rule of law and parliamentary democracy.[120]

In its unpublished judgment, the Court held that the Parliament has a duty to have sittings and conduct vote of no confidence motions when instituted. The Court rejected the actions of the Speaker as 'an affront to the rule of law and a real threat to Parliamentary democracy in this country'.[121] The Court's judgment clearly demonstrated an understanding of the judicial role that includes policing the workings of the parliament.

In response, Governor Kelly Naru of the Morobe Provincial Government, requested for 'Parliament and the executive to seek a judicial review on the matter' in regards to the 'principle of separation of powers provision'.[122] Governor Naru argued that 'Courts have no power to interfere with the way in which Parliament goes about to conduct its businesses'. Naru's opinion, significant due to his background as a member of parliament and as a senior constitutional lawyer, underscores the differing views on the judiciary's role and the separation of powers doctrine in Papua New Guinea. It represents the extent to which the differing views have permeated both the political and the legal institutions in the country.

3 Supreme Court's Responses to a Traditional Separation of Powers Argument

The case studies discussed illustrated that both the Executive and Parliament envisioned a limited role for the judiciary, with Parliament expected to hold dominance in Papua New Guinea. As the subsequent chapter will elaborate, this expectation is deeply rooted in the traditional interpretation of the doctrine of separation of powers. The tension surrounding the understanding of the doctrine of separation of powers

---

117 Ibid [108]–[110].

118 S 124; Eric Tlozek, 'PNG court orders the recall of Parliament to hear no-confidence motion in Prime Minister', *ABC News* (online) 12 June 2016.

119 Ibid.

120 Ibid.

121 Ibid.

122 Isaac Nicholas, 'PNG Governor Calls for Judicial Review on Separation of Powers', *Pacific Islands Report* (online) 24 July 2016.

extends beyond these specific cases, permeating all major constitutional disputes in Papua New Guinea with the potential to 'trigger controversy and produce political chaos [and] civil strife.[123]

Justice Sakora described the doctrine of separation of powers as being on a list of 'tired legal, constitutional and political principles' that public officials 'have become good at mouthing-off…rendering them mere platitudes that are respected more in their breach than observance'.[124] That was apparent in the *Marat Case* where the Court further found that Parliament made 'very forceful criticisms of the Supreme Court of exceeding its jurisdiction in violation of…the [doctrine] of separation of powers'.[125]

Central to this doctrinal argument is the assertion of parliamentary supremacy. However, that argument not only expose the deep misunderstanding of the judicial character, but also serve as a façade to conceal political interests. As Justice Kirriwom countered, 'the argument on separation of powers and sovereignty or supremacy of Parliament that was forcefully advanced by the referrers…were mere smokescreens' to conceal their political interests to remain in power.[126] Justice Kirriwom went further to confront the misconceptions evident in Parliament's submission:

> Just because Parliament is constituted by Members directly elected by the People and is the supreme law making body does not empower it with greater power than the other two arms. *That is only wishful thinking and a misconception of a bygone era... No longer are we tied down with that colonial legacy.*[127] (emphasis added)

Other judges echoed similar concerns in the *Marat Case*, albeit less explicitly. These exchanges underscored the pervasive nature of misconceptions regarding the judiciary's role and the doctrine of separation of powers, which often serve political agendas more than an interest in substantive constitutional inquiry. In both the ESP and Marat cases, the judges in the majority demonstrated that their opposition to the executive and parliament did not undermine the doctrine of separation of powers. Rather, they emphasised that adherence to constitutional directives should supersede concerns for traditional interpretations of judicial power. Those directives, as will be discussed further in Chap. 7, intends for a departure from the traditional understanding of judicial power and the doctrine of separation of powers.

---

[123] *Reference by Allan Marat & Reference by the National Parliament* [2012] PGSC 20, [34], [42], [39], [363], [373], [443]; *In the Matter of the Organic Law on the Nomination of Governor-General* [2004] PGSC 3.

[124] *Reference to Constitution Sect. 19(1) by East Sepik Provincial Executive* [2011] PGSC 41, [522].

[125] *Reference by Allan Marat & Reference by the National Parliament* [2012] PGSC 20, [200].

[126] Ibid [363]–[64].

[127] Ibid (emphasis added). His Honour went on to reverse the charge that in fact, the country is witnessing 'a deliberate and calculated breach of the separation of powers principle by members of Parliament…with ulterior motive to cause a collision between two arms of government to suit their own selfish ends while hiding behind the pigment (sic) of parliamentary supremacy over the judiciary' [376]–[78].

Signaling the need for a rethink and a departure from a culture of uncritical adherence to colonially influenced legal framework, Justice Kirriwom firmly held in the Marat Case that '[n]o longer are we tied down with that colonial legacy.'[128]

The judicial stance on 'parliamentary supremacy' is particularly relevant in the context of Papua New Guinea, where traditional leaders or 'bigmen' wield significant influence and enjoy a superior position among the rest of the people. The 'bigmen' impose their superiority mentality on to the modern parliamentary system, which is then reinforced by the colonial ideas of parliamentary supremacy. The Court has shown itself to be aware of this reality. However, the Supreme Court has maintained that

> [t]he Constitution is the supreme authority and even the Parliament is subservient to it and neither the Parliament nor the elected representatives in the Parliament have the power to pass or make laws that diminishes that authority...of the Constitution.[129]

These responses reject the assumption inherent in traditional interpretations of the doctrine of separation of powers, which often accord parliament as superior. Instead, they advocate for the primacy of the Constitution and a more liberal interpretation of judicial authority. These insights necessitate a reevaluation of how the doctrine of separation of powers is understood and applied in Papua New Guinea.

4 Conclusion

The case studies presented reveal the contrasting views on the judiciary's role and the doctrine of separation of powers within Papua New Guinea. The different understandings have, on occasion, escalated into significant conflicts between the judiciary and the other branches of government. Moreover, these cases underscore the judiciary's steadfast commitment to maintaining their broad judicial review functions. The responses from the Supreme Court underscore the necessity of reassessing the judiciary's role and the doctrine of separation of powers within the Papua New Guinea context. Having established the liberal character of the judiciary, the next chapter undertakes the reassessment of the doctrine of the separation of powers as applied in Papua New Guinea.

This chapter further highlights the undesirability of tension between the government branches. In his address to the new Parliament following the 2011–2012 constitutional crisis, Governor-General Sir Michael Ogio urged leaders '[to] correct the mistakes of the past, heal the wounds of political infighting and resolve never to repeat these difficult and challenging times'.[130] However, as evidenced by the cases,

---

[128] *Reference by Allan Marat & Reference by the National Parliament* [2012] PGSC 20, [363–364].

[129] In *re Constitutional (Amendment) Law 2008, Reference by the Ombudsman Commission of Papua New Guinea* [2013] PGSC 67, [51].

[130] Firmin Nanol, 'PNG's Governor-General opens Parliament with a call for reconciliation', *Radio New Zealand* (online), 21 August 2012.

achieving Ogio's aspirations for the future may prove elusive if conflicting perspectives on the judiciary's role and the doctrine of separation of powers persist in Papua New Guinea.

Chapter 7
Rethinking the Doctrine of Separation of Powers

Abstract Drawing from the contestations about the doctrine of separation of powers in Chap. 6, Chap. 7 contends that Papua New Guinea has a modified model of separation of powers doctrine. It argues that the liberal role of the judiciary not only departs from the traditional tripartite model of the doctrine of separation of powers, in which the role of the judiciary is restricted, but also asserts that the drafters of the Constitution have also embedded a set of independent constitutional institutions that do not fall under any of the conventional three arms of government—legislature, executive and judiciary. The chapter argues that the correct model of the doctrine of separation of powers under the Papua New Guina Constitution is a quadripartite or four arms of government model instead of the traditional three arms of government. It describes this model as the 'home-grown' model of separation of powers and argues that the judiciary, with its unusually liberal judicial powers, is best suited to and needs to be understood within that modified model of the separation of powers doctrine as opposed to the traditional tripartite model.

Keywords Doctrine of separation of powers · Fourth arm of government · Constitutional innovation · Constitution-making · New separation of powers · 'homegrown' constitution

1 Introduction

The constitutional structures under the 'home-grown' Constitution point to the existence of a modified version of the doctrine of separation of powers, or what could be referred to as the 'home-grown' or autochthonous model of the doctrine.

There are two distinct elements that characterise this 'home-grown' model—the liberal character of the judiciary and the independent constitutional institutions. Together, they indicate a constitutional framework that does not fit into the traditional three arms of government model of the doctrine. By incorporating the independent constitutional institutions, the 'home-grown' model establishes a new separation of powers doctrine that could be described as the 'fourth arm' of government.

B. Kama, *Rethinking Judicial Power in Papua New Guinea*,
https://doi.org/10.1007/978-981-97-2946-3_7

This chapter will establish these arguments by firstly, discussing the historical development of the doctrine of separation of powers to demonstrate that the doctrine is amendable to modification to suit local contexts and intents; and secondly, how this modification is reflected in the 'home-grown' Constitution of Papua New Guinea. The discussion will urge for a rethink of the doctrine of separation of powers beyond the tripartite model to a quadripartite model, with the judiciary having a dominant role in this new formulation.

2 Early Development of the Doctrine of Separation of Powers

The doctrine of separation of powers has been widely regarded as a cornerstone of democracy and constitutional government. It asserts that laws should be administered through three distinct and separate branches of government—the legislature, the executive, and the judiciary—each charged with the separate responsibility of making, executing and judging the laws. Initially advanced to counter the concentration of power in a single branch of government or the monarch.

Its application of the doctrine in practice is far from its idealised form.[1] Its evolution is shrouded with adaptations and inconsistencies, with no democracy yet exercising its pure form.[2] Additionally, in some context, it has been an obstructive ideological instrument employed to advance certain interests and work against political and legal innovations.[3] Its value in political and constitutional settings is, therefore, contested. As Professor MJC Vile noted, the doctrine

> is by no means a simple and immediately recognisable, unambiguous set of concepts. On the contrary, it represents an idea of political thought in which there has been an extraordinary confusion of definition and use of terms.[4]

A review of the doctrine's development and usage demonstrates how it has been used to suit local contexts and drafting intentions—a case, as will be argued, that occurred in Papua New Guinea.

---

[1] Jeremy Waldron, 'Separation of Powers in Thought and Practice?' (2013) 54 *Boston College Law Review* 433, 434.

[2] J. M Finnis, 'Separation of Powers in the Australian Constitution' (1968) 3(2) *Adelaide Law Review* 159, 162–3.

[3] Joerg Chet Tremmel, 'An extended separation of powers model as the theoretical basis for the representation of future generations' (Discussion Paper No. 11, Future Justice London, 2013) 6; McMillan John, 'Re-thinking the Separation of Powers' (2010) 38 *Federal Law Review* 423, 424.

[4] M. J. C Vile, *Constitutionalism and Separation of Powers* (Clarendon Press, 1967) 2.

2.1 Formulations of Locke, Montesquieu, Blackstone, and the American Federalists

John Locke (1632–1704) is widely credited with providing the earliest prescription of the doctrine in the parliamentary era.[5] Locke asserted in his *Treatises*:

> Whoever has the Legislative or Supream(sic) Power of any Commonwealth is bound to govern by established standing laws, promulgated and known to the people, and not by Extemporary Degrees; by indifferent and upright judges who are to decide Controversies by those Laws; And to employ the force of the Community at home only in the Execution of such Laws…[6]

Writing in an era of growing conflict over governmental power between the monarch and the parliament (Stuart era, 1603–1714), Locke's main concern was to address the risks of monarchical tyranny. Locke argued that sovereignty is derived from the consensus of the people and that a system of accountability is needed to prevent its abuse.[7]

Locke elevated people as the repository of all governmental power and argued that the people's power is vested in the legislature through their representatives. Locke therefore viewed the legislature as supreme over the other arms of government, including the monarch.[8] However, Locke's ideas of parliamentary supremacy, displayed during the Long Parliament era (1640–60), saw the English Parliament challenging the monarch and becoming a tyranny as it exerted both the legislative and executive powers, with firm control over the judicature.

Learning from the failings of the English Constitution, Baron de Montesquieu (1698–1755) proposed a different approach to the separation of powers doctrine for France, advocating a system of government with three branches that are specialised and independent.[9] Like Locke, Montesquieu acknowledged people as the repository of all governmental powers but refused Locke's proposition that the legislature should be supreme or for any arm of government to be exercising dual functions as it breeds tyranny.[10] For Montesquieu, a complete separation between all three arms of government was the best guarantee of checked power and the preservation of rights and liberties.

However, Montesquieu's proposal fell short in its prescription of the judicial arm. He viewed judges as 'no more than the mouth that pronounces the words of the law, mere passive beings, incapable of moderating either its force or rigour'.[11]

---

[5] Although, some may argue its genesis goes further to Aristotle in Fourth Century B.C in his thesis *Politics*.

[6] John Locke, *Two Treatise of Government* 1689 (compiled by P. Laslett, Cambridge University Press, 1970) 371.

[7] Ibid 343.

[8] Ibid 348, 385–86.

[9] Baron de Montesquieu, The Spirit of Laws (Complete Works, Vol. 1, 1748) (online) Chapter 6, 199.

[10] Ibid 202.

[11] Ibid 208.

Montesquieu therefore argued that 'of the three powers, the judiciary is, in some measure, next to nothing: there remain, therefore, only two'.[12]

In Montesquieu's view of the doctrine of separation of powers, the judiciary is the weakest of the three separate arms of government, having neither the power to interpret the laws nor the right to scrutinise the two arms of government.[13]

Following Montesquieu, the views of William Blackstone (1723–1780) on the doctrine of separation of powers has had a profound influence on British legal thinking and colonialism. There were two significant contributions. First, like Locke, Blackstone advocated for the supremacy of parliament. However, unlike Locke who advocated for people as the ultimate sovereign, Blackstone declared the supremacy of parliament as 'absolute and without control'.[14]

Blackstone's conception of parliamentary supremacy, later carried on by influential jurists such as John Austin (1790–1859) and Albert Dicey (1835–1922), would become a cornerstone of English constitutionalism and imperial influence.[15] Dicey for instance, contended that this supremacy means '[a]ny Act of Parliament...will be obeyed by the courts [and that]...no person or body [has] a right to override or set aside the legislation of Parliament'.[16]

Second, in contrast to Locke and Montesquieu, Blackstone articulated a clear function for judges—to determine the law 'not according to his own private judgment, but according to the known laws and customs of the land'.[17] Blackstone prescribed the role of judges as not 'to pronounce a new law, but to maintain and expound the old one'.[18]

He argued that while expounding the law, judges may develop the common law, but that development should strictly adhere to precedents.[19] The subsequent judges therefore 'do not pretend to make a new law, but to vindicate the old one from misrepresentation'.[20] In this regard, Blackstone limited the role of the judges to only declaring the law and apply precedent, without delving into reviewing the constitutionality or legality of the legislative instrument under consideration.

---

[12] Ibid 205.

[13] Michel Troper, 'Constitutional Justice and Democracy' (1995) 17 *Cardozo Law Review* 273, 273–74.

[14] William Blackstone, 'Commentaries on the Laws of England' (1765–1769), Book 1, Chapter 2 of the Parliament, Lonang Institute (online). https://lonang.com/library/reference/blackstone-commentaries-law-england/.

[15] Roy Stone de Montpensier, 'The British Doctrine of Parliamentary Sovereignty: A Critical Inquiry' (1966) 26(4) *Louisiana Law Review* 753, 766.

[16] Albert V. Dicey, *Introduction to the Study of the Law of the Constitution* (first published 1885, 10th ed, 1959), 39–40.

[17] Blackstone, above n 14, Vol 1:14.

[18] Ibid.

[19] Ibid; William S. Brewbaker III, 'Found Law, Made Law and Creation: Reconsidering Blackstone's Declaratory Theory' (2006–07) 22 (1) *Journal of Law and Religion*, 255, 265–67.

[20] Blackstone, above n 14, Vol 1:15.

While Locke conceived the judiciary as a construct of the executive, Blackstone agrees with Montesquieu that it is an independent entity but with a limited function. All three, therefore, promoted the common theme that governmental power is primarily divided between the legislature and the executive branches, with the judiciary holding a subordinate position.

The American Revolution against the British Empire (1775–1783) provided the first real opportunity for the adoption of the doctrine of separation of powers in a constitution in a way that challenges the British conception of the doctrine and would inspire many post-colonial constitutions globally.

Thomas Madison, a leader of this constitutional revolution resulting in the American Constitution, considered Montesquieu's strict application of the doctrine as 'totally misconceived and misapplied'.[21] Although he resented '[t]he accumulation of all powers, legislative, executive, and judiciary, in the same hands,' he conceded that the structure of representative democracies means some dual functions are inevitable without necessarily resulting in tyranny.[22]

Similarly, another influential constitutional thinker of the Revolution era, James Hamilton, advocated for judicial independence. However, like Montesquieu, he conceded that 'the judiciary, from the nature of its functions, will always be the least dangerous' as it '[has] neither force nor will, but merely judgment…'.[23]

The American Federalists departed from Locke, Montesquieu, and Blackstone, by rejecting the idea of a supreme parliament, instead affirming popular sovereignty and constitutional supremacy, and recognising the importance of a separate and independent judiciary.[24] Yet, like their predecessors, the judiciary was still considered the 'weakest' compared to the other two branches of government.

At least, that was the prevailing view until the case of *Marbury v Madison* (1803), which firmly established the doctrine of judicial review, elevating the judicial branch of government to a co-equal status.[25] It challenged the general perception up to that point of judges as mere passive actors whose duty is only to declare the law given to them by the legislature or congress.[26] This contrast with the early formulations of the doctrine of separation of powers demonstrates that the doctrine is open to modification to suit different political and social contexts.

---

[21] James Madison, *The Federalist Papers: No. 47* (1788) (online) Yale Law School Avalon Project. http://avalon.law.yale.edu/18th_century/fed78.asp.

[22] Ibid; Harry Gibbs, 'The Separation of Powers—A Comparison' (1987) 17 *Federal Law Review* 151, 160–61.

[23] Alexander Hamilton, The Federalist Papers: No. 78 (1788) (online) Yale Law School Avalon Project http://avalon.law.yale.edu/18th_century/fed78.asp. That, according to Hamilton, is because the judiciary 'has no influence over either the sword or the purse; no direction either of the strength or of the wealth of the society; and can take no active resolution whatever'.

[24] John Adams, The Political Writings of John Adams: Representative Selections 1785–1826 (Hackett Publishing, 2003) 94.

[25] *Marbury v Madison* (1803) 5 U.S 137; Peter Cane, 'Reconceptualising separation of powers' (2015) 101 *Amicus Curiae* 2, 5.

[26] Erwin Chemerinsky, 'In Defense of Judicial Supremacy' (2017) 58 *William & Mary Law Review* 1459, 1461.

2.2 *Adaptations of the Doctrine in Australia*

The early understanding of the doctrine of separation of powers in Papua New Guinea was influenced by Australia's formulations during the colonial period. Australia constructed its Constitution based on both the British Westminster system of parliament and the United States model of federalism and constitutionalism.[27]

Australia advances Thomas Madison's notion of duality further by not strictly adhering to the distinct separation envisaged by Montesquieu, particularly between the executive and the legislature. While the first three chapters of the Australian Constitution appear to embody the doctrine, the High Court of Australia has interpreted the separation as a flexible relationship between the executive and legislature, and a robust independence for the judiciary.[28] Judicial independence is elevated as providing 'a safeguard against arbitrary power',[29] and as 'one of the bulwarks of liberty'[30] and fundamental to the preservation of Australia's federalism.

The hybrid nature of the doctrine as applied in Australia suggests there was some local innovation of the doctrine. Andrew Inglis Clark, a draftsman of the Australian Constitution, for instance, noted that he had 'followed very closely the Constitution of the United States, with such alterations and additions as the local circumstances of the Colonies' permit.'[31]

Australia's modification of the doctrine indicates not only its adaptability but also that Australia's version, which retains the traditional three branches of government, was tailored to its specific context and intentions. Colonialism meant it was extended to Papua New Guinea without regard for Papua New Guinea's contexts and intentions.

3 The Doctrine Under the Papua New Guinea Constitution

The drafting of the Papua New Guinea Constitution was informed by an awareness of the historical evolution of the doctrine of separation of powers and its adaptability to local contexts. The colonial legacy instilled a general skepticism towards Western legal frameworks, and the process of decolonisation necessitated a reimagining of society to establish Papua New Guinea's own constitutional identity. It became

---

[27] A. R. Butterworth, 'Australian Constitution' (1901) 17 *Law Quarterly Review* 381, 382–3; Brian Galligan, *A Federal Republic: Australia's Constitutional System of Government* (Cambridge University Press, 1995) 45–7.

[28] *Huddart, Parker and Co Pty Ltd v Moorehead* (1909) 8 CLR 330; *Victorian Stevedoring and General Contracting Company v Dignan* (1931) 46 CLR 73; James Stellios, *The Federal Judicature: Chapter III of the Constitution* (LexisNexus Butterworths, 2010) 79–6.

[29] William Harrison Moore, *The Constitution of the Commonwealth of Australia* (Sweet and Maxwell, 2nd ed, 1910) 322.

[30] *Wilson v Minister for Aboriginal and Torres Strait Islander Affairs* (1996) 189 CLR 1, 10–11, 13.

[31] 'Inglis Clark's Memorandum to Delegates' in John M Williams, *The Australian Constitution: A Documentary History* (Melbourne University Press, 2005) 65, 67.

evident that simply replicating the Australian model would not only contradict this objective but also ignore the inherent flaws and inconsistencies of the doctrine.

These considerations, fundamental to the 'home-grown' constitutional endeavour, led to the development of a unique version of the doctrine of separation of powers. As the following discussion will contend, this 'home-grown' rendition envisioned a governmental structure with 'four arms' of government, where the judiciary assumed a dominant role.

3.1 Basis of the Framework of Government

Before delving into the analysis of the 'home-grown' framework, it is crucial to grasp the foundational intentions behind its formation. The Constitutional Planning Committee (CPC) emphasised that '[i]n planning a constitution we are concerned above all else with these very questions—who shall have what powers and in what manner shall they be exercised'.[32] They articulated:

> We see the planning of our own constitution as a vital aspect of the process of self-determination. It is not just a matter of our people determining that they should govern themselves. We have the opportunity of determining *how* we shall govern ourselves.[33]

In shaping the mechanisms for 'how' to govern, their intention was to devise a system of government focused on the 'development of the people rather than development of the country'.[34] They advocated for 'a fundamental re-orientation of the institutions of government' towards two distinct goals—firstly, reflecting 'Papua New Guinean forms of participation, consultation, and consensus' and secondly, establishing a framework that fosters greater accountability and checks and balances.[35]

Addressing the first objective, the CPC stressed that 'unless we revitalise those practices of participation, of consultation and consensus...we are continuing the colonial process of holding our people subservient'.[36] Concerning the second objective, the CPC was determined to counteract the despotic tendencies within colonial government institutions and the emerging abuse of power among local political elites.[37] Historian Ian Downs observed that the CPC 'wanted a truly 'home-grown' constitution to be established with an emphasis on restraint of executive power wielded by heads of departments'.[38]

---

32 CPC Report 1974, Chapter 1 [11].

33 Ibid [12] (emphasis added).

34 Ibid [14].

35 Ibid Chapter 2 [153].

36 Ibid [112].

37 Anthony J Regan, 'Protection of the Independence of Constitutional Office-Holders' in Anthony J Regan, Owen Jessep and Eric L Kwa (eds), *Twenty Years of the Papua New Guinea Constitution* (University of Papua New Guinea Press, 2001) 233–4.

38 Ian Downs, *The Australian Trusteeship: Papua New Guinea 1945–1975* (Canberra, 1980) 493.

In response, the CPC conferred an array of expansive judicial review powers upon the judiciary and established a set of independent constitutional institutions. As will be discussed, these independent constitutional institutions exist outside of the three traditional branches of government. Intended to provide oversight of the three branches of government, they constituted the 'fourth arm' of government. This framework transcended the traditional tripartite model of the separation of powers doctrine, giving rise to what could be termed as a 'home-grown' quadripartite model.

The innovative restructuring of established colonial institutions and ideologies is apparent in the CPC Report:

> Our colonisers have...imposed their "government", their democracy, their institutions and their will with little or no regard to our own values and institutions. This way is a blatant denial of our humanity. By their practices, they have to some extent changed the natural growth of our human development and our organizations and forced them into positions of subservience.[39]

By referring to 'their "government", their democracy [and] their institutions', the CPC underscored the necessity to construct 'our' government, 'our' conception of democracy and 'our' institutions that are suited 'to meet [our] needs and circumstances'.[40]

The Supreme Court affirmed this quest for autonomy and constitutional reimagining, asserting that being 'a "home-grown" constitutional document [meant it was] not one "made in Canberra" or anywhere else'.[41] Reference to 'Canberra' not only signified an intent for institutional disconnection between the colonial power and its former colony, but also ideological discontinuity and rejection of the power structures, ideas and practices that conflicted with the 'home-grown' intentions and expectations.

3.2 *Reconfiguration of the Doctrine in the Constitution*

The CPC's insistence on designing a 'home-grown' constitution did not imply overlooking the importance of the tripartite framework of government. Chaps. 6, 7 and 8 of the Constitutional Planning Committee 1974 Final Report extensively discuss the functions and expectations of the three arms of government.[42] This discussion was materialised into the Constitution, with section 99 establishing the tripartite structure of government:

> 99. Structure of Government

---

[39] CPC Report 1974 Chapter 2 [109].xx

[40] Ibid Chapter 15 [2–3].xx

[41] *Reference by the Ombudsman Commission of Papua New Guinea* [2010] PGSC 10, [80].

[42] CPC Report 1974. http://www.paclii.org/pg/CPCReport/main.htm.

1. Subject to and in accordance with this Constitution, the power, authority and jurisdiction of the People shall be exercised by the National Government.
2. *The National Government consists of three principal arms*, namely:
   (a) the National Parliament, which is an elective legislature with, subject to the Constitutional Laws, unlimited powers of law-making; and
   (b) the National Executive; and
   (c) the National Judicial System, consisting of a Supreme Court of Justice and a National Court of Justice, of unlimited jurisdiction, and other courts.
3. In principle, the respective powers and functions of the three arms shall be kept separate from each other.
4. Subsection (2) is descriptive only and is non-justiciable.

A literal interpretation of this provision unveils three significant insights. Firstly, subsection 99(1) emphasises that the 'People' are the custodian of all governmental powers. The notion is reinforced throughout the Constitution, delineating the functions of each arms of government: 'the legislative power of the People is vested in the National Parliament'[43]; 'the executive power of the People is vested in the Head of State'[44]; 'the judicial authority of the People is vested in the National Judicial System'.[45]

The emphasis on popular sovereignty will be further discussed in Chap. 9, analysing its implications for judicial power. For the purpose of this discussion, this aspect of the provision suggests that the authority exercised by the three arms of government derives entirely and directly from the people.[46] The drafters of the Constitution affirms that '[t]he principle that power derives from the people provides the basis of the *Constitution*.'[47] The Supreme Court reinforced this in the *Marat Case*:

> The *Constitution* being autochthonous and home grown makes it unique and rare, it is the embodiment of the will of the people to whom all power belongs. Thus the authority of the *Constitution* is original and it does not derive from any other source.[48]

Consequently, Parliament is not the sole institution with popular mandate as each arm of government inherently possesses a form of popular sovereignty.

Secondly, subsection 99(2) delineates the structural and functional separation of the branches of government but cautions in subsection 4 that this delineation 'is descriptive only and is non-justiciable'. This implies that the doctrine, as represented in the Constitution, serves solely for describing the governmental framework and cannot be litigated or judicially enforced.

---

[43] S 100(1).

[44] S 183.

[45] S 158(1).

[46] *Wari v Ramoi and Dibela* [1986] PNGLR 112 (Amet J) (unnumbered judgment); *Wonom, The State v* [1975] PGLawRp 311 (Frost CJ) (unnumbered judgment).

[47] CPC Report 1974, Chapter 7 [1].

[48] *Reference by Allan Marat & Reference by the National Parliament* [2012] PGSC 20, [427] (emphasis added).

Third, subsection 99(3) reinforces the notion that the separation envisaged between the arms of government is only 'in principle'. Schedule 1.6 elucidates that '[w]here a provision is expressed as "in principle", it means that 'an act (including a legislative, executive or judicial act) that is inconsistent with [that provision] is not, by reason of that inconsistency alone, invalid or ineffectual'.

Interpretations of these provisions have resulted in two sets of viewpoints. The first set of interpretations is that section 99 establishes a tripartite system of government in Papua New Guinea, contemplating 'a general separation of powers' between the legislature, executive, and judiciary.[49] The second set of interpretation suggests that section 99 envisages an expansive framework of government beyond the traditional tripartite system of government.

The first point in this second set of interpretations was underscored, for instance, in *Southern Highlands Provincial Government v Somare* (2007). In that case, Sakora J, in discussing the phrase 'in principle', favoured an expansive role of the judiciary, stating that 'the Constitution goes beyond just vesting the traditional "law-finding and law-application" functions of the superior courts. Vested are also law-making powers'.[50] This aligns with the discussion in Chap. 5, which elaborates on the liberal powers of the judiciary, indicating a broad definition of judicial power beyond the expectations of the traditional tripartite framework.

The second point in the second set of interpretations of section 99 was firmly advanced by Pritchard J in *Re Ombudsman Commission Investigations of the Public Solicitor* (1978).[51] After establishing that a set of autonomous constitutional institutions were established equally alongside the three traditional arms of government under the Constitution, His Honour observed that '[i]f our Constitution-makers envisaged the traditional English concept of three arms of Government only, the word "principal"(sic) need never have appeared in s. 99'.[52]

His Honour asserted that there are, in fact, 'six bodies' that constitute the 'arms of the National Government', including the three traditional arms.[53] Anthony Deklin argued that the provision possibly allows for multiple arms of government, while Professor Michael Ntumy contended that section 99 'merely requires a separation of the powers...as a matter of principle'.[54]

---

[49] *Motor Traffic Act 1950, S138A District Courts Act 1963 and S38A Local Courts Act 1963, Re* [1982] PNGLR 122, [134]; *Ombudsman Commission of PNG v Denis Donohoe* [1985] PGLawRp 348.

[50] *Southern Highlands Provincial Government v Somare, Chairman of the National Executive Council* [2007] PGSC 2, [119].

[51] [1978] PGSC 7.

[52] *Re Ombudsman Commission Investigations of the Public Solicitor* [1978] PGSC 7 (Prtichard J) (unnumbered judgment).

[53] Ibid.

[54] Tony Deklin, *Legal Control of the Executive under the Papua New Guinea Constitution* (PhD Thesis, Australia National University, 1985) 95; Michael A Ntumy, 'Separation of Powers' in Anthony J Regan, Owen Jessep and Eric L Kwa (eds), *Twenty Years of the Papua New Guinea Constitution* (University of Papua New Guinea Press, 2001) 194–5.

As will be argued later, this second set of interpretations appears to be consistent with the intents and structure of the Constitution. The terms 'non-justiciable' and only 'in principle' affords expansive latitude and do not intend a strict application of the doctrine.[55] The wording of this provision was deliberately chosen to limit the application of the traditional tripartite model and to promote a 'home-grown' framework of government that envisaged a liberal judiciary and other non-traditional branches of government.

The subsequent discussion will elaborate on the two indicators referred to in the second set of interpretations—liberal judiciary and independent constitutional institutions—to demonstrate that the doctrine of separation of powers was modified in Papua New Guinea.

3.2.1 Liberal Character of the Judiciary

Chapter 5 discussed the indicators in the Constitution that point to the entrenchment of the liberal character of the judiciary. The indicators strongly suggest that many of the traditional functions of the legislature and the executive were either subsumed by or shared with the judiciary, which possessed an expansive role beyond the conventional limits assumed under the typical understandings of the doctrine of separation of powers. Without restating the indicators, the extensive liberal character of the judiciary discussed constitutes a fundamental reconfiguration in the traditional conception of the doctrine in terms of judicial power.

It is acknowledged that some judges have cautioned against the 'frightening' prospect of the liberal judicial powers under this doctrine.[56] For instance, in *Marat v Hanjung Power Ltd* (2014), a three member Supreme Court panel, which included Justice Collier of the Australian Federal Court, who was seconded to Papua New Guinea, held that the Court 'cannot interfere with a valid legislative enactment [because] this principle is rooted in the doctrine of separation of powers which is entrenched in the *Constitution*'.[57] Deputy Chief Justice Injia (as he then was) also cautioned in *Lupari v Somare* (2008) that '[t]he Court must always be mindful that in exercising its discretion, it does not overstep the limits imposed by the constitutional doctrine of separation of powers'.[58]

However, as demonstrated by case studies in Chap. 6, the prevailing view supports the liberal and expansive role of the judiciary as an accepted feature of the doctrine of separation of powers in Papua New Guinea. For instance, in the *Marat Case* (2012), the Supreme Court firmly rejected the arguments for a restrictive use of judicial power. It found that the doctrine of separation of powers has been misused

---

55 John Goldring, *The Constitution of Papua New Guinea* (Lawbook Co, 1978) 78.

56 *Peter v South Pacific Brewery* [1976] PNGLR 537, 555 (Frost CJ).

57 [2014] PGSC 33, [25].

58 [2008] PGNC 121, [63]; In *Peter v South Pacific Brewery Ltd* [1976], for instance, the Court held that 'this court has no function in relation to the legislative power which is vested in the National Parliament' ([1976] PNGLR 345, 546).

and exploited as a shield to conceal Parliament's illegal actions and rejected its use to limit the legitimate actions of the Court.[59]

In *Southern Highlands Provincial Government v Somare* (2007), Justice Sakora, declared that the Court is bestowed the 'traditional "law-finding and law-application" functions [as well as] law-making powers', and also possesses 'supervisory and controlling powers over exercise of both legislative and executive powers [and] functions'.[60]. This character of the judiciary goes beyond the role expected under the traditional tripartite model. In *Aihi v The State* (1981), the Supreme Court held that its inherent jurisdiction to do justice may sometimes appear to contradict the doctrine of separation of powers—by usurping the function of the legislature—but is constitutionally founded.[61] Furthermore, in *Calling of the Parliament* (1999), the Court rejected arguments on the non-justiciability of parliamentary proceedings. While, affirming the general value of the doctrine of separation of powers upon which the non-justiciability arguments were sustained, the Court found the doctrine's strict application contrary to the intents of the Constitution:

> The independence of each of the three arms of government is fundamental. However, the Constitution of Papua New Guinea is unique in many respects. *It has subjected many political or policy issues to the scrutiny of the Courts.* It is the duty of this Court to take up these issues without fear and favour within the strict confines of the powers given by the Constitution.[62]

The Court made it very clear that it has 'a proud tradition of addressing such [political] issues [and] becoming involved in the policy decisions' in Papua New Guinea.[63]

In *Enforcement Pursuant to Constitution section 57, Application by Gabriel Dusava* (1998), Justice Sakora, with whom the other members of the Supreme Court agreed, used a common charge for breaching the separation of powers doctrine—judicial law-making—to distinguish firmly between the traditional model and the modified 'home-grown' model of the doctrine under the Constitution.[64] His Honour responded to the argument that 'judicial law-making would somehow affect the doctrine of separation of powers,' by stating that, 'this argument certainly does not hold water in PNG where the Constitution confers on the judiciary specific law reform and law-making and developing powers.'[65]

---

[59] *Reference by Allan Marat & Reference by the National Parliament* [2012] PGSC 20, [283], [455].

[60] *Southern Highlands Provincial Government v Somare, Chairman of the National Executive Council* [2007] PGSC 2, [119]–[20].

[61] *Aihi v The State* (No 1) [1981] PGSC 9 (Kidu CJ, Kearney DCJ and Andrew J) (unnumbered judgment).

[62] *SC Reference No 3 of 1999; Re Calling of the Parliament* [1999] PNGLR 285 (25 June 1999) (Kapi DCJ) (accepted by the Court of Amet CJ, Woods, Los, Sheehan, Sakora & Sevua JJ) (unnumbered judgment) (emphasis added).

[63] Ibid; See also, *The State v. NTN Pty Ltd & Another* [1992] PNGLR 1; *Haiveta v Wingti* (No 3) [1994] PNGLR 197.

[64] *Enforcement Pursuant to Constitution Section 57, Application by Gabriel Dusava* [1998] PGSC 59.

[65] Ibid.

He Honour also responded to another argument on 'usurpation of legislative powers of the Parliament if the judiciary attempted to change laws or introduce new ones by its decisions…' by further stating:

> Unlike its counterparts in other countries, the judiciary in Papua New Guinea (PNG) has an explicit and far-reaching law-making responsibilities to discharge. We have to do more than just perform our traditional (inherited) functions of applying the law. Pursuant to the powers vested in us by ss.18 and 19 *Constitution* we are in a unique position to participate fully in the overall development of the country.[66]

Justice Sakora's statements profoundly identify not only the unique character of the Papua New Guinea judiciary that distinguishes it from other judiciaries, but also that these unique features mean the judiciary does not adhere to the conventional understanding of a judiciary under the traditional doctrine of separation of powers and its tripartite framework.

The authorities highlighted further demonstrate that with the expansive and liberal role of the judiciary envisioned under the 'home-grown' Constitution, the traditional tripartite model of the separation of powers doctrine have been reconfigured. The contrasting viewpoints underscore the imperative for judges and litigants to accurately understand the true nature, intent, and scope of the doctrine of separation of powers in the 'home-grown' Constitution, without readily resorting to adopting interpretations influenced by principles and assumptions developed elsewhere.

3.2.2 Independent Constitutional Institutions

The second indicator in the Constitution supporting the assertion of a reconfigured doctrine of separation of powers outside the tripartite model in Papua New Guinea is the establishment of independent constitutional institutions. These institutions include the Ombudsman Commission, the Public Solicitor and the Public Prosecutor, the Public Service Commission, the Judicial and Legal Service Commission, the Auditor-General, and the Electoral Commission.[67] The Constitution designates the heads of these offices as 'constitutional office-holders' and explicitly states that these institutions are 'not subject to direction or control by any person or authority'.[68]

The Supreme Court has interpreted this to mean that these office-holders have a constitutionally guaranteed independence, separate from any control or administration by the three arms of government.[69] This was emphasised by Pritchard J in *SCR No 1 of 1978* regarding the Public Solicitor:

---

[66] Ibid.

[67] See the composition of these institutions, for instance, in ss 183, 221.

[68] Ss 126(6), 176(3)(a), 192, 183(4), 213(3), 217(1)(5).

[69] *Application by Herman Joseph Leahy* [2006] PGSC 21, 148; *Re Ombudsman Commission Investigations of the Public Solicitor* [1978] PGLawRp 345 (Prentice CJ); *Ombudsman Commission of PNG v Ellis, Constituting the Poreporena Freeway Commission of Inquiry* [1992] PNGLR 437, (Hinchliffe, Konilio, Andrew JJ).

> The Public Solicitor is not so created [by] an Act of Parliament. He is created by the *Constitution*, his is an independent office, he is responsible to the people in his specialized field and is a separate arm of the National Government not an instrumentality responsible or subservient to any one of the three principal arms.[70]

His Honour further suggested that multiple bodies, in addition to the traditional three arms of government, constitute the governance structure under the Constitution.[71]

This perspective is also supported in *Re Constitutional (Amendment) Law 2008* (2013) where the Ombudsman Commission (OC) challenged constitutional amendments aimed at limiting its power. The Supreme Court held that any amendments made by parliament to the Constitution to dictate

> what powers it [the OC] has and what powers it does not have, or what it can do in the performance of its constitutional functions and what it cannot do...is clearly not in harmony with section 217(5) of the *Constitution* that mandatorily prescribes that "in the performance of its functions…the Commission is not subject to direction or control by any person or authority".[72]

The protection of these institutions as 'not subject to direction or control' does not imply that they operate as rogue entities; their functions are strictly bound by the Constitution.[73] The unique constitutional arrangement for these institutions reflects a widespread public opinion noted by the the CPC that favoured making these institutions 'constitutionally independent of the executive government'.[74] Professor Yash Ghai, who advised the CPC, later reflected that the Constitution contains an 'unusual number of safeguards' because the drafters 'did not necessarily trust politicians'.[75]

Part XI of the Constitution further safeguards these constitutional institutions by preventing the suspension or dismissal of their heads except as specified in the Constitution. It further prohibits reductions in their total remunerations except as part of a general reduction applicable equally to all constitutional office-holders.[76] The government is obligated to provide necessary facilities and support for their proper functioning.[77]

---

[70] *SCR No 1 of 1978; Re Ombudsman Commission Investigations of the Public Solicitor* [1978] PGSC 7 (Prtichard J).

[71] Ibid.

[72] *In re Constitutional (Amendment) Law 2008, Reference by the Ombudsman Commission of Papua New Guinea* [2013] PGSC 67, [50].

[73] Schedule 1.19; *SCR No 9 of 1990, Application by the Principal Legal Adviser Bernard M Narokobi* [1991] PNGLR 239; *The State v Patrick Saul* [1988–89] PNGLR 337; *The State v Jack Gola and Mopana Aure* [1990] PNGLR 206.

[74] CPC Report 1974, Chapter 8 [110].

[75] Yash Gai, 'Establishing a Liberal Political Order through a Constitution: the Papua New Guinea Experience' (1997) 28 *Development and Change* 303, 308.

[76] S 223.

[77] Ss 223 and 225; See discussion in Chaps. 5 and 8 on the enforceability of these provisions.

The Constitutional Office-holders Rights Tribunal, mandated to handle matters concerning their removal from office, ensures additional protection for their independence.[78] The Supreme Court consistently supports these institutions, recognising their critical roles and independence within the government structure:

> [The] constitutional office-holders in Papua New Guinea stand in a unique position in the structure of government...They form an exclusive group... [They] are few in number (presently 32) but great in power and independence. The *Constitution* demands that their critical roles be recognised and protected.[79]

The independence of these institutions is further fortified by the composition of the appointing bodies that appoints the heads of the institutions. The appointing bodies are bipartisan and diverse in affiliation. For instance, the Ombudsman Appointments Committee (OAC) includes the Prime Minister, Chief Justice, Leader of the Opposition, Chairman of the Parliamentary Appointments Committee, and Chairman of the Public Services Commission.[80] While the Chief Justice is an appointee of the executive,[81] the Chairman of the Public Services Commission is appointed by the Public Services Commission Appointments Committee, which consists of the Prime Minister, the Chief Justice, the Leader of the Opposition, the Chairman of the Parliamentary Appointments Committee and the Chief Ombudsman.[82]

The Judicial and Legal Service Commission (JLSC) is the body that appoints the Public Prosecutor, the Public Solicitor and all judges (other than the Chief Justice) and the Chief Magistrate.[83] The JLSC comprises the Minister for Justice, the Chief Justice, the Deputy Chief Justice, the Chief Ombudsman and an appointee of the Parliament.[84] The involvement of these partisan and nonpartisan members in the appointment process underscores their status as independent bodies subject solely to the Constitution and not to any other arm of government. The composition of the appointment committees ensures a high level of independence and transparency in the appointments, consistent with the drafters' intent that the institutions' 'independence must be real'.[85]

These independent constitutional institutions are a unique design compared to other democracies in the Pacific region including Australia and New Zealand where

[78] *Organic Law on the Guarantee of the Rights and Independence of Constitutional Office-holders* (PNG) s 5. Given that the Organic Laws are an extension of the Constitution, and not an ordinary Act of Parliament, these protections are entrenched (Schedule 1.2).

[79] *Review Pursuant to Constitution Section 155(2)(b): Application by Herman Joseph Leahy* [2006] PGSC 21, [146], [148]; *Alleged Improper Borrowing of AUD1.239 Billion Loan, In re* [2017] PGSC 8, [49] (emphasis added).

[80] S 217(2).

[81] S 169.

[82] S 192(2).

[83] Ss 170, 175, 176.

[84] S 183.

[85] CPC Report 1974, Chapter 14 (37).

all state bodies fall under one of the three arms of government. They have constitutionally guaranteed independence and exists outside the traditional tripartite model.[86]

Their independent place in the Constitution not only 'ensure a high degree of accountability in government'[87] but also, as Pritchard J observed, illustrates that they are not on the fringes, nor do they operate as 'subsidiary arm[s] of the principal arm[s] of government'.[88] They are part of the main 'structure of government' in Papua New Guinea.[89]

Similar to the three branches of government, the independent constitutional institutions are creatures of popular sovereignty manifested through the Constitution.[90] According to Australian jurist Chief Justice Prentice, they are 'creature[s] of the people not of Parliament'.[91] In *Nilkare v Ombudsman Commission* (1995), the National Court described the Ombudsman Commission as 'the People's administrative watchman'.[92] The CPC viewed the constitutional office holders as 'leaders' who 'have a different role from others' and whose 'first responsibility is to the people.'[93]

These features and the cases affirming the high degree of independence of these institutions entrenched in the Constitution firmly demonstrate that they exist outside the traditional three arms of government under the conventional separation of powers doctrine. As Anthony Regan aptly noted, these independent constitutional institutions spread 'power horizontally, at the national government level, far beyond the limits of the separation of powers doctrine'.[94] Their entrenched position in the Constitution firmly signals the existence of a distinct model of the doctrine of separation of powers in Papua New Guinea, extending beyond the traditional confines of the tripartite separation of powers doctrine.

---

[86] *SCR No 1 of 1978; Re Ombudsman Commission Investigations of the Public Solicitor* [1978] PGSC 7 (Pritchard J) (unnumbered judgment).

[87] CPC Report 1974 Chapter 1 [22], [23].

[88] *SCR No 1 of 1978; Re Ombudsman Commission Investigations of the Public Solicitor* [1978] PGSC 7 (Pritchard J) (unnumbered judgment).

[89] *Alleged Improper Borrowing of AUD1.239 Billion Loan, In re* [2017] PGSC 8, [49].

[90] *SCR No 1 of 1978; Re Ombudsman Commission Investigations of the Public Solicitor* [1978] PGSC 7 (Pritchard J) (unnumbered judgment).

[91] Ibid.

[92] *Nilkare v Ombudsman Commission* [1995] PGNC 29 (unnumbered judgment).

[93] CPC Report 1975, Chapter 3 [3]–[5].

[94] Anthony J Regan, '*Protection of the Independence of Constitutional Office-Holders*' in Anthony J Regan, Owen Jessep and Eric L Kwa (eds), *Twenty Years of the Papua New Guinea Constitution* (University of Papua New Guinea Press, 2001) 233–4.

4 A New Separation of Powers in Papua New Guinea: The 'Fourth Arm' of Government

The innovative approach taken by the constitutional drafters in designing the Papua New Guinea Constitution comes as no surprise when considering their intentions, as stated in their Final Report:

> [O]ur Report recommends the *establishment of a number of new institutions* in Papua New Guinea and the *reconstitution of some existing ones*…[W]e are in general opposed to the concentration of power in too few hands...Both power and responsibility should be distributed among our leaders.[95]

The Constitutional Planning Committee (CPC) was not only committed to establishing 'a number of new institutions' and reconstituting 'some existing ones' but also defined the 'leaders' in these institutions to include 'members of the National Parliament' as well as 'constitutional office-holders, judges and magistrates'.[96] Placing 'constitutional office holders' in the same group of 'leaders' as parliamentarians and judges reflects a deliberate effort to establish a separate arm of government led by individuals with comparable leadership stature to those leading the three traditional arms of government.

The existence of multiple arms of government in Papua New Guinea was first significantly observed by Australian colonial judge Justice Pritchard in 1978.[97] Anthony Deklin further developed Justice Pritchard's findings in his 1982 thesis, proposing a 'multi-governmental arms theory' that argued the separation of powers in Papua New Guinea does not adhere to a 'strict separation in the traditional sense'.[98] Deklin's focus, however, was limited to the intertwined relationship between the executive and the legislature.

Australian David Cannings, who later became a judge, in his capacity as the lawyer for the Papua New Guinea Ombudsman Commission, appeared to make the earliest reference to the constitutional institutions and their firm independence as indicative of a 'fourth arm of government'.[99] Noting though that Chief Justice Gibbs Salika, in a discussion on this topic, indicated that Bernard Narokobi might have made the earliest reference to the 'fourth arm'. However, any relevant literature indicating Narokobi's assertion was not available to be verified at the time of research for this book. To the present, there is no evidence that Cannings' assertion has been accepted or thoroughly explored by the judges or deliberated by practitioners and scholars in Papua New Guinea.

---

[95] CPC Report 1975, Chapter 14 [2] (emphasis added).

[96] Ibid Chapter 3 [2].

[97] *Re Ombudsman Commission Investigations of the Public Solicitor* [1978] PGSC 7 (Pritchard J) (unnumbered judgment).

[98] Anthony P. W. Deklin, 'The Legal Control of the Executive in Papua New Guinea' in P Sack (ed), *Pacific Constitutions* (Australia National University, 1982) 173, 195.

[99] David Cannings, 'The Ombudsman Commission: Jurisdiction, Functions and Performance' in Anthony J Regan, Owen Jessep and Eric L Kwa (eds), *Twenty Years of the Papua New Guinea Constitution* (University of Papua New Guinea Press, 2001) 196, 201.

The disinterest or silence is likely due to a lack of critical judicial and legal thinking in Papua New Guinea on this subject rather than a rejection of Cannings' assertion. It needs to be revisited considering the discussion in this book. Recognising that a 'fourth arm' of government exists under the Constitution is critical to properly understanding the imperatives, workings and contexts of the Constitution. It would ensure that the Constitution is appropriately interpreted and applied, showcasing a constitutional innovation ahead of its time compared to other jurisdictions, including Australia.

There has been increasing international interest in recent years regarding the concept of the 'fourth arm' of government. For example, American Professor Bruce Ackerman, in his seminal thesis *The New Separation of Powers* (2000), questioned the efficacy of the traditional tripartite model of separation of powers in addressing contemporary challenges such as corruption. Ackerman proposed a reconfigured model to include 'constitutional watchdogs' in two primary branches—the 'integrity branch' and the 'democracy branch'—each constitutionally entrenched, independent, and specialized in promoting accountability and protecting democratic rights.[100]

Ackerman highlighted the growing politicisation of bureaucracy and lack of impartiality in modern parliaments as necessitating this restructuring.[101] He argued that the 'integrity branch' deserves a place in the modern separation of powers despite not being part of the traditional 'Holy Trinity'.[102]

In Canada, David Smith and Andrew Bell argues that a 'new separation of powers' is emerging as democracies trend towards an 'audit society'.[103] They described this as an increase in relatively independent agencies auditing government operations, such as the Auditor-General, Privacy Commissioner, and Electoral Commissioner, transforming them from 'being parliament's servants to being parliament masters.'[104] Underlying their submissions is the need for these 'agents of parliament' to be constitutionally entrenched to consolidate their place as a 'new branch of government'.

The notion of the 'fourth arm' of government was initially explored in Australia at the 1898 Constitutional Convention Debate when assessing whether the Australian Constitution should provide for an independent Inter-State Commission to administer and adjudicate disputes on interstate trade.[105]

---

[100] Bruce Ackerman, 'The New Separation of Powers' (2000) 113 *Harvard Law Review* 634, 694.

[101] Ibid 641, 694.

[102] Ibid 641, 695.

[103] David Smith, 'A Question of Trust: Parliamentary Democracy and Canadian Society' (2004) *Canadian Parliamentary Review* 25, 27; Jeffery Graham Bell, 'Agents of Parliament: A New Branch of Government?' (2006) Canadian Parliamentary Review 13, 13–7.

[104] Jeffery Graham Bell, 'Agents of Parliament: A New Branch of Government?' (2006) *Canadian Parliamentary Review* 13, 13–7.

[105] Sir William McMillan (25 February 1989) cited in Andrew Bell, 'The Elusive Promise of the Inter-State Commission' in James Stellios (ed), *Encounters with Constitutional Interpretation and Legal Education* (The Federation Press, 2018) 38.

Andrew Bell observed that 'in short, it was to be the fourth arm of government'.[106] However, Isaac Isaacs, one of the constitutional convention delegates, objected:

> We have the Parliament, the Executive, and the High Court, and now a fourth branch is created independent of all the rest – the Inter-State Commission…I want to eliminate the constitutional creation of the Inter-State Commission. *I think it is a great mistake that we should erect this body – a fourth branch of the Constitution.*[107]

Isaacs, who would later become a judge of the High Court, feared upsetting the tripartite framework of government, advocating strict adherence to traditional separation of powers principles.[108]

According to Professor J.M Finnis,

> the linchpin of his [Isaacs'] argument was precisely that there could be no "fourth branch" under the Constitution; that every institution must conform itself to one or other of the three exhaustive categories of power, but never to more than one.[109]

In his 2010 paper *Re-thinking the Separation of Powers*, Professor John McMillan differed from Isaacs in proposing a reconfiguration of Australia's tripartite model of the separation of powers doctrine to accommodate the rise of non-judicial accountability bodies like the Commonwealth Ombudsman and Auditor-General.[110] McMillan argued that these institution should collectively constitute a distinct branch of government. McMillan observed the limitations in the separation of powers doctrine:

> [T]he growth of non-judicial accountability bodies [in Australia] has not been constrained by the doctrine of separation of powers, but equally this new system of government accountability does not fit easily within that doctrine.[111]

According to McMillan, the same accountability function traditionally afforded to the courts is increasingly performed by a range of independent and specialised institutions, sometimes performing 'more effectively than the courts', that these institutions should form a distinct branch of government.[112] McMillan pertinently concluded:

> It is necessary to "rethink the separation of powers" [doctrine], to build a more accurate picture of legal and political accountability and to question longstanding beliefs that impede a proper appreciation of how people are protected in relation to government.[113]

---

[106] Ibid 39.

[107] Federal Convention Debates (1989) 2279, 2391 quoted in Finnis, 'Separation of Powers in the Australian Constitution: Some Preliminary Consideration' (1968) 3(2) *Adelaide Law Review* 159, 174–5 (emphasis added).

[108] Ibid.

[109] Ibid 164.

[110] John McMillan, 'Re-thinking the Separation of Powers' (2010) 38 Federal Law Review 423.

[111] Ibid.

[112] Ibid.

[113] Ibid.

In Europe, Frank Vibert has argued that interest driven politics and supranational institution penetration have led to 'unelected bodies' overseeing governmental oversight, constituting a new branch of government. Vibert posited that these bodies strengthen democratic systems by enhancing public accountability.[114] Vibert argued that these 'unelected bodies...compos[e] a new branch of government and [are] forming the basis of a new separation of powers'.[115] Contrary to fears that this may mark a decline in democracy or constitutionalism, Vibert contended that 'their rise has the potential to make democratic systems of government more robust'.[116]

In a most recent and substantive study on the subject, Harvard Professor Mark Tushnet, contended that the 'fourth arm' of government is a phenomenon in twenty-first century constitutions.[117] While it is a correct assessment, considering the nineteenth to twentieth century constitutions generally did not have a fourth branch as a common feature of constitution-making, the Papua New Guinea Constitution, enacted in 1975, was clearly ahead of its time and peers.

These literature from a range of jurisdictions further demonstrates that the proposal for the 'fourth arm' of government is re-emerging in light of contemporary challenges to democracies.[118] However, the challenge for these jurisdictions, as demonstrated in the case of Australia, is for the fourth arm to be entrenched in the constitution and to overcome the reluctance of the courts to recognise a potential rival to their functions.[119]

Conversely, Papua New Guinea, having understood its constitutional history, context and intent, presents a different case. While the concept of a fourth arm of government may be emerging in other jurisdictions as a matter for constitutional reform, the Papua New Guinea 'home-grown' Constitution anticipated the role of the fourth arm of government at its beginning in 1975. In that respect, the drafters of the Constitution were profoundly innovative and forward thinking.

The comparisons provide further insights between Papua New Guinea and other jurisdictions. Firstly, Papua New Guinea's independent constitutional institutions do not fit neatly into the traditional 'integrity branch' model, as some of them, such as the Ombudsman Commission and the Public Prosecutor, possess substantive investigative, prosecutorial, and legal aid powers.

Secondly, these institutions are constitutionally entrenched and explicitly independent of the three traditional arms of government. Thirdly, many of the institutions have standing under section 19 of the Constitution to challenge constitutional amendments or enactments, thereby enhancing their accountability function against

[114] Frank Vibert, *The Rise of the Unelected: Democracy and the New Separation of Powers* (Cambridge University Press, 2007) 1–3, 6–9, 129.

[115] Ibid 2.

[116] Ibid.

[117] Mark Tushnet, *The New Fourth Branch* (Cambridge University Press, 2021).

[118] International Institute for Democracy and Electoral Assistance (IDEA), 'Fourth Branch Institutions' (Paper presented at the Workshop on the Tuvalu Constitutional Reform, University of New South Wales, 27 February 2018) 4–5.

[119] Finnis, above n 107, 164.

other branches of government. Fourthly, Papua New Guinea's judiciary is supportive and encouraging of the establishment of these institutions, contributing to a unique accountability landscape, in contrast to Australia's High Court, for instance.

These distinctions underscore that the textual references to the separation of powers doctrine in the Papua New Guinea Constitution discussed earlier only partially apply within the country's constitutional context. In Papua New Guinea, the doctrine has evolved beyond the traditional tripartite model to encompass a 'fourth arm' of government. While other democracies argue for a 'new' separation of powers to incorporate their conceptions of the fourth arm, it is, in fact, an 'old' concept for Papua New Guinea under its 'home-grown' constitutional framework. This innovation was thus ahead of its time and its peers globally, serving as a hallmark of the Constitution's 'home-grown' character.

The traditional conception of the separation of powers doctrine, which limits to three arms of government with the judiciary prescribed as having a restricted role, is therefore not applicable in Papua New Guinea. The doctrine has been reconfigured to include four arms of government and a judiciary with a clear mandate to exercise a more expansive and liberal role in Papua New Guinea.

5 Conclusion

The doctrine of separation of powers, as a fundamental constitutional principle of democracies, has undergone various adaptations and modifications to suit different contexts and drafting intentions. Papua New Guinea was no different in contextualising and reconfiguring the doctrine.

While the traditional model of the three arms of government may appear entrenched in the Constitution, this is only in principle and inadequate to meet the demands for a governmental framework based on a high degree of accountability. Although Papua New Guinea inherited aspects of the British Westminster system of government, the liberal character of the judiciary with its expansive powers and the establishment of independent constitutional institutions operating outside the traditional tripartite model of government, firmly indicate a deliberate reconfiguration of the traditional doctrine of separation of powers. The outcome of this reconfiguration is a 'home-grown' model of separation of powers doctrine with a liberal judiciary and a fourth arm of government.

As interest in the 'fourth arm' mechanism emerges globally in response to issues of democratic decline and good governance, the framers of the Papua New Guinea Constitution foresaw its need at the time of drafting. The Supreme Court attested to the innovation and foresight of the drafters in the following way:

> The wisdom and ingenuity of our founding fathers, many of them with limited knowledge of constitutionalism, is remarkable; they foresaw a global movement towards a decline in

> Parliamentary sovereignty and supremacy; and the evolution of a Parliamentary democracy of limited power, limited by a written Constitution.[120]

There should, therefore, be a rethinking of how the separation of powers doctrine is understood in Papua New Guinea, so that it represents a more accurate portrayal of legal and political accountability and the 'home-grown' constitutional design. This reevaluation should also challenge longstanding ideologies and practices, often uncritically accepted, in understanding Papua New Guinea's political and constitutional systems.

As Justice Pritchard argued in rejecting submissions on the 'three traditional' arms of government, 'there is no such tradition in Papua New Guinea.'[121] The call for a reevaluation in the understanding of the separation of powers doctrine firmly aligns with the clarion call by Justice Pritchard that 'in Papua New Guinea we do not call on traditions of government from anywhere in the world at all; we look to our own constitutional laws and them alone'.[122]

Looking 'to our own constitutional laws and them alone' firmly demonstrates that the intended separation of powers doctrine for Papua New Guina was never meant to follow the traditional model of Anglo-Australian or any other model elsewhere. A significant benefit of such rethinking would be to prevent misunderstandings of the role of the courts, which could lead to mitigating the kind of tensions between the judiciary and the other two arms of government discussed in the preceding chapter.

---

[120] *In re Reference to Constitution Section 19(1) by East Sepik Provincial Executive* [2011] PGSC 41, [89].

[121] *Ombudsman Commission Investigations of the Public Solicitor* [1978] PGSC 7 (Pritchard J) (unnumbered judgment).

[122] *Re Ombudsman Commission Investigations of the Public Solicitor* [1978] PGSC 7 (Pritchard J) (unnumbered judgment) (emphasis added).

Chapter 8
Judges as Guardians of Papua New Guinea's Democracy

Abstract Chapter 8 delves deeper into how the liberal judicial powers of the judiciary have been applied in addressing socially and politically embedded issues, arguing that the role of the judges has expanded beyond their traditionally assigned role as 'guardians of the Constitution' to that of 'guardians of Papua New Guinea democracy.' The analysis highlights various judicial approaches and textual indicators in the Constitution to demonstrate that Papua New Guinea judges have unprecedented and critical political and social oversight and supervisory roles. Properly considered, these powers elevate the role of the judges to a broader societal guardianship role. Embracing this position not only enhances understanding of the Papua New Guinea judiciary's character but also underscores the legitimate function of courts and judges as agents of social and political development in the country.

Keywords Guardians of the constitutions · Judicial power · Liberal judiciary · Papua New Guinea judges

1 Introduction

Judges of the Supreme Court of Papua New Guinea have frequently described their role through various court rulings as 'the guardian of the Constitution', asserting their 'constitutional duty to guard and defend the Constitution'.[1] This perspective is shared by many superior courts in other jurisdictions.[2] However, as this chapter will discuss, in Papua New Guinea, judges are not merely 'guardians of the Constitution' in the traditional sense but also guardians of the Papua New Guinea democracy. The expanded role signifies that the courts have a function that extends beyond the legal sphere to the socio-political arena. Their role is as much political as it is legal.

[1] *Reference by Allan Marat & Reference by the National Parliament* [2012] PGSC 20, [429]; *In re Reference to Constitution Section 19(1) by East Sepik Provincial Executive* [2011] PGSC 41, [397]; *Christopher Haiveta v Pius Wingti (No 3)* [1994] PNGLR 197 (Amet CJ) (unnumbered judgment).

[2] Lady Hale, *The Supreme Court: Guardian of the Constitution?* (Speech delivered at the Sultan Azlan Shah Lecture, Kuala Lumpur Malaysia, 2016) 2.

B. Kama, *Rethinking Judicial Power in Papua New Guinea*,
https://doi.org/10.1007/978-981-97-2946-3_8

The implication of reframing judicial actors as guardians of the country's democracy, rather than solely guardians of the Constitution, is that it clarifies their position under the 'home-grown' Constitution as legitimate socio-political actors. The following analysis starts with a conceptual overview of the traditional 'guardian of the constitution' role. It is then followed by a substantive discussion, arguing that the guardianship role of the courts in Papua New Guinea needs to be understood differently, encompassing guardianship of the country's democracy. Their role includes a distinct political function that co-exists with their judicial responsibilities.

2 Orthodox View as Guardian of the Constitution

One of the earliest references to the 'guardian' role of the courts was by Alexander Hamilton in the *Federalist Papers* (1788), where he described judges as 'faithful guardians of the Constitution'.[3] The decision of the United States Supreme Court in the famous *Marbury v Madison* (1803) case, which upheld the principle of judicial review, consolidated the notion of superior courts being the 'guardians of the constitution'.[4] This concept is widely evident in constitutions influenced by the American constitutional system. But what does this role of guardianship involve?[5]

Hamilton envisioned the 'guardians' as having a role limited to upholding the 'constitutional intentions of the legislature'.[6] Chief Justice Marshall in *Marbury v Madison* maintained that perspective, stating:

> The province of this court is, solely, to decide on the rights of individuals, not to inquire how the executive or executive officers, perform duties in which they have discretion. Questions, in their nature political, or which are, by the constitution and laws, submitted to the executive can never be made in this court.[7]

This limitation was also approved, for instance, by the High Court of Australia in *Victoria v Commonwealth* (1975) where it held that 'as the guardian of the Constitution, [we are] charged...with the responsibility of determining whether legislative powers conferred by the Constitution are validly exercised in accordance with its requirements'.[8]

Aligned with the traditional restrictive role of judges, the concept of 'guardian' in these jurisdictions typically does not go beyond resolving the legal disputes to acting

[3] Alexander Hamilton, *The Federalist Papers: No. 78* (1788) (online) Yale Law School Avalon Project, http://avalon.law.yale.edu/18th_century/fed78.asp.

[4] (1803) 5 US (1 Cranch) 137.

[5] Above n 2. Lady Hale of the United Kingdom Supreme Court noted, regarding her Honour's jurisdiction: 'it is accepted that we are the guardians of the Constitution [but] if only we knew what it meant'.

[6] Hamilton, above n 3.

[7] *Marbury v Madison* (1803) 5 US (1 Cranch) 137, 170.

[8] *Victoria v Commonwealth* (1975) 134 CLR 81, 182 (Mason J).

as 'guardians of the society'[9] or 'to be involved in political matters'.[10] It further advocates that 'the authority of the court is enhanced only by maintaining silence on constitutional questions that engender political controversy'.[11] This position was evident, for instance, in *Attorney-General (Cth) v The Queen* (1957), where the Privy Council emphasised that the executive government of Australia should not seek 'advisory opinions' from the High Court as it had the potential 'to sap [the Court's] independence and impartiality'.[12]

As Professor Loughlin observed, in jurisdictions where the restrictive role of the judiciary is applied, courts tend to use 'a number of strategies to avoid being dragged into [the socio-political] arena, including doctrines of non-justiciability, ripeness, standing, and refusal to determine moot questions'.[13] These strategies are argued to be necessary to prevent the courts from being engaged in political controversies and 'contaminate judicial power'.[14]

However, as discussed in Chap. 5 (textual indicators of a liberal judiciary with expansive powers) and Chap. 6 (mandate of the Supreme Court to engage in politically contentious cases), none of these 'strategies' typically associated with the traditional conception of judges as 'guardians of the constitution' are intended to be applied in the case of Papua New Guinea. In fact, quite the opposite is observed, noting the 'home-grown' Constitution envisioned a broader societal role of judges. The courts in Papua New Guina are thus open and constitutionally mandated to deal with political questions and have actively limited the application of the traditional barriers to judicial review such as standing and non-justiciability principles.

3 Guardians of Democracy: Beyond the Orthodox View to a Political Function in Papua New Guinea

In a revealing paper to his Australian audience on the character of the Papua New Guinea judiciary in 1996, Chief Justice Arnold Amet acknowledged that the judiciary 'is vested with very powerful roles to play in the shaping' of the country and 'in the overall shaping of developments and the future of the constitutional democracy of the young independent Papua New Guinea'.[15] The phrase 'shaping of developments' in

[9] Edward Corwin, 'Marbury v Madison and the Doctrine of Judicial Review' (1914) *12 Michigan Law Review* 538, 559.

[10] Peter Mulhern, 'In Defence of Political Question Doctrine' (1988) 137 *University of Pennsylvania Law Review* 97, 102.

[11] Martin Loughlin, 'The silences of constitutions' (2019) 17 *International Journal of Constitutional Law* 18, 27.

[12] *Attorney-General (Cth) v The Queen* (1957) 95 CLR 529, 541; James Stellios, *The Federal Judicature: Chapter III of the Constitution* (LexisNexis, 2010) 95.

[13] Loughlin, above n 11.

[14] Ibid.

[15] Sir Arnold Amet, 'Issues facing the Supreme Court of Papua New Guinea' in Cheryl Saunders (ed), *Courts of Final Jurisdiction: The Mason Court in Australia* (The Federation Press, 1996), 261.

the country suggests a role for the judiciary that extends beyond legal to political. This will be explored further below with two sets of indicators supporting the assertion that the role of the judges in Papua New Guinea transcends their traditional role as guardians of the Constitution to encompass guardianship of the Papua New Guinea's democracy, thereby entailing a political role.

The first set of indicators consists of judicial approaches evident in court judgements. The second set includes specific constitutional provisions as interpreted by the courts that uphold these judicial approaches, thus permitting greater judicial role in the political sphere.

3.1 Judicial Approaches

There are five judicial approaches evident, especially in the opinions of the judges in the constitutional crisis cases discussed in Chap. 6, and others of a similar nature, demonstrating that superior courts in Papua New Guinea have a socio-political function.

Open criticism of and passing judgement on internal parliamentary matters

The first judicial approach is the tendency of the courts to openly criticise Parliament and their readiness to pass judgement on its internal workings.[16] A significant critique by the judiciary against Parliament is that it has been 'a mere rubber stamp for the policies and decisions of the executive government' without 'debate and meaningful discourse'.[17] Justice Sakora denounced in the *ESP Case* the 'growing dominance of and over parliament by the executive' as 'a creeping tyranny'.[18]

This view contrasts with the general understanding of a Westminster parliament, where a ruling party or a coalition government with a majority of seats, supported by party discipline, typically leads to a compliant parliament.[19] Such a parliament could rightfully be described as a 'rubber-stamp' parliament or 'a legislature on its knees'.[20] The dominance of the executive is thus accepted as an inherent feature of the Westminster parliament and a compliant parliament tolerated as a normal political condition.

---

[16] See for instance, *In re Reference to Constitution Section 19(1) by East Sepik Provincial Executive* [2011] PGSC 41, [85], [533]; *Re Calling of the Parliament* [1999] PNGLR 285 (unnumbered judgment); *Namah v O'Neill* [2015] PGSC 77, [46].

[17] *In re Reference to Constitution Section 19(1) by East Sepik Provincial Executive* [2011] PGSC 41, [65].

[18] *In re Reference to Constitution Section 19(1) by East Sepik Provincial Executive* [2011] PGSC 41, [604].

[19] Meg Russell, Daniel Gover and Kristina Wollter, 'Does the Executive Dominate the Westminster Legislative Process?' (2016) 69 *Parliamentary Affairs* 286.

[20] Anthony King and Ivor Crewe, *The Blunders of Our Governments* (Oneworld Publications, 2013) 36.

Yet, in Papua New Guinea, the drafters of the Constitution rejected this practice of Westminster parliament,[21] and the Court was mindful of that drafting history in its criticism. For instance, Justice Sakora, explained that '[a]t independence, we adopted what can be described as a "modified version" of the *Westminster* model of parliamentary executive government system'[22] with the expectation that the

> national parliament, the highest political forum in the land, should never be a 'rubber stamp' of or for the executive, and that any legislative programme of the executive should be subjected to the closest scrutiny. No legislation should, therefore, be, colloquially speaking 'steamrolled' or 'bulldozed' through parliament.[23]

Chief Justice Injia further reiterated this point in a direct rejection of party politics or party discipline in *Namah & Geno v O'Neill* (2015):

> [O]ur politicians must, by now, understand and fully appreciate, that they are in Parliament at their people's behest and that party politics should not dictate their actions, rather, the people they represent and the platforms that got them into Parliament in the first place.[24]

These cases highlight that the Constitution, as interpreted by the Court, mandates the legislators to perform their functions without pressure or constraints from their political parties or the executive. In the Court's view, any deviation from this principle, although consistent with Westminster practices, conflicts with the intents of the 'home-grown' Constitution. By taking this stance, the Court exercises its judicial power beyond strictly legal issues to make judgments on political matters and the type of political culture that should shape Papua New Guinea.

The second set of criticism indicative of the Court's political role involves its interactions with the Speaker of Parliament. In both the *ESP* and *Marat Cases*, the Court openly criticised the Speaker of Parliament, holding him responsible for the constitutional crisis.[25] Justice Kirriwom, for instance, stated that 'the Speaker contributed enormously to this [constitutional] crisis… [by] collaborating with the proponents of this motion to over-throw a legitimate government'.[26]

According to the Constitution, the Speaker of Parliament is responsible for 'upholding the dignity of the Parliament, maintaining order in it, regulate its proceedings and administering its affairs'.[27] Despite this, numerous cases exist where the Court has openly rebuked the Speaker for actions deemed improper and contrary to the functions of the Speaker.[28] For instance, in *Re-Election of the Governor*

---

[21] CPC Report 1974, Chapter 6 [1].

[22] *Reference by the Ombudsman Commission of Papua New Guinea* [2010] PGSC 10, [83].

[23] Ibid [85].

[24] *Namah & Geno v O'Neill* [2015] PGSC 77, [192].

[25] *In re Reference to Constitution Section 19(1) by East Sepik Provincial Executive* [2011] PGSC 41, [153], [159], [744]; *Reference by Allan Marat & Reference by the National Parliament* [2012] PGSC 20, [100], [151], [189].

[26] *In re Reference to Constitution Section 19(1) by East Sepik Provincial Executive* [2011] PGSC 41, [734], [744].

[27] S 108.

[28] *In re Reference to Constitution Section 19(1) by East Sepik Provincial Executive* [2011] PGSC 41, [159], [744]; *In re Re-Election of the Governor General* [2010] SC1085, [130]; *Reference by the*

General (2010), the Court scrutinised the Speaker's conduct during the election of the Governor-General by Members of Parliament and questioned the Speaker's commitment to the Constitution.[29] In 2016, the Supreme Court condemned the Speaker's decision to defer scheduled parliament sittings for political conveniences as 'an affront to the rule of law'.[30]

What is particularly significant in Papua New Guinea is that some of the Court's criticisms of the Speaker involve actions that would typically be considered internal parliamentary proceedings and ordinarily excluded from judicial review due to non-justiciability (discussed later). In the Westminster system, the Speaker is considered to occupy 'the foremost place in the body that expresses the national will' and is the 'physical embodiment of the Assembly'.[31] Consequently, judges elsewhere typically exercise restraint in reviewing intramural parliamentary proceedings or criticising the parliament's administration beyond any legal issues arising in dispute.[32]

However, Papua New Guinea presents a distinct case. The judiciary's determination to denounce the Speaker, even regarding matters of internal parliamentary procedure, underscores its broader and unique guardianship role to shape Papua New Guinea's society and democracy.

Accountability of constitutional institutions and personnel

The second indicator of a socio-political guardian function of the superior courts, evident in the case studies is their tendency to criticise and hold accountable the performance of other constitutional institutions and personalities, even if they are not part of formal court proceedings.[33] For instance, in the *ESP Case*, Justice Sakora described the weaknesses and abusive attitudes within constitutional institutions and their personnel as an 'adverse assault on the integrity of the public office(s)', which 'diminish[ed] international respect for our system of government'.[34]

In *Re Application by Ila Geno* (2014), the Supreme Court lamented that 'five different [constitutional] authorities under Section 19(1) expressed no interest' in initiating a constitutional reference against a controversial constitutional amendment.[35] As a result, the Court extended standing to challenge constitutional

---

Ombudsman Commission, Re Section 19 of the Constitution [2010] PGSC 43; *Special Reference Pursuant to Constitution Section 10, Calling of the Parliament* [1999] PGSC 21.

[29] *In re Re-Election of the Governor General* [2010] SC1085, [144].

[30] It was an unpublished judgement, but journalists present at the court house cited the decision. See, for instance, Eric Tlozek, 'PNG court orders the recall of Parliament to hear no-confidence motion in Prime Minister', *ABC News* (online), 12 July 2016.

[31] Georges Bergougnous, *Presiding Officers of National Parliamentary Assemblies: A World Comparative Study* (Inter-Parliamentary Union, 1997) 35.

[32] Robert French, 'The Courts and the Parliament' (Speech delivered at the Queensland Supreme Court Seminar, Brisbane, 04 August 2012) 5.

[33] See, for instance, *In re Reference to Constitution Section 19(1) by East Sepik Provincial Executive* [2011] PGSC 41, [211]—[12]; *Namah v O'Neill* [2015] PGSC 77, [83].

[34] *In re Reference to Constitution Section 19(1) by East Sepik Provincial Executive* [2011] PGSC 41, [520].

[35] *In re Application by Ila Geno* [2014] PGSC 2, [39].

amendments to a retired public servant.[36] The Court criticised these constitutional institutions for failing to invoke their powers to hold the government accountable:

> This is disappointing but perhaps it is not surprising. It is a reflection of a certain degree of constitutional apathy that has been developing for some time. The authorities that would be expected to take a great deal of interest in constitutional issues appear to be sleeping at the wheel.[37]

Regarding constitutional personnel, including members of the legislature and the executive, the courts have been critical of their interferences with the constitutional system's general functioning. For instance, in *Somare v Manek* (2011), where former Prime Minister Sir Michael Somare sought interim injunctive orders to prevent trial by a Leadership Tribunal for breaches of the Leadership Code,[38] the Court refused to intervene. It stated that ongoing investigations and properly constituted trials needed completion before judicial review could proceed.

In a revealing response indicative of the Court's role in political accountability, it went beyond the legal issue to emphasize the importance of responsible leadership and the integrity of constitutional offices:

> Good leadership requires a ready acceptance of responsibility for one's actions and try to minimize any harm or damage that can be done to themselves, interest of the institutions they are part of and that of the nation, by allowing the process to take its course. Most of the harm and damage is caused by people who chose to take all sorts of unnecessary issues with the process without merit most of the time, which results in unnecessary costs and delay. Usually, such steps are taken to divert attention from the real issues.[39]

The Court continued its assessment of the political realities that justified its response, going beyond the legal issue to address deep political and governance issues:

> [I]t is unfortunately fast becoming the norm for most leaders in PNG who are the subject of allegations and investigations for misconduct in office and or criminal offences to continuing to occupy their respective offices and continue to function and are readily applying for stay or injunctive orders. Some of them are even interfering into the proper conduct of investigations and proper conclusions of such investigations. Others are doing everything they possibly can to remain in office, continue to function and in most instances are either committing more misconduct in office from tampering with evidence, interfering with witnesses, swindling of funds or otherwise seriously abusing their powers knowing that, they may not last long in those offices.[40]

The Court also expressed similar sentiments earlier in *Pruaitch v Manek* (2010).[41] In that case, the appellant, who was the Minister for Treasury and Finance, appealed a National Court decision that refused his application for interim injunction and

---

[36] Ibid.

[37] Ibid [39], [40].

[38] *Somare v Manek* [2011] PGSC 17.

[39] Ibid [59].

[40] Ibid [66].

[41] *Pruaitch v Manek* [2010] PGSC 7, [82], [87].

stay orders against investigations conducted by the Ombudsman Commission.[42] The Court rejected the appeal and emphasised that if courts allow leaders to

> tak[e] out stay orders at will against the tribunals from inquiring into their alleged misconduct, [it] will [not only] make a mockery of the *Leadership Code*...[but] will also make a mockery of the *Constitution* and the leaders will continue to act in contempt and defiance of the *Constitution*.[43]

These judicial opinions illustrate the courts' use of their judicial power to address profound socio-political issues of accountability and good governance beyond mere legal matters. They firmly demonstrate the superior courts as having an expansive constitutional guardianship role, encompassing both institutional policing and political accountability functions.

Political commentary in judicial opinions

The third indicator of the courts having a socio-political function stem from judicial statements that extend beyond the legal issues to include explicit political commentary. This was clearly demonstrated in the cases discussed in Chap. 6, where judges made statements that arguably had purely political implications.

For example, in the *ESP* case, Justice Sakora described the usurpation of the Somare regime not as an isolated event but as something preceded by 'tell-tale signs [and] the writing on the wall'.[44] His Honour identified these 'signs' as simmering political rivalries within Somare's government, 'mounting social and economic evils [and the] perennial allegations of official corruption'.[45] His Honour continued with a political assessment of the country:

> Goods and services were not reaching the people they were or ought to be intended for. In a country of rich mineral resources, neglect and poverty were everywhere. Run-down social services infrastructure remained unattended to. We seemed to be quite content with a general air of neglect, decay and deterioration that were evident everywhere in the country.[46]

Justice Sakora concluded that these issues created 'a political environment that was causing widespread frustration and uncertainty... [among] the long-suffering people of this country' and thus, created a 'state of necessity' for intervention against Somare's government.[47]

Another example of political assessment discussed in Chap. 6 involves the memo allegedly from Justice Kirriwom to all judges in the country. The memo called for judges 'to demonstrate more collegiality in this war' against the Executive and denounced the criminal charges against the Chief Justice as being 'politically

[42] Ibid.

[43] Ibid [87] (emphasis added).

[44] *In re Reference to Constitution Section 19(1) by East Sepik Provincial Executive* [2011] PGSC 41, [540].

[45] Ibid [605].

[46] Ibid.

[47] Ibid [554], [602]–[35].

motivated'.[48] The memo condemned the O'Neill government in politically explicit terms:

> This regime is in a way like a puppet that is dancing to the tune that somebody else (Prime Minister) is playing, somebody who wants this institution (judiciary) under current CJ dismantled permanently.[49]

The memo invited judges to a 'call to arms', to not be 'too passive, very inactive and so complacent' but to 'rise up now against [the Executive] in the best and long-term interest of the judiciary' and to 'defend the institution that our oath of loyalty demands of us'.[50]

These examples illustrate that the constitutional guardianship role of judges extends beyond the narrow confines of simply adjudicating on legal issues to contributing vigilantly to the political culture and in shaping the development of the country. It requires them to engage deeply with socio-political issues, enlighten the public, influence political discourse, and potentially impact regime change. Such actions are consistent with their constitutional position as 'leaders' in Papua New Guinea society and as guardians of its democracy.

Circumventing the traditional non-justiciability barrier

The fourth judicial indicator of the Court's expansive guardianship role is its tendency to apply broad interpretations to contentious constitutional provisions to address underlying socio-political issues. Chapters 6 and 7 discussed how this is applied in terms of departing from the narrow application of the separation of powers doctrine and promoting constitutional supremacy as opposed to parliamentary supremacy.

Another contentious example is the principle of non-justiciability of parliamentary proceedings. Section 134 of the Constitution states:

> Except as is specifically provided by a Constitutional Law, the question, whether the procedures prescribed for the Parliament or its committees have been complied with, is non-justiciable.

In other constitutional systems, the principle of non-justiciability is intended to shield the internal matters and proceedings of parliament from judicial review.[51]

However, in the *Marat* case, the Supreme Court held that the non-justiciability defence should not be taken to 'permit Parliament to commit breaches of Constitutional provisions...with impunity [leading to] political instability'.[52] This followed the decision in *Haiveta v Wingti* (No 1) (1994), that

---

48 'Is Papua New Guinea's judiciary no longer independent?' on *PNG Exposed Blog* (13 March 2012). http://pngexposed.wordpress.com/2012/03/13/is-papua-new-guineas-judiciary-no-longer-independent/ (A purported copy of the memo can be viewed from this publicly accessible blog).

49 Ibid 2.

50 Ibid 1–3.

51 Appleby, Gabrielle and Adam Webster, 'Parliament's Role in Constitutional Interpretation' (2013) 37(2) *Melbourne University Law Review* 255, 269.

52 *Reference by Allan Marat & Reference by the National Parliament* [2012] PGSC 20, [48].

> issues raised in the [constitutional] Reference were of National interest and justice demanded that the Court needed to go behind or past the immunity wall of the non-justiciability doctrine.[53]

The Court in the *Marat* case reaffirmed this expansive view that the

> court's inherent powers and jurisdiction must not be subdued by section 134 of the *Constitution* in its inquiry into what happened on the floor of Parliament...in the interest of good governance and in the interest of justice.[54]

This position was further upheld in *Namah v Poole* (2016), where the judges held that 'the Court is permitted, despite a question being labelled non-justiciable, to hear argument that the power, function, duty or responsibility was exercised or performed unlawfully'.[55]

These broad interpretations clearly distinguished itself from the non-justiciability principle accepted in other democracies, reflecting the distinct 'home-grown' constitutional intents for the judiciary to address deep socio-political issues underlying legal disputes. The Court in these cases took the approach fully aware of its broader societal role to transcend beyond the confines of the legal issues.

In fact, in *Matter of the Organic Law on the Nomination of Governor-General* (2004), the Court went so far as to overturn traditional barriers against the exercise of its judicial power, declaring that 'any argument that the Parliament and or the Executive are free from the directives of the Court are misconceived'.[56] This reflects the Court's unwavering stance on its 'inherent power to do justice,'[57] which includes 'supervisory and controlling powers over exercise of both legislative and executive powers'.[58]

These examples illustrate the judiciary's function as extending beyond mere adjudication of legal disputes to actively engaging with and supervising the interactions of political entities to ensure the welfare of the Papua New Guinea's democracy.

Declaration of unconstitutional constitutional amendments

The fifth indicator of an expansive guardianship role of superior courts, which encompasses a political function, is the exercise of judicial power to declare 'validly' enacted constitutional amendments unconstitutional. Establishing the Court's authority to do so in Papua New Guinea is significant, as this area of constitutional law is not widely

---

[53] *Haiveta v Wingti (No 1)* [1994] PNGLR 160 (Amet CJ); *In re Reference to Constitution Section 19(1) by East Sepik Provincial Executive* [2011] PGSC 41, [719].

[54] *Reference by Allan Marat & Reference by the National Parliament* [2012] PGSC 20, [724].

[55] *Namah v Poole* [2016] PGSC 34, [37].

[56] *In the Matter of the Organic Law on the Nomination of Governor-General* [2004] PGSC 3 (Kapi CJ, Injia DCJ, Hinchliffe, Salika & Sawong JJ) (unnumbered judgment).

[57] *Bebi v Fox* [2010] PGNC 158 (unnumbered judgment).

[58] *Southern Highlands Provincial Government v Somare, Chairman of the National Executive Council* [2007] PGSC 2, [120]; Accepted in *Reference by Allan Marat & Reference by the National Parliament* [2012] PGSC 20, [72].

accepted, even in countries that embrace judicial review.[59] Jurist Aharon Barak, for instance, observed that while superior courts tend to accept that their functions include 'judicial review of the constitutionality of a statute', it remains contentious 'whether that judicial review also covers an amendment to the constitution that has been made pursuant to the provisions of the constitution regarding amendment of the constitution'.[60]

The controversy arises because constitutional amendments, unlike ordinary legislation, involve a high degree of 'constituent power', either directly through referendum or indirectly through consultation with the constituency, where parliament is the sole amending body.[61] The latter process applies to the case of Papua New Guinea, where the Constitution mandates that MPs receive at least one month's notice of proposed amendments before tabling in parliament, and at least two months between readings of amendment bills.[62] According to the Supreme Court, these time periods are intended for MPs to facilitate 'consultation with members of their constituency'.[63]

However, the Constitution has been interpreted as providing the Supreme Court power to review the substantive aspects of a constitutional amendment despite it being validly enacted.[64] For example, in the landmark case of *Re Organic Law on Integrity of Political Parties and Candidates* (2010) (OLIPAC Case),[65] a Supreme Court reference was brought against a set of constitutional amendments passed by the Somare government that were aimed at disciplining MPs and their political parties for frequently changing political allegiances.[66] Shifting political allegiances is an unsettling political issue in Papua New Guinea as it often results in frequent vote of no confidence motions and political instability among other consequences.[67]

However, despite the policy merits and procedural compliance of these amendments, the Supreme Court deemed parts unconstitutional because they unduly restricted MPs' rights to make decisions and form alliances freely.[68]

---

[59] Yaniv Roznai, 'Unconstitutional Constitutional Amendments: The Migration and Success of a Constitutional Idea' (2013) 61 *The American Journal of Comparative Law 657*.

[60] Aharon Barak, 'Unconstitutional Constitutional Amendments' (2011) 44 *Israel Law Review* 321.

[61] Yaniv Roznai, *Unconstitutional Constitutional Amendments:* The Limits of Amendment Powers (Oxford University Press, 2017) 107–111.

[62] Ss 13, 14; *Standing Orders of the National Parliament* Part XIXA.

[63] *In the Matter of Constitutional Validity of Constitutional Amendment (Provincial Governments and Local-Level Governments)* [1995] PGLawRp 714 (unnumbered judgment).

[64] Sections 18 and 19.

[65] *Special Reference By Fly River Provincial Executive Council, Re Organic Law on Integrity of Political Parties and Candidates* [2010] PGSC 3.

[66] Ibid [4].

[67] David Kavanamur, Charles Yala and Quinton Clements, *Building a Nation in Papua New Guinea: Views of the Post-independence Generation* (Pandanus Books, 2003) 38; Bal Kama, 'The Supreme Court's 'vote of no confidence' decision: game on in Waigani' on Australian National University Development Policy Centre, *DevPolicy Blog* (online) (12 Oct 2015).

[68] *Special Reference By Fly River Provincial Executive Council, Re Organic Law on Integrity of Political Parties and Candidates* [2010] PGSC 3, [165], [169], [172], [209], [268].

Another significant case was *Namah v O'Neill* (2015), where the Opposition Leader challenged amendments extending the 'grace period' from 18 to 30 months before a no-confidence vote could be triggered after forming a new government.[69] The government argued that the amendments were intended 'to maintain political stability' and 'to defend against motions of no confidence' that often interrupts government business.[70]

The Court acknowledged the amendments' policy objectives and procedural validity but invalidated them, citing 'inconsistency with the principle of responsible government'.[71] The principle of 'responsible government' is not explicitly entrenched in the Constitution, although it is part of the basic structure of any Westminster system. It is largely a principle in political theory than for constitutional enforcement. For the Court to rely on the principle to invalidate validly enacted constitutional amendments firmly underscores its role as a political guardian. [72]

To substantiate its findings, the Court went beyond traditional interpretative tools, to requesting and accepting affidavits from former prime ministers and members of the Constitutional Planning Committee (CPC) such as Sir Michael Somare, Sir Julius Chan, Pais Wingti, Peter O'Neill and John Momis. These affidavits affirmed that responsible government is foundational to the Constitution, influencing the Court's interpretation.[73] This approach resonated with Chief Justice Barak's observations that 'protecting the constitution does not only involve protection against statutes that violate the constitution but also against amendments to the constitution that violates its foundations'.[74]

However, the process of obtaining the evidence was unconventional. The Supreme Court not only requested the affidavits from these political actors to aid its interpretation of the legal issues, but importantly, the named persons were all politically active and occupied various political role in the society, including having views that were contrary to the government that passed the constitutional amendments. In engaging them, the Court demonstrates that assessing the constitutionality of validly enacted amendments in Papua New Guinea involves not only legal but also broader constitutional and political considerations. By engaging with these perspectives, the Court positioned itself as a guardian of democracy, ensuring the integrity and stability of the country's political framework.

---

[69] *Namah v O'Neill* [2015] PGSC 77 (4 September 2015).

[70] Ibid [78].

[71] Ibid [53].

[72] John Uhr, 'Parliament and the Executive' (2004) 24 *Adelaide Law Review* 51, 53–4.

[73] *Namah v O'Neill* [2015] PGSC 77, [24], [28]—[32].

[74] Aharon Barak, 'Unconstitutional Constitutional Amendments' (2011) 44 *Israel Law Review* 321, 336.

3.2 Textual Indicators

The judiciary's broader socio-political guardianship role is bolstered by several textual indicators in the Constitution. Chapter 5 provided a detailed discussion of these provisions, focusing mainly on demonstrating the liberal character of the Papua New Guinea judiciary. Building on this foundation, the following discussion delves deeper into how specific textual indicators, as interpreted by the courts, underscore the assertion that the courts have a distinct political function.

Standing for the Opposition Leader—Section 18(1)

The first textual indicator is Section 18(1), which establishes the Supreme Court's 'original jurisdiction' to adjudicate 'any question relating to the interpretation or application of any provision of a Constitutional Law'.[75] This provision has been interpreted by the Court to grant standing to the Opposition Leader to challenge legislative and constitutional amendments on grounds of public interest.

In landmark cases, *Re Petition of MT Somare* (1981)[76] and *Namah v Pato* (2014),[77] the Opposition Leader successfully petitioned the Supreme Court for constitutional review, arguing that certain legislative and constitutional reforms were unconstitutional. The Supreme Court granted standing to the Opposition Leader in these cases and proceeded to reviewing the legislative and constitutional amendments in question.

This is significant within the context of the Westminster parliamentary system, where the Opposition Leader holds a distinctly political position. The role of the Opposition Leader includes criticising government performance and advocating for alternative policies with an interest in regime change, traditionally within the parliamentary arena rather than the courts. Moreover, parliament is the expected forum under the Westminster system, as opposed to the courts, for elected representatives in the Opposition to provide their political challenge, including opposing legislative and constitutional reforms brought by the government. In Australia and other Pacific countries, for instance, the standing rules are not broadened to allow the Opposition Leader the opportunity to challenge constitutional or legislative amendments outside of parliament.

Nevertheless, reflecting the 'home-grown' nature of the Constitution, the Supreme Court expanded the criteria for standing to include the Opposition Leader. This decision was accompanied by observations on parliamentary inefficiencies and shortcomings in the democratic process, justifying the Court's intervention.[78]

---

[75] A fuller discussion on the provision is in Chap. 5.

[76] *Re Petition of MT Somare* [1981] PNGLR 265.

[77] *Namah v Pato* [2014] PGSC 1.

[78] See further discussion in Chap. 5. These broad rules on locus standi are accepted as part of the underlying law of Papua New Guinea, see *Re Petition of MT Somare* [1981] PNGLR 265; *Southern Highlands Provincial Government v Somare, Chairman of the National Executive Council* [2007] PGSC 2, [13], [15]; *Namah v Pato* [2014] PGSC 1, [23].

The Court's decisions hold profound implications, creating the possibility for an Opposition Leader, unable to block government initiatives in Parliament, to turn to the Court to achieve political objectives. While this prospect exists, granting standing to the Opposition Leader under Section 18(1) does not imply a ticket for misuse for political gain. The Court has demonstrated resilience against frivolous lawsuits. Instead, by enlarging political accountability through Section 18(1) and engaging directly with political figures and their interests for constitutional governance, the Court asserts a critical aspect of its role as a guardian of Papua New Guinea's democracy. The interpretation of Section 18(1) by the Court strongly suggests that the judiciary in Papua New Guinea assumes a political function, using judicial power to uphold democratic principles and foster accountability among political leaders and constitutional institutions.

Law making powers—Sections 20, 21, 60 and schedule 2.3

The second set of textual indicators supporting the judiciary's political function is found in the constitutional directive for judges to develop an indigenous jurisprudence referred to as the 'Underlying Law'.[79] As discussed in Chap. 5, this directive empowers judges similarly to legislators, enabling them to develop laws in response to societal changes. In addition to drawing upon relevant common law principles, judges are instructed to use customs and traditional norms, ensuring that the development of this 'indigenous jurisprudence' responds 'to the changing circumstances of Papua New Guinea.'[80]

The scope of the phrase 'circumstances of Papua New Guinea' is expansive, encompassing various aspects of the nation's legal, socio-cultural and political contexts. As Justice Sakora observed, this directive to develop the Underlying Law not only empowers courts with 'traditional law-finding and application functions' but also confers 'law-making powers.'[81]

The Underlying Law framework thus equates the judiciary's role with that of the legislature in law-making, firmly illustrating that the judiciary's constitutional guardianship role includes a political function.

Powers for judges to act on their own volition to enforce human rights and to protect constitutional institutions—Sections 57 and 225

The third compelling set of textual indicators suggesting that courts in Papua New Guinea have an inherently political function can be found in Sections 57 and 225. These provisions empower judges to voluntarily enforce human rights and safeguard the operations of constitutional institutions from external interferences. As highlighted in Chap. 5, under Section 57, judges may voluntarily initial human rights proceedings such as summon the police to investigate alleged breach of human rights,

[79] Ss 20, 21, 60 and schedule 2.3.4; *Underlying Law Act 2000* (PNG) s 5.

[80] S 21; *Underlying Law Act* (PNG) s 3, 5.

[81] *Southern Highlands Provincial Government v Somare, Chairman of the National Executive Council* [2007] PGSC 2, [119] (Sakora J); Bernard Sakora, 'Judicial Law-making' in Peter Sack (ed), *Pacific Constitutions* (Australian National University, 1982) 257–270.

order the closure of prisons due to inhumane conditions, and direct the Commissioners of Police and Correctional Services to maintain police cells and correctional facilities.[82]

Similarly, Section 225 mandates judges to voluntarily issue orders requiring statutory bodies, ministerial departments, public service providers, and private entities to support constitutional institutions, including funding and logistical support for their proper functioning.[83] This provision diverges from the traditional Westminster model of government, where issues of funding and facilities for constitutional institutions are typically administrative matters influenced by government policy agendas and budget allocations. The effect of Section 225 is therefore unusual and goes beyond the orthodox understanding of judicial function to the courts directly intervening in and impacting the political processes, agenda-setting and policy administration.

The proactive stance taken by judges under these provisions is further unconventional, as judicial practice generally in common law jurisdictions is limited to cases being brought before the court rather than judges acting on their own initiative to instigate a case. By identifying failures in government or private sector service delivery or holding the executive accountable through its proactive measures, judges in Papua New Guinea assume a role akin to parliamentary oversight under the principle of responsible government. The interpretation of these provisions by the courts strongly suggests they fulfill a unique political function as part of their constitutional guardianship role under the 'home-grown' Constitution.

Power to install and supervise democratic institutions—Sections 22 and 23

The fourth persuasive set of textual indicators that firmly suggests the superior courts in Papua New Guinea have an inherently political role is found in Sections 22 and 23. Section 22 grants the National Court discretion to formulate procedures, policies and mechanism where they are lacking or insufficient in the Constitution or statutes to implement the rights and duties recognised in the Constitution.[84] This provision essentially empowers the Court to address gaps in the constitutional framework, including deficiencies in the operation and administration of parliament and the executive.[85]

The significant extent of this authority was demonstrated in the *Moresby Northeast Parliamentary Election Petition* (1977), where the Supreme Court ruled that if

[82] Cases include *Re Section 57 of the Constitution of Papua New Guinea, Enforcement of Basic and Human Rights* [2006] PGNC 201; *In the matter of enforcement of Basic Rights under the Constitution re conditions of detention at Bialla Police Lock-up* (2006) N3022; *Lack of Correctional Service (CS) Facilities in Enga Province, In re* [2010] PGNC 251.

[83] Cases include, *PNG Power Ltd v Augerea* [2013] PGSC 53, [70] (Kandakasi, Manuhu and Kawi JJ); *In re Constitution Section 225; Re National Court circuit to Bali and Vitu Island* [2011] PGNC 266 (Kawi J).

[84] See a fuller discussion on the whole of the provision in Chap. 5.

[85] *Re Rights of Person Arrested or Detained* [1977] PGSC 15 (Frost CJ) (unnumbered judgement); *In re Reference to Constitution Section 19(1) by East Sepik Provincial Executive* [2011] PGSC 41, [397].

parliament fails to revise election laws in time for the next election, thereby jeopardising citizens' voting rights and representation, the National Court could intervene to ensure electoral procedures and mechanisms were in place.[86] While the National Court cautioned against frequent use of this power, it emphasised that the judiciary must act if parliament undertake certain actions that threaten the exercise of people's rights.[87] The Court stated:

> [T]he rights and duties conferred by the Constitution are not meant to be illusory, ephemeral or just feel-good principles, but real, tangible, powerful and enforceable obligations capable of immediate effect through court orders and declarations.[88]

The approach under Section 22 allows courts to intervene in and shape public policy, influencing political institutions directly.

Section 23, in contrast, empowers the National Court to prohibit actions or impose duties on individuals or agencies when their actions breach or are likely to breach their constitutional duties and prohibitions. This section includes an anticipatory element, allowing courts to issue orders proactively and pre-emptively.

The use of Section 23 against the Parliament exemplifies the broader societal and constitutional guardianship role assumed by the courts. For example, in *Re Calling of the Parliament* (1999),[89] the Supreme Court used Section 23 to compel Parliament to reconvene sitting after it failed to meet the required number of sitting days.[90] Similarly, in July 2016, amidst civil unrest, the Court invoked this provision to order the Speaker of Parliament to recall a parliamentary session to consider a motion of no confidence vote, after the Speaker postponed as a political maneuver.[91]

While directing the national parliament in its internal affairs is a drastic exercise of judicial power that touches at the core of representative democracy and notions of parliamentary sovereignty, it is firmly consistent with the role of the judges as guardians of democracy. It demonstrates how the 'home-grown' Constitution has expanded the role of the judiciary beyond its traditional sphere to include supervision of political institutions.

Review of proposed laws and binding judicial opinion—Section 19

The fifth textual indicator suggesting that the courts in Papua New Guinea have an inherently political function is Section 19, which, as discussed in Chap. 5, provides automatic standing to over three hundred public institutions to bring constitutional

---

[86] *Moresby Northeast Parliamentary Election Petition; Lowa v Damena* [1977] PGSC 11 (unnumbered judgement).

[87] *In the Matter of Enforcement of Basic Rights Under the Constitution Section 57* [2006] PGNC 29 (unnumbered judgment). I.

[88] Ibid.

[89] *SC Reference No 3 of 1999; Re Calling of the Parliament* [1999] PNGLR 285, [7]–[10].

[90] Ibid.

[91] Eric Tlozek, 'PNG court orders the recall of Parliament to hear no-confidence motion in Prime Minister', *ABC News* (online) 12 July 2016.

references.[92] There are two important aspects of this provision that highlight the Supreme Court's political role.

First, the provision allows constitutional reference applications to be brought not only against enacted laws but also 'proposed laws'.[93] A 'proposed law' is defined as 'a law that has been formally placed before the relevant law-making body'.[94] The Supreme Court has interpreted that

> a proposed law could even include a draft law that is awaiting or has gone through the required number of readings by the Parliament or a law that was passed by the Parliament except it is still awaiting certification.[95]

The Court took this to mean that it can conduct anticipatory reviews of legislation still in its draft stage or awaiting certification.[96] This effectively grants the Court the power to preemptively invalidate legislation, thereby intervening in the legislative process typically reserved for the political arena.

The second significant aspect is the allowance for seeking judicial opinions on any constitutional issue, including for advisory opinion and on 'hypothetical questions'.[97] Any opinion rendered by the Court is binding.[98] The binding nature of advisory opinions is even more profound when considering the authorities under Section 19 'need not wait until an actual dispute arises between parties…[or] even wait until the proposed law comes into force before seeking the court's opinion'.[99]

This provision empowers the Court to be part of the political and democratic processes of law-making, actively guiding even before an issue crystallises into legal contest. It allows for the Court to assume a profoundly preventative role akin to legal advisory as opposed to its traditional arbiter function. This was evident, for instance, in *Re Re-Election of the Governor General* [2010], where the Court urged the Parliament to actively use Section 19 'to seek opinions from the Supreme Court…*before* decisions are made…to enhance the prospects of compliance with the law and to reduce the risk of constitutional errors being made.'[100] These two aspects under Section 19 underscore the political nature of the judicial function,

---

92 See a fuller discussion on the provision in Chap. 5.

93 Ss 19(1)(2)(3), 156 ('law officers').

94 S 19(5).

95 *In re Constitutional (Amendment) Law 2008, Reference by the Ombudsman Commission of Papua New Guinea* [2013] PGSC 67, [21].

96 *Somare, Re* [1981] PGSC 23 (Miles J) (unnumbered judgment). A later decision held that the limited 'proposed law' period meant a month period from when it is gazetted to it being introduced in Parliament. After that, the Court should not interfere until the law is passed, see *Reference by the Ombudsman Commission; Re Section 19 of the Constitution* [2010] PGSC 43, [34]–[36] (Injia CJ, Kirriwom and Gavara-Nanu JJ). However, this view remain unsettled, see in *In re Constitutional (Amendment) Law 2008, Reference by the Ombudsman Commission of Papua New Guinea* [2013] PGSC 67, [21].

97 *Special Reference by the Morobe Provincial Executive* [2005] PGSC 32, [50]–[67]; *Reference by Allan Marat & Reference by the National Parliament* [2012] PGSC 20, [34].

98 Ibid.

99 *Somare, Re* [1981] PGSC 23; [1981] PNGLR 265 (Miles J) (unnumbered judgment).

100 *In re Re-Election of the Governor General* [2010] PGSC 32, [147].

as reviewing proposed laws can directly influence government policy-making, and advisory opinion or answers to questions with hypothetical bearing can address politically charged issues.

Political documents and views as aids to interpretation—Section 24

The sixth textual indicator supporting the courts in Papua New Guinea as having a political function is Section 24, which list certain materials to be used as 'aids to [the] interpretation' of the Constitution.[101] These include politically significant documents with strong political aspirations such as submissions from political parties during the Constitution's drafting and the Constitutional Planning Committee (CPC) Report, which outlines the National Goals and Directive Principles (NGDPs) and Basic Social Obligations (BSOs).[102] Professor John Goldring notes that the NGDPs are 'a general statement of policy' and

> [while] it is not unusual for a constitution to contain a statement of political aims... [w]hat is unusual...is the degree of detail with which the political aims are set out and also the fact that to some extent, at least, those political aims are made enforceable.[103]

The CPC specifies that the NGDPs and the BSOs 'should not be regarded by any court...as being of less weight than other directly justiciable provisions'.[104] The Supreme Court interpreted that the NGDPs and the BSOs are not to be used 'only when there is some deemed ambiguity or uncertainty'.[105] Instead, the Court directed that they be used concurrently with any interpretation approaches 'in every question relating to the interpretation or application of any provision of a constitutional law'.

This means these politically charged documents forms part of the interpretative tools the courts must consider in interpretating laws and responding to legal issues. As seen in *Namah v O'Neill* (2015), the Supreme Court has expanded its 'aids to interpretation' by voluntarily requesting and accepting affidavits from former prime ministers and serving politicians to inform its constitutional interpretation.[106]

The effect of this provision, allowing the Court to engage extensively with political materials and personalities in its key interpretive function, firmly demonstrates the expectation of the 'home-grown' Constitution for the judiciary to exercise a form of judicial power that is socio-politically informed. This requirement necessitates judges to wield judicial power in ways that impact the broader socio-economic and political culture and institutions as part of their constitutional guardianship role.

---

[101] See a fuller discussion on the whole of the provision in Chap. 5.

[102] *Constitutional Documents (Manner of Proof) Act 1976* (PNG). The *Act* governs how the documents can be proved before the Court and what version is to be accepted where there are multiple versions or copies etc.

[103] John Goldring, *The Constitution of Papua New Guinea* (Law Book, 1978) 39; Ss 25, 63 (non-justiciability of NGDPs and BSOs but Court has made exceptions, see Chap. 5).

[104] CPC Report 1974 Chapter 3 [153(3)].

[105] *Supreme Court Reference by the Western Highlands Provincial Executive* [1995] PGSC 6 (unnumbered judgment, Amet CJ).

[106] *Namah v O'Neill* [2015] PGSC 77, [23]–[24].

4 Conclusion

The judicial approaches and the textual indicators discussed firmly indicate that the constitutionally expected role of the judiciary in Papua New Guinea extends beyond the judiciary's traditional scope of adjudicating legal issues to engaging with broader socio-political issues. This involves applying judicial power in ways that instigate reform and impact socio-political processes and institutions that shape society. It is a responsibility expected to be central to judges as leaders of Papua New Guinea society and to their judicial oath and loyalty to the 'home-grown' Constitution.

As Deputy Chief Justice Kapi declared in *Re Calling of the Parliament* (1999), there 'is no reason for this Court to turn a blind eye and come to the view that it should not enter the arena of politics'.[107] This statement aligns with the views of the Constitutional Planning Committee, firmly placing the role of the courts in Papua New Guinea not only within the legal and judicial arena but also squarely within the 'arena of politics'.

Acknowledging the judiciary as having a political function is not unique to Papua New Guinea. Judiciaries in other decolonised jurisdictions are increasingly observed to assume broader governance function, performing 'essential governance functions when other institutions are weak or ineffective'.[108] While intervening for weak institutions resonates with Papua New Guinea, the judiciary's constitutional mandate goes beyond this to impact the larger political and social sphere and overall state of democracy.

Deputy Chief Justice Kapi envisaged that special role when he remarked that the Supreme Court has 'a proud tradition of addressing [political] issues [and] becoming involved in the policy decisions' in Papua New Guinea.[109] It is critical that this 'tradition' is better framed and appreciated so that the broader role of judges in Papua New Guinea in shaping society is not misunderstood. In conceptualising judicial role, judges in Papua New Guinea need to be seen not only as the guardians of the Constitution but also as guardians of the country's democracy.

This chapter thus reinforces the argument (previously discussed in Chap. 7) to reconsider traditional conceptions of the role of the judiciary and the separation of powers. It also strengthens the assertion (as developed in Chap. 4) that the judiciary possesses a transformative character and is therefore a constructive partner in the broader socio-political development of Papua New Guinea.

The arguments in this chapter does not suggest that the courts should overlook the need for restraint or ignore the contextual challenges in effectively enforcing their liberal functions. Rather, the courts should be understood as appropriately having a

[107] *SC Reference No 3 of 1999; Re Calling of the Parliament* [1999] [1999] PNGLR 285 (Kapi DCJ) (unnumbered judgment).

[108] Tom Ginsburg, 'Courts and New Democracies: Recent Works' (Public Law & Legal Theory Working Paper No.388, University of Chicago, 2012), 2–3.

[109] *SC Reference No 3 of 1999; Re Calling of the Parliament* [1999] PNGLR 285 (unnumbered judgment).

dual function as 'a court of law and a political court'[110] in the context of Papua New Guinea.

[110] Mark Mina Mikhaiel, 'The Dangers of the Reference Question: SCC v SCOTUS' (2016) 40 *Canada-US Law Journal* 71, 72.

Chapter 9
Maintaining the Liberal Character of the Judiciary: Challenges and Impetuses

Abstract The judiciary not only faces potential tensions with an unyielding executive and legislative arms of government in the implementation of its liberal powers but it also faces other challenges, both internal and external, that threatens to undermine its role. Internal challenges include judicial appointments and tenure, judicial philosophy of foreign judges, and the practice of singular judgements, which are susceptible to overbearing legalistic approaches. External challenges encompass inefficiencies in police investigations, incompetent and unethical lawyering, and deficiencies in the country's lone law school, which fails to foster research that supports judges and instills in law students a deeper appreciation of the liberal character of the Papua New Guinea judiciary. This chapter analyses these challenges against three core imperatives for maintaining the judiciary's liberal character: the serious decline and paralysis of deliberative and accountability institutions, the lack of a constitutional culture, and the legitimate expectation of the people for the judiciary to respond to these conditions. It argues that these imperatives outweigh the challenges and underscore the urgent need for the judiciary to maintain its liberal and interventionist role.

Keywords Judicial tenure · Judicial appointment · Composite judgements · Unethical lawyering · Papua New Guinea law school · Papua New Guinea legal system · Democratic decline · Constitutional culture · Judicial governance

1 Introduction

The central argument of this book is that the judiciary in Papua New Guinea was intended to have a liberal and transformative function, and that the traditional understandings about the judiciary's place in the separation of powers doctrine need to be reconsidered. The analysis so far has highlighted some persisting doctrinal challenges to this argument. This chapter aims to address some key institutional and contextual challenges that impact or are likely to impact the judiciary's liberal character and the need to maintain this character nowithstanding the challenges.

B. Kama, *Rethinking Judicial Power in Papua New Guinea*,
https://doi.org/10.1007/978-981-97-2946-3_9

This discussion will begin with an analysis of the conventional argument against judges having a broader role in shaping society, arguing that conventional assumptions about judicial restraint should not be uncritically applied to Papua New Guinea.

2 Considering Judicial Restraint

American constitutionalist and statesman Thomas Jefferson once insisted that 'it is a very dangerous doctrine to consider the judges as the ultimate arbiters of all constitutional questions'.[1] Speaking in the context of Australia, Justice Dyson Heydon of the Australian High Court described the 'furthering of some political, moral or social programme' by judges as an 'illegitimate function' of judicial power.[2] His Honour went on to reject the so-called 'activist judges' as 'ambitious, vigorous, energetic and proud [who] think that they can not only right every social wrong, but achieve some form of immortality in doing so'.[3] Others have gone further to condemn judges who exercise broad judicial powers as guilty of 'judicial dictatorship'[4] and even 'treason' against the constitution.[5] According to Professor Ronald Dworkin,

> [t]he program of judicial restraint…[thus] argues that courts should allow the decisions of other branches to stand, even when they offend the judges' own sense of principles required by the broad constitutional doctrines.[6]

Entrenched in the concerns for restraint is an assumption that there are some inherent dangers in giving broad powers to unelected judges.[7] Judges are therefore expected to act in devotion to the dictates of parliament, irrespective of its justness or conformity to broader constitutional principles.

These concerns may be argued to have relevance in Papua New Guinea considering the behaviour of some of the judges as evidenced in Chap. 6. For instance, the overtly political criticisms against the Somare and the O'Neill governments in the *ESP* and *Marat* cases; the explicit memo alleged to be from Justice Kirriwom that declared 'war' on the executive; and the staunch refusal by Chief Justice Injia and Justice Kirriwom to recuse themselves may suggest the need for judicial restraint.

---

[1] Thomas Jefferson letter to William Jarvis (1820) cited in William Quirk and Randell Bridwell, *Judicial Dictatorship* (Transaction Publishers, 1995) 3.

[2] Heydon, Dyson, 'Judicial Activism and the Death of the Rule of Law' (2004) 10, *Otago Law Review* 493, 495.

[3] Ibid 501.

[4] Quirk and Bridwell, above n 1, xiii, 3.

[5] Tom Campbell, 'Judicial Activism—Justice or Treason?' (2003) 10 *Otago Law Review* 307, 311–313.

[6] Ronald Dworkin, *Taking Rights Seriously* (Harvard University Press, 1977) 137.

[7] Stanley C. Brubaker, 'Reconsidering Dworkin's Case for Judicial Activism' (1984) 46 *The Journal of Politics* 503, 507–8.

However, these incidents are isolated and rare. They also need to be understood within the context of cases in which the executive government showed considerable and unprecedented hostility towards the judiciary. More importantly, the context of the Papua New Guinea Constitution must also be considered. As demonstrated in the preceding chapters, judges are leaders and have a political role—to undertake a value-laden, politically infused, and expansive adjudicative approach consistent with the transformative intents of the 'home-grown' Constitution.

For Papua New Guinea, readily relying on externally developed assumption that there are dangers in giving too much power to judges risks undermining and abrogating clear constitutional directives tailored for its own intents and context. While the caution for restraint, may merit some consideration, it must not be the default position or unquestioningly applied as some sort of enlightened *modus operandi* for use of judicial power. As Professors Bilchitz and Landau argued, 'courts in the global south [should not be pressured] to reference and implement doctrines that are not clearly applicable in their contexts'.[8]

Further, there are sufficient mechanisms to prevent judges from abusing their powers in the case of Papua New Guinea. The Constitution establishes two primary bodies to scrutinise the conduct of judges: the Judicial and Legal Services Commission and the Ombudsman Commission. As discussed in Chap. 7, both bodies are highly independent institutions.[9]

Under the Constitution, judges are subject to the Leadership Code administered by the Ombudsman Commission, recognizing them as constitutional office holders.[10] Any member of the public can lodge complaints against judges related to the Leadership Code.[11] The Ombudsman Commission has the power to investigate judges and recommend their trial by the Leadership Tribunal, with penalties including dismissal from office, similar to any other public office holder.[12]

Another accountability mechanism allowing public complaints against judges is the Judiciary Complaints Committee (JCC), which was set up in 2014. Comprising the Chief Justice, a fellow judge, the Deputy Registrar, and the Deputy Secretary of the National Judicial Staff Services, the JCC investigates complaints concerning both judicial and non-judicial members of the judiciary and makes recommendations to the appropriate disciplinary authority, including the Ombudsman Commission and the police.[13] The option of accessing both the JCC or directly through the Ombudsman Commission provides a dual-layered scrutiny, further enhancing the standard of accountability for judges. [14]

---

[8] David Bilchitz and David Landau (eds), *The Evolution of the Separation of Powers between the Global North and the Global South* (Edward Elger, 2018), 19.

[9] Ss 178–182, 217; See discussion in Chap. 7.

[10] Ss 26(1)(e), 218, 221.

[11] S 219(1)(a).

[12] S 28(1)(g).

[13] National Judiciary Services, *Judiciary Complaints Procedure* (Port Moresby, 2014) 8, [3].

[14] Ibid 3–4, 8.

These mechanisms compliment standard 'inbuilt restraints' for judges, such as the obligation to give reasons for decisions, the court appeal system, professional reputation among colleagues, and personal ethics.[15]

The Supreme Court in Papua New Guinea has also demonstrated awareness for judicial restraint. For examples, in the *Marat Case,* the Court noted it is 'conscious of the potential risk of politicisation of the Court in deciding politically charged cases and [have] taken great care in staying within the limits of law and reason'.[16] It affirmed that this 'has always been the approach of this Court and this Court will continue that path'.[17]

The Court's awareness of the need for restraint, together with its inbuilt restraining and steadying factors and the accountability mechanisms within the Constitution and the judicial system, firmly demonstrates that there are measures established to restrain any judicial overreach or rogue judge.

3 Challenges to Maintaining the Liberal Character of the Judiciary

Moving away from traditional assumptions of judicial restraint, there are significant structural and contextual challenges to maintaining the liberal character of the judiciary in Papua New Guinea. These challenges can be categorised into internal and external factors affecting the judiciary's exercise of its liberal role.

3.1 *Internal Challenges*

Appointment and tenure of judges

The first internal challenge concerns the appointment and tenure of judges.[18] The Judicial and Legal Service Commission (JLSC) appoints all judges of the National

[15] P. N. Bhagwati, 'The Role of the Judiciary in the Democratic Process: Balancing Activism and Judicial Restraint' (1992) 18 *Commonwealth Law Bulletin* 1262, 1267; Ronald Sackville, 'Judicial Law Making' (2011) 5 *University of Western Sydney Law Review* 59, 67.

[16] *Reference by Allan Marat & Reference by the National Parliament* [2012] PGSC 20, [318]; See also *Special Reference By Fly River Provincial Executive Council, Re Organic Law on Integrity of Political Parties and Candidates* [2010] PGSC 3, [108].

[17] *Reference by Allan Marat & Reference by the National Parliament* [2012] PGSC 20, [318].

[18] Remuneration of judges has not been a signficant issue. An independent body established by the Constitution, the Salaries and Remuneration Commission, comprising members including the Prime Minister, the Opposition Leader and the Chief Justice, sets the remuneration for the judges (Constitution s 216A). See discussions in Chap. 7.

and the Supreme Court, except the Chief Justice. As discussed in Chap. 7, the composition of the JLSC is relatively independent.[19] However, the same cannot be said of the body that appoints the Chief Justice—the National Executive Council (NEC)—which is a purely political entity chaired by the Prime Minister.

Permanent appointment tenure for citizen judges is ten years, and for non-citizen judges, is three years, both renewable for the same term.[20] Acting judges can also serve for a maximum of twelve months, with the possibility of renewal for another twelve months if not confirmed for a permanent position after their initial term.[21]

This appointment and tenure framework raises significant questions about judicial independence and its potential impact on the exercise of the judiciary's liberal functions. The fixed tenure of ten years for national judges and three years for foreign judges also raises concerns that considerations for reappointments may influence judges' conduct.

While the JLSC, as the appointing body, is relatively independent, the prospect of reappointment after short-term tenure may sway judges' behavior, potentially affecting their inclination to depart from conservative judicial approaches in enforcing liberal powers. Deputy Chief Justice Gibbs Salika (as he then was in an interview), acknowledged this as a potential problem and quipped: '[t]hose of us who have been on the bench for some time, I think you grow thick skin'.[22]

Similar concern applies to the appointment of acting judges. While the acting period may be a test for prospective judges, it could pressure acting judges to adopt behaviors that do not necessarily reflect their usual judicial outlook during that period.[23] The frequent use of acting judges could also lead to compromising the judiciary's institutional integrity.[24]

Judicial appointments, security of tenure, and remuneration are not only essential for maintaining judicial independence,[25] but in the context of Papua New Guinea, they also empower judges to engage with and uphold the judiciary's liberal character. Sir Harry Gibbs of the Australian High Court aptly noted that a critical condition for the effective discharge of judicial function is 'that no judge should have anything to

[19] Ss 170, 175, 176.

[20] *Organic Law on the Terms and Conditions of Employment of Judges* (PNG) s 2.

[21] PNG Constitution, s 170(3); Interview with Deputy Chief Justice Salika (now CJ), Papua New Guinea Supreme Court (Port Moresby, 31 March 2016).

[22] Interview with Deputy Chief Justice Salika (now CJ), Papua New Guinea Supreme Court (Port Moresby, 31 March 2016).

[23] Alysia Blackham, 'Judges and Retirement Ages', (2016) 39 *Melbourne University Law Review* 738, 750-2.

[24] Anna Dziedzic, 'Forge v Australian Securities and Investments Commission: The Kable Principle and the Constitutional Validity of Acting Judges' (2007) 35(1) *Federal Law Review* 129, 143.

[25] Rebecca Ananian-Welsh and George William, 'Judicial Independence from the Executive: A First-Principles Review of the Australian Cases' (2014) 40 *Monash University Law Review* 593, 598.

hope or fear in respect of anything which he or she may have done properly in the course of performing judicial functions'.[26]

The current framework in Papua New Guinea for the appointment and tenure of judges stands as a potential barrier for judges to effectively implement the judiciary's liberal functions.

Engagement of foreign judges

The second internal challenge to maintaining the liberal character of the judiciary arises from the use of foreign judges. Foreign judges have been part of Papua New Guinea's judicial system since the nation was colonised. The engagement of foreign judges offers various benefits to a local judiciary, especially in cases of a small legal profession or the need for impartiality in contexts of strong local interconnectedness.[27] In the context of Papua New Guinea, the engagement of foreign judges has ensured legal and comparative expertise on the judicial bench in certain areas of law where local experience is lacking or local practitioners are unwilling to take judicial positions. However, they present two significant challenges to the maintenance of the liberal character of the judiciary.

First, foreign judges from the dominant sourcing jurisdictions, Australia and New Zealand, often come from professional backgrounds rooted in traditional constitutions and constitutional arrangements where the role of the judiciary is relatively restrictive and legalisitic. Unless they understand and appreciate the constitutional context of Papua New Guinea that permits an expansive judicial function, they are likely to default to their conservative perceptions and instincts regarding judicial power, shaped by their experiences and sense of propriety in their own jurisdictions, and refrain from exercising the liberal powers of the judiciary. This has been apparent in many cases in Papua New Guinea.[28]

An example of hesitation from foreign judges was demonstrated by Justice John Logan of the Australian Federal Court who was on secondment to Papua New Guinea. In a paper presented at the Underlying Law Conference in 2017 that was intended to encourage Papua New Guinean judges to actively develop the Underlying Law, his Honour expressed scepticism of such an endeavour on the basis of the doctrine of separation of powers and noted that '[h]aving regard to the separation of powers for which the PNG Constitution provides, it is difficult to see why the principle…does not apply with equal force in Papua New Guinea'.[29]

[26] Sir Harry Gibbs cited in G Sturgess and P Chubb, *Judging the World, Law and Politics in the World's Leading Courts* (Butterworths 1988) 353.

[27] Anna M. Dziedzic, 'The use of foreign judges on courts of constitutional jurisdiction in Pacific island states' (PhD Thesis, University of Melbourne, 2018).

[28] For examples of cases, see Bal Kama, 'Expectations for Foreign Judges in the Implementation of Papua New Guinea's "Home-Grown" Transformative Constitution' (2022) 24 *Asian-Pacific Law & Policy Journal* 1.

[29] Justice John Logan, 'Executive Intervention in Judicial Functions and Judicial Encroachment into Executive Functions—Defining the Boundaries' (Paper presented at the National Conference on Development of the Underlying Law on Administrative Law, Port Moresby, 27 November 2017) 36.

His Honour went on to insist that the Papua New Guinea 'judiciary acknowledge and observe the limits of [its] constitutional remit' if it is to avoid the inevitability of tension with the executive.[30] Purporting to draw lessons from the execution of King Charles I after his quarrel with the Parliament of England in 1649, his Honour explicitly warned the Papua New Guinea judges: 'We are not elected...a King lost his head'.[31]

It could be argued that Logan's paper demonstrated a lack of understanding of the constitutional context in which the purported doctrine of separation of powers was intended to apply. It not only promoted a contrary understanding of the role of the judiciary in Papua New Guinea but undermined the intention of the 'home-grown' Constitution for the judiciary to exercise liberal and expansive powers.

The paper arguably promoted legal positivism and a conservative judicial attitude, which, while prevalent in Australia, is clearly incompatible with the judicial character under the Papua New Guinea Constitution. The paper epitomised the general challenge posed by the judicial thinking of foreign judges, some of which is evident in controversial judgments,[32] and an underlying assumption often made that certain Western legal thought and principles should unquestionably apply to Global South countries such as Papua New Guinea.

In her rebuttal of the hesitations by foreign judges to depart from 'legal positivism', American Professor Jean Zorn noted that '[t]he Papua New Guinea Constitution authorises the adoption in Papua New Guinea of a jurisprudential style grounded in the insights and methods of legal realism'.[33] Zorn further noted that this means the Constitution demands that all judges, including foreign judges, 'adopt a jurisprudential philosophy and method that contradicts positivism, one that gives judges broader scope for the exercise of their discretion'.[34] The importance of judging within the constitutional context was reinforced by Professor John Nonggor in his assessment that appointments to judicial positions should require

> not merely the formal qualification but also the capacity to understand Papua New Guinea as a young country with people, cultures and aspirations different from other, especially western societies.[35]

Foreign judges are expected to understand the constitutional context and purpose of judicial power in Papua New Guinea in the same way they would in their own jurisdictions. Resorting to their preconceived conceptions and biases and promoting their uncritical allegiance to the Anglo-Australian common law and its ideology not

---

[30] Ibid 39.

[31] Ibid (comment).

[32] Bal Kama, 'When police try to arrest the Prime Minister' on Lowy Institute, *The Interpreter* (22 December 2017).

[33] Jean Zorn, 'Common Law Jurisprudence and Customary Law' in R.W. James and I. Fraser, *Legal Issues in a Developing Society* (University of Papua New Guinea, 1990) 104–5.

[34] Ibid.

[35] John Nonggorr, 'The Maintenance of Judicial Independence and Integrity in Papua New Guinea: Some Recent Developments' (1992) 18 *Commonwealth Law Bulletin* 1181.

only hinders the full realisation of the liberal character of the judiciary, but also amount to abdicating their constitutional responsibilities and judicial oath.

The benefits of employing foreign judges must therefore be balanced with the risk of their influence diluting the constitutionally founded liberal role of the Papua New Guinea judiciary.

Lack of separate judgments

The third challenge to the fuller realisation of the liberal character of the judiciary in Papua New Guinea is the tendency of the superior courts to issue single judgments. This trend appeared in the 1990s when separate assenting or dissenting judgments were criticised for lacking clarity and authoritativeness.[36] It was argued that '[c]larity could be best achieved if judges were prepared to subordinate and subsume their pride of authorship to one written opinion of the court—the single joint opinion'.[37]

This practice is supported in other jurisdictions. For instance, Lord Neuberger of the Supreme Court of United Kingdom, described multiple judgments as 'vanity judgments' which are 'at best a waste of time and space, and, at worst, confusion and uncertainty—although they are popular with academics'.[38] Chief Justice Kiefel of the Australian High Court remarked that '[a] single judgment of the Court or of the majority carries greater authority, not only for its precedential value. It instils confidence in the Court's decision'.[39] These reasons are advanced alongside others, such as better coherence in judicial opinions, efficiency in producing judgment and greater collegiality.[40]

However, in the case of Papua New Guinea, this practice risks stifling the growth of its indigenous jurisprudence and the judicial creativity mandated by its Constitution. A single judgment may be fitting for Australia or the United Kingdom, where the scope for judicial creativity is limited. In Papua New Guinea, the liberal character of the judiciary was intended to allow individual judges to be dynamically involved in shaping society. One of the surest ways to foster such dynamism is through individual judgments, where judges can be creative and take greater responsibility in offering different perspectives and judicial reasoning that could lead to the development of the law. Given the issues in the appointment and tenure of judges as well as the subtle influence of conservative foreign judges, a culture of single opinion judgments is likely to pressure judges to conform to a single dominant opinion that may have conservative leanings.

---

[36] James, R. W and I. Fraser, *Legal Issues in a Developing Society* (University of Papua New Guinea, 1990), 11.

[37] Ibid.

[38] Lord Neuberger, 'Sausages and the Judicial Process: the Limits of Transparency' (Speech delivered at the Annual Conference of the Supreme Court of New South Wales, Sydney, 1 August 2014), [32].

[39] Hon. Kiefel Susan, 'Judicial Methods in the 21st Century' (Speech delivered at the Supreme Court Oration, NSW Supreme Court, 16 March 2017), 8.

[40] A.W.B. Simpson, 'Lord Denning as Jurist' in J. L. Jowell and J.P.W.B. McAuslan (eds), *Lord Denning: The Judge and the Law* (Sweet & Maxwell, 1984) 450–51.

A significant case in point was the Supreme Court judgment in *O'Neill v Eliakim* (2017), that dismissed an arrest warrant issued against Prime Minister Peter O'Neill as 'defective' and invalid.[41] It was a singular judgment issued by a three-member Supreme Court comprised of Justices Higgins, Foulds and Yagi. Justices Higgins and Foulds were Australian judges and Justice Yagi was a local judge who was a recent appointee. Justice Higgins was a former Chief Justice of the Australian Capital Territory Supreme Court.

The judgment, led by Higgins, followed various court cases over a three-year period, including a controversial Supreme Court reference filed by the Prime Minister in 2014 to dispute the powers of the police to effect an arrest warrant against him. In that 2014 Supreme Court case, Prime Minister O'Neill argued that 'an arrest warrant is not a court order and should not be regarded as being the equivalent of a court order' by the police.[42]

However, the Full Court of the Supreme Court comprised of four local judges and one foreign judge, unanimously dismissed his arguments. They held that the arrest warrant against the Prime Minister was not 'simply an administrative authority for an arrest'—it was 'something more than an authorisation: it is an order, demanding obedience' and that the warrant was validly issued.[43] This 2014 judgment remained authoritative until the Higgins-led decision in *O'Neill v Eliakim* (2017) to reject the arrest warrant issued against the Prime Minister as 'defective'.[44]

There were two main grounds to the decision of the Higgins-led Court. First, regarding the technical aspects of the warrant, their Honours found that the information provided on the arrest warrant form was insufficient and 'did not follow the form set out in the Arrest Regulations'.[45] Second, their Honours found that it was unreasonable and therefore an abuse of police powers to compel the Prime Minister, through an arrest warrant, to attend a police interview. They held that there was no evidence to suggest that the Prime Minister would have failed to attend a police interview without a warrant.[46] This latter ground was found to be 'the more fundamental defect'.[47]

Their decision was based solely on the evidence presented by the lawyers of the Prime Minister and the police, both of whom consented to the dismissal of the warrant. There was no opposing party at the trial after the Prime Minister, prior to the trial, disbanded the Investigative Task Force Sweep (ITFS), a special investigative agency responsible for obtaining the arrest warrant.[48] The Attorney-General further

---

41 *O'Neill v Eliakim* [2017] PGSC 53, [43], [49].

42 *In re Powers, Functions, Duties and Responsibilities of the Commissioner of Police* [2014] PGSC 19, [109]—[112].

43 Ibid [127], [129].

44 *O'Neill v Eliakim* [2017] PGSC 53, [43, 49].

45 Ibid.

46 Ibid [47–49].

47 Ibid.

48 Bal Kama, 'When police try to arrest the Prime Minister' on Lowy Institute, *The Interpreter* (22 December 2017).

withdrew funding for the independent legal service provided to ITFS.[49] Another judge, Justice Makail, observed worryingly in one of the earlier proceedings that 'the parties represented at trial all wanted the warrant of arrest set aside'.[50]

The apparent serious interferences in police functions by the Prime Minister, who was the subject of the police warrant, gave rise to the need to take a liberal approach that is consistent with the judicial character and with precedents in Papua New Guinea in cases of great conflict. A liberal approach would have included taking judicial notice of the adverse actions by the Prime Minister and going beyond the traditional approach of simply adjudicating or relying on submissions from consenting lawyers. The Higgings-led Court could have requested previous court files and used the Court's 'inherent powers to do justice' by possibly granting special leave for members of the ITFS to appear and offer their evidence. None of that took place.

The findings of the Higgins-led Court on the technical aspects of the warrant of arrest form was thus restrictive and legalistic. They were not only contrary to the decision of the Supreme Court in 2014[51] but also contrary to a subsequent judgment in the National Court by Chief Justice Injia, who ruled that the technical aspects of the warrant were intact.[52] Injia CJ also relied on the 2014 Supreme Court reference, which the Higgins-led Court largely overlooked, to reach his conclusion. In their unusually short singular judgment for a case of great national and political significance, Higgins, Foulds and Yagi JJ offered very little reasoning for their departure from these existing precedents.

Their findings on the unreasonableness of using an arrest warrant to compel the Prime Minister to attend a police interview, was also contrary to the *Criminal Code Act,* which provides that in cases of 'official corruption,' 'a person shall not be arrested without warrant'.[53] There have been precedents where the police, to question public officials suspected of official corruption under this provision, have used arrest warrants.[54] The National Court has held that an arrest warrant is an exception made for suspects of official corruption, in that 'a formal interview is not a pre-condition to effecting an arrest of such a suspect'.[55]

Another unusual aspect of the case and the judgment was that all the opposing parties to the Prime Minister were being sacked or disbanded, including the prosecutors. As a result, the new prosecutors consented for the warrant to be quashed. The three judges failed to inquire into or discuss in their judgment the political undercurrents as to why the pleadings had changed to a unanimous consent, which, among other consequences, have grave implications for the rule of law.

---

[49] *Marape v O'Neill* [2016] PGSC 4, [27].

[50] Ibid.

[51] *In re Powers, Functions, Duties and Responsibilities of the Commissioner of Police* [2014] PGSC 19, [130].

[52] *Damaru v Vaki* [2015] PGNC 308, [40].

[53] *Criminal Code Act 1974* (PNG) s 87(2).

[54] Bal Kama, 'Some clarification from the courts in PNG PM's 'fight to the very last breath' on Australian National University Development Policy Centre, *DevPolicy Blog* (04 July 2014).

[55] *Marape v Paraka* [2014] PGNC 118, [34].

A further unusual aspect of their singular judgment in *O'Neill v Eliakim* (2017) was that it only referred to cases in the Australian Capital Territory (ACT) as the sole body of international case law. It may have reflected the Bench, given two of the three judges were Australians, especially Higgins being a former Chief Justice in the ACT. However, such an approach did not assist the development of the law in Papua New Guinea.

While it may be difficult to draw firm conclusions, it could be said from this case example that there are risks for singular or composite judgments to be dominated by those with conservative inclination, especially the overbearing influence of senior conservative foreign or domestic judges. Where such influence is present, composite judgements also have the potential to suppress independent judicial thinking and influence the development of law away from its transformative intents under the 'home-grown' Constitution.

As research in the United States noted, 'some judges join a majority opinion, not because they agree with it, but because to dissent will magnify the effect of the majority opinion by drawing attention to it.'[56] The research further noted that most judges do not like to dissent because it 'frays collegiality'.[57] The domineering influence of foreign judges in such cases and the perception of them as experts with specialist skills and knowledge increases the likelihood of falling into this trap and of them advancing a contrary understanding of judicial role in Papua New Guinea.

Former High Court Judge Dyson Heydon captured these issues in a notable essay that questioned the practice of giving a singular judgment:

> Composite judgments raise questions. Who did the work? Did every judge understand the judgment? Did every judge closely examine it? Did a confident "specialist" assume dominance over nervous "generalists"? What, if any, compromises were made?[58]

Justice Heydon went on to argue the risks of having 'a spurious expression of solidarity' in unanimous opinions that camouflage disagreement.[59]

Salika DCJ (now CJ) noted that judges in Papua New Guinea have 'post-hearing conferences' to discuss the decision and if a consensus is reached, a judge is selected to draft the judgment and later circulate it for comments.[60] Kiefel CJ reported a similar practice in Australia.[61] Such post-hearing conferences could explain the increase in the trend for single opinion judgments in Papua New Guinea. However, Heydon J warned of 'strong judicial personalities in conjunction with judicial herd behaviour' permeating such 'judicial conferences' and argues that it is contrary to the notion that 'judicial independence [which involves] independence from one's colleagues'.[62]

---

[56] J. D. Heydon, 'Threats to Judicial Independence: the Enemy Within (2013)' 129 *Law Quarterly Review* 205, 213; R.A. Posner, *How Judges Think* (Harvard University Press, 2008) 10, 30, 32.

[57] Ibid.

[58] Heydon, , above n 57.

[59] Ibid.

[60] Interview with Deputy Chief Justice Salika (now CJ), Papua New Guinea Supreme Court (Port Moresby, 31 March 2016).

[61] Kiefel, above n 39, 2–5.

[62] Heydon, above n 56, 217.

The practice of composite or single majority judgments raises questions about whether there has been 'uneasy compromise and intellectual fudge'.[63] It encourages a judicial culture of uncritically following the majority.[64] Former Australian High Court Chief Justice Harry Gibbs therefore considered a singular judgment in appellate court as 'not wise'.[65]

Justice Heydon's reflection is particularly pertinent to the case of PNG:

> It is wrong, then, for judges to abstain from disagreement merely because it is convenient to drift along with the majority view, or to submit to raw power, or to avoid unpleasantness, or to escape the work involved in explaining why a majority is wrong, or to avoid lowering the public reputation of the institution, or to seek to achieve the appearance of unity and uniformity for its own sake.[66]

Moreover, unlike members of the other two branches of government who have access to the media and other communication outlets, convention dictates that judges only speak through judgments, which serves as their primary platform of communication.[67] Unlike Australia, Papua New Guinea lacks a periodic law journal in which judges can engage in extrajudicial writings. Only a few judges have endeavoured to write law books. A court judgment is the primary outlet which judges can engage deeply and intellectually with an issue, demonstrating not only their awareness of the law but also the broader societal concerns that permeate legal issues.

The CPC's view of judges as 'leaders' carries with it the unique expectation that they shape politics and society, as discussed in the preceding chapter. Multiple voices through judgements are likely to assist the judiciary in performing this important liberal role. However, congregating under a singular judgment could have the opposite effect. It has the potential to not only diminish the significance of individual judicial voices entrusted to shape the society, but also entrench precedents that may be contrary and detrimental to the liberal judicial architecture.

Inconsistencies in judgment

The fourth internal challenge for the maintenance of the liberal character of the judiciary is the inconsistency in judicial decisions in Papua New Guinea. Practitioners interviewed for this book have raised concerns of inconsistent judgments, which have led to confusion among judges, lawyers, and the public at large. The decision in *O'Neill v Eliakim* (2017) could be seen as an example of such inconsistencies.[68]

A primary cause of inconsistent judgments and enunciation of legal principles appears to be the overcrowding of the Supreme Court as all the full-time judges, currently thirty-seven judges, are eligible to sit on both the National and the Supreme Courts. Maintaining consistency in the opinion of the different compositions of the

---

[63] Roderick Munday, 'Judicial Configurations' (2002) 61 *Cambridge Law Journal* 612, 637.

[64] Cass Sunstein, *Why Societies Need Dissent* (Harvard University Press, 2003) 4, 23.

[65] Harry Gibbs, 'Judgment Writing' (1993) 67 *Australian Law Journal* 494, 501.

[66] Ibid 221.

[67] Enid Campbell and H.P. Lee, *The Australian Judiciary* (Cambridge University Press, 2013) 285.

[68] *O'Neill v Eliakim* [2017] PGSC 53.

Bench of both the National and Supreme Courts is challenging.[69] There are two potential implications of this trend, which could impede the liberal functions of the judiciary. The first issue is lack of expertise. Appointing all the judges to the Supreme Court overlooks the fact that some are not sufficiently experienced to sit on appellate matters. Given their inexperience, they tend to cautiously maintain a legalistic approach to their decision-making.[70]

The second issue with inconsistent judgments is the potential for confusion, both in judicial decisions and the public perception of those decisions. Multiple judges deliberating on different aspects of a single case or at different stages, have produced differing opinions of the relevant facts and legal principles, which then confuses lawyers and the public as to the authoritativeness of the judgements.[71]

Salika DCJ (now CJ) acknowledged the issue of inconsistency, noting that 'there are some judges who will refuse applications…[b]ut there are other judges [who] will readily grant the relief', attributing this to 'different levels of understanding'.[72] Former Attorney-General Kerenga Kua emphasised the seriousness of this issue, noting that 'the judiciary is responsible for creating the confusion' and that '[t]hey need to pretty smartly come forward and reconcile' this tendency for inconsistencies in their judgments.[73]

These concerns suggest that while multiple judgments are important for the expression and development of liberal views as noted in the preceding discussion, there must be better discipline for consistency in the judgements to ensure the principles developed towards the realisation and fulfilment of the liberal character of the judiciary remain secured.

These issues are likely to escalate with the judiciary's aim to increase the number of judges.[74] Having faced with the challenge of operating in one of the most litigious societies, some urgent rearrangement in the set-up and administration of the courts is required. The recent development towards the establishment of a Supreme Court of Appeal as an appellate court may assist in addressing this issue, ensuring specialisation, certainty, and consistency in the development of legal principles.

---

[69] Interview with Deputy Chief Justice Salika (now CJ), Papua New Guinea Supreme Court (Port Moresby, 31 March 2016).

[70] Ibid.

[71] Interview with CL6, Constitutional and Law Reform Commission (Port Moresby, 29 April 2016).

[72] Salika DCJ, above n 69.

[73] Interview with Kerenga Kua, Member of Parliament (Port Moresby, 12 April 2016).

[74] Tony Sii, 'PNG records 38 judges, highest in Commonwealth', *Post Courier* (online) 05 March 2018.

3.2 External Challenges

Institutions and actors outside of the judiciary but important to the running of the legal system also pose challenges to the realisation and maintenance of the liberal character of the judiciary. Two of the primary external actors considered in the preceding chapters were the parliament and the constitutional institutions. The former has a restrictive perception of the role of the judiciary, while the latter has shown lethargy in implementing the transformative intents of the Constitution, described by the Supreme Court as them 'sleeping at the wheel'.[75] The following discusses the challenges posed by other notable actors within the legal system, namely police, lawyers, academic institutions and the public.

Inefficiencies and politicisation of the police force

The first external challenge to implementing the liberal character of the judiciary is the inefficiencies and politicisation of the police force in Papua New Guinea. As a highly tribal and heterogeneous society, Papua New Guinea is often prone to conflict. The country further has one of the highest crime and corruption rates in the region. While these conditions pose serious challenges for policing, they also constitute the very 'circumstances of Papua New Guinea', which the CPC urged the judges to actively engage with and to 'use judicial ingenuity' to address.

However, the courts' ingenious accountability role is often hampered with poor investigations and lack of compliance from the police, resulting in significant cases, including those involving societal elites, escaping from judicial scrutiny. This tendency is compounded by a growing trend of direct political interference in the functions of the police, which compromises its independence. A case in point was *Aigilo v Prime Minister Morauta* (No 2) (2001), where the National Court condemned what it deemed as 'direct political interference and collusion between' the Police Commissioner, the Police Minister and the Prime Minister in pursing 'activities outside of the Police functions in their desire to reinforce themselves in power, and in some cases avoid the law'.[76]

This issue was reinforced in the 2011–2012 constitutional crisis where the Somare and the O'Neill governments appointed their own police commissioners and had their own police brigades. Consequently, legitimate police investigations and prosecutions of some of the criminal aspects of the crisis, as well as the enforcement of the Supreme Court's decision against Prime Minister O'Neill, were prevented.

A more extensive situation ensued in 2014 under Prime Minister Peter O'Neill where he replaced two police commissioners and sacked senior police officers that were involved in investigating corruption allegations against him. The police prosecutors and the Police Commissioners newly appointed by the O'Neill government went on to make formal applications to the courts to discontinue the case against the Prime Minister.[77] The Police Commissioners even refused to execute the arrest

---

[75] *In re Application by Ila Geno* [2014] PGSC 2, [39].

[76] *Aigilo v Prime Minister* Morauta (No 2) [2001] PGNC 115, [4].

[77] See for instance, *Damaru v Vaki* [2015] PGNC 308, [14].

warrant against the Prime Minister and opted, instead, to set up a 'vetting committee' within the police force, comprised of both civilians and police officers, to examine requests for investigations and arrests against any member of the political elite before they could be executed.

These developments demonstrated the risks that court decisions against influential political elites or decisions of a liberal nature aimed at addressing broader issues of political accountability might not have the threat of enforcement by the police, which could ultimately render court decisions futile.

The potential for the courts to use their broad powers and to instigate social change when there are effective police investigations was firmly demonstrated in the landmark case of *State v Tiensten* (2014).[78] In that case, Deputy Chief Justice Salika (now CJ) sentenced a senior sitting Member of Parliament and former Minister for National Planning to nine years of imprisonment 'with hard labour' for misappropriating K10 million.[79] The decision was reached despite the Court finding that the Minister did not directly benefit from the public funds. Salika DCJ justified the punishment on the basis that

> unless drastic steps such as imposition of stiff penalties are taken against such persons, the ordinary people of this country will continue to be manipulated and...suffer at the hand of the very people they appointed or elected to assist them.[80]

His Honour's intention to vindicate the suffering of 'the ordinary people' through harsh penalty is demonstrative of the reformist and accountability-focused, liberal role of the judiciary. Further, the successful criminal prosecution of the case by the investigators allowed his Honour to go beyond the legal issue to take a principle approach to addressing the broader social implications of corruption.

As discussed in Chap. 2, the drafters intended for a high standard of accountability of governmental power as a fundamental constitutional objective. Competency in enforcement and investigative agencies is critical to realising this objective. Unlike those in other jurisdictions, Papua New Guinea police therefore have a special function beyond the mere enforcement of the law. Their role is to assist the judiciary in actively bringing into fruition the broader 'home-grown' constitutional goal of institutional, social and political accountability. Inefficiencies and politicisation within the police force undermine that function and thus diminish the impact of the liberal powers of the judiciary.

Incompetent and unethical lawyering

The second external challenge for the judiciary in effectively exercising its liberal character is incompetent and unethical lawyering. This issue was starkly demonstrated in the *Marat Case* (2012). The Supreme Court noted that allegations of the Court acting contrary to the doctrine of separation of powers were propagated by

[78] *State v Tiensten* [2014] PGNC 224.

[79] Ibid [58].

[80] *State v Tiensten* [2014] PGNC 224, [7].

'lawyers advising the Parliament and lawyer-cum politicians,' aimed at misleading the public.[81] The Court condemned that acting with

> pride, egoism, arrogance and bad advice, Parliament and their lawyers opted for a confrontational approach, treating the highest court with contempt in such manner never seen in this country since Independence.[82]

Citing 'bad advice' as the root cause of the constitutional crisis, the Court asserted that the lawyers 'recklessly approached the whole issue for their own selfish gains and not in the best interest of the nation by not ensuring that any likelihood of collision between different arms of government was minimised or prevented'.[83] The Court rejected the multiple court proceedings that constituted the crisis as vexatious and criticised the lawyers as having a 'day of harvest…at the People's expense', and failing in their 'duty…to assist the court'.[84] The Supreme Court continued its condemnation of the role of the lawyers in the constitutional crisis:

> [H]ad Parliament been given proper legal advice, no issue of public perception of judicial impartiality and integrity of the judicial system ought to have cropped up or come under public scrutiny. They became issues because lawyers wanted to promote their own ideologies and favoured a confrontational approach.[85]

The Court found that its orders were 'shunned, ridiculed and trampled on [due to] the advice of lawyers'[86] and that the lawyers were advising the Parliament and the Executive Government differently from the Supreme Court.[87]

These are extraordinary judicial rebukes of the lawyers involved and the legal profession at large. They raise serious questions regarding competency and professional ethics, highlighting how lawyering can undermine the judiciary's liberal character.

Deputy Chief Justice Salika (now CJ) candidly observed that professional ethics among lawyers in Papua New Guinea have become 'very loose now,' and that 'the ethical aspect of lawyering is now being lost to too much lawyering'.[88]

Alois Jerewai, a Papua New Guinean senior lawyer who earned his law degree in 1978, just three years after Independence, went further to observe a 'general decadence in the rule of law' in the country, attributing lawyers as 'the worst culprits in driving this decadence'.[89] Jerewai argued that lawyers bear a responsibility to ensure the nation's future by correctly interpreting laws to their clients, thereby upholding rather than undermining the constitutional system.[90]

---

[81] *Reference by Allan Marat & Reference by the National Parliament* [2012] PGSC 20, [210].

[82] Ibid [235].

[83] Ibid.

[84] Ibid [220].

[85] Ibid [239].

[86] Ibid [349].

[87] Ibid [347].

[88] Interview with Deputy Chief Justice Salika (now CJ), Papua New Guinea Supreme Court (Port Moresby, 31 March 2016).

[89] Interview with Alois Jerewai, Senior Counsel (Port Moresby, 22 April 2016).

[90] Ibid.

These perspectives underscore the pervasive influence of social, financial, and political factors on lawyers' conduct and emphasize their critical role in affecting the implementation of the Constitution's transformative objectives.

An anonymous judge from the National and Supreme Courts echoed concerns about the competence of lawyers in a personal interview, stating, the 'challenge I face is that the court does not get well-researched submissions—there is no challenge to my intellect'.[91] The judge lamented that the 'Constitution gives so much leeway [to me in terms of my judicial powers] but I am not given much support by counsel' in terms of the quality of their submissions.[92] The judge's reflection demonstrates firmly how lawyer incompetence undermines the judiciary's exercise of its liberal powers.

The nexus between incompetent lawyering and its impact on the liberal role of the judges underscores the need for lawyers in Papua New Guinea, similar to the police force, to go beyond conventional lawyering to conscientiously assist the judiciary to invoke its liberal powers to shape society. This demands a standard of lawyering that promotes rather than stifles the liberal judicial functions—a standard ground, as Professor Zorn argues, 'in the insights and methods of legal realism'.[93]

Shortcomings in the Law School

The third external challenge to discovering and enforcing the liberal character of the judiciary is the deficiencies within the Law School at the University of Papua New Guinea (UPNG), the nation's sole legal academic institution. The deficiencies in the standards of competency and professional ethics among lawyers are, in large part, a reflection of the academic institution. As Professor Felix Frankfurter noted regarding the link between the quality of a law school and the standards of lawyering in a society, 'the law is what the lawyers are [a]nd the law and the lawyers are what the law schools make them'.[94] Two important deficiencies at the UPNG Law School presents challenge in maintaining the judiciary's liberal nature.

The first challenge arises from issues in the training of law students. Commenting on the content of the courses in regard to ethics and competency in the legal profession, Stephen Pokawin, a senior law lecturer at UPNG noted a failure to prioritise law subjects that deal with ethics and professional conduct over more conventional law subjects.[95] The observation aligns with that of Justice Edward of the United States Circuit Court, who argues that 'law school[s] must work all the harder to

---

[91] Interview with Judge A1, Papua New Guinea Supreme Court (Port Moresby, 27 November 2017). The judge wish to remain anonymous.

[92] Ibid.

[93] Zorn, above n 33, 104–5.

[94] Felix Frankfurter (1927) cited in Harry T. Edwards, 'The Growing Disjunction between Legal Education and the Legal Profession' (1992) 91 *Michigan Law Review* 34.

[95] Interview with Stephen Pokawin, Law Lecturer, University of Papua New Guinea (Port Moresby, 21 April 2016).

create ethical graduates' or else 'their only model of the practicing lawyer may well be crudely materialistic'.[96]

Professor Michael Coper expanded on this argument, asserting that 'law schools are not just professional schools, they are institutions of moral purpose'.[97] In the context of Papua New Guinea, this implies instilling in law graduates a dynamic understanding of law as a tool for social and political reform. Such understanding of the law would enable law graduates to better appreciate and engage with law in ways that enliven the liberal functions of the judiciary and the Constitution's transformative objects and mechanisms.

The second significant challenge posed by the UPNG Law School is its lack of academic research and intellectual output. Aside from sporadic individual publications, there is no legal journal or other periodic legal publications within the country. This absence stifles robust discussions on legal principles developed by the courts and limits judges from engaging in extrajudicial writings critical to a fuller understanding of judicial decisions.

Senior lecturer Samson Kaipu acknowledged the need for the Law School to support the judges with 'well researched opinions'.[98] This view is similarly supported in Australia and elsewhere.[99] Justice Bastarache of the Supreme Court of Canada, for instance, highlighted the importance of the connection between academic research and judicial decisions:

> [T]he contribution of academics is invaluable to the development of legal principles and coherent judicial decisions. The nature of the law itself is being transformed. The work of academics serves to provide a contextual social background for legal disputes, helps to make judges aware of the underlying reasons for the decisions that they make and offers useful suggestions for reform. No principled approach to decision-making can ignore the role of academics.[100]

Kaipu also pointed out how the lack of research affects the quality of law graduates:

> The majority of the graduates that we put out go into the profession with some writing skills but I think they're still missing in the quality of research. Consequently, when they write submissions in the courtroom situation, they may not be producing what the court is requiring. So I think it also reflects on the law school. What quality of graduates are we putting out? The quantity is there, but is the quality also there?[101]

---

[96] Edwards, above n 94, 73.

[97] Michael Coper, 'Legal Knowledge, the Responsibility of Lawyers, and the Task of Law Schools' (2008) 39 *University of Toledo Law Review* 251, 260.

[98] Interview with Samuel Kaipu, Law Lecturer, University of Papua New Guinea (Port Moresby, 22 April 2016).

[99] Hon. Michael Kirby, 'Welcome to Law Reviews' (2002) 26 *Melbourne Law Review* 1, 7, 10-11; Russel Smyth, 'Academic Writing and the Courts: A Quantitative Study of the Influence of Legal and Non-legal Periodicals in the High Court' (1998) 17 *University of Tasmania Law Review* 164.

[100] Justice Michel Bastarache, 'The Role of Academics and Legal Theory in Judicial Decision-Making' (1999) 37 *Alberta Law Review* 739, 746.

[101] Interview with Samuel Kaipu, Law Lecturer, University of Papua New Guinea (Port Moresby, 22 April 2016). Kaipu also points to the low 'command of the English language' among the students as a contributing factor for the lack of quality legal submissions.

It becomes evident from Kaipu's observations that the lack of research at UPNG Law School affects the ability of graduates to understand and engage with the unique constitutional history and framework, including the liberal role of the judiciary, and to critically evaluate imported assumptions.

Furthermore, the absence of an academic research environment means judges lack an informed audience to critique their approaches or encourage their liberal function consistent with the Constitution. For example, a conservative judicial approach contrary to the liberal constitutional mandate and intents may go unchallenged due to weak submissions from counsel or a lack of rigorous academic debate. These shortcomings in training and research at the UPNG Law School present a significant obstacle to realising and maintaining the liberal character of the judiciary.

Public perceptions and local allegiances

The fourth external challenge for the judiciary in effectively enforcing or realising its liberal character is the influence of strong localised tribal allegiances and groupings. As Chaps. 2 and 3 demonstrated, the highly heterogeneous nature of Papua New Guinea society, with over 6000 social groups and about 837 languages, contributed to the establishment of a 'home-grown' Constitution.

However, this intensely diverse society also fosters strong kinship ties and tribal enclaves that sometimes challenge the legitimacy and influence of unitary state institutions, including the national judiciary. This influenced is often manifested in court decisions that impact the status of local leaders or involve issues of resource ownership and land titles. For instance, court decisions regarding election disputes are particularly contentious, as deep political rivalries often accompany the threat of violence, which can overshadow judicial outcomes.[102]

A notable case is the Supreme Court's decision in *Kobol v Powi* (2018), where an election petition against the respondent, the Governor of Southern Highlands Province, following the 2017 general election, was dismissed.[103] The supporters of the aggrieved applicant reacted to the Court's decision by burning a passenger aircraft at the local airport, as well as destroying various infrastructure in the Province, including the National Court building, the governor's residence and properties belonging to the Prime Minister.[104]

The severity of these reactions underscores the significant pressure on judges, indicating that in certain cases, strong localised groups may reject and undermine the legitimacy of the courts. There are some limitations, however, as such incidents are generally isolated and localised, and do not represent the typical response to judicial decisions. In fact, many people in Papua New Guinea, distrustful of the political structures and leaders amidst high levels of corruption, view judicial interventions as

---

[102] Graeme Orr, 'Integrity on the Line: Judicial Power Over Elections in Papua New Guinea' (2017) *LAWASIA Journal* 65, 75.

[103] *Kobol v Powi* [2018] PGSC 51. Related cases are *Kobol v Powi* [2018] PGNC 1 and *Kobol v Powi* [2018] PGSC 68.

[104] Eric Tlozek, 'Angry protesters burn passenger plane after PNG Highlands' election result', *ABC News* (online) 14 June 2018.

the 'last beacon of hope'.[105] As Justice Davani articulates this sentiment, 'the courts are the last bastion in a sea of uncertainty'.[106]

Nevertheless, despite the absence of a more widespread resistance to judicial decisions, ethnic diversity and strong tribal allegiances pose a persisting challenge to the liberal role of the judiciary. This challenge underscores the importance of considering wider cultural, social, and political contexts in judicial deliberations. It necessitates courts to employ broad, open, and expansive methods of judicial analysis and to develop legal principles that are suitable to the local context, rather than relying readily on externally developed legal principles incongruent to local realities.

4 Impetuses for Maintaining the Liberal Character of the Judiciary

Despite the challenges identified above to effectively maintaining the liberal character of the judiciary, they are compelling reasons why courts in Papua New Guinea should continue to uphold this liberal character, even if some challenges warrant judicial restraint.

Decline of deliberative and accountability institutions

The first reason why the judiciary should not retreat from maintaining its liberal character is the serious decline of the democratic deliberative and accountability institutions in the country, exacerbated by the increasingly dominant executive government. This issue, as discussed in preceding chapters, saw the courts criticised Parliament for becoming a 'mere rubber stamp for the executive' and described constitutional institutions as 'sleeping at the wheel'.[107]

This decline adds to a global trend towards a general 'decline in democracy' under the weight of both international and domestic forces such as increase influence of multinational corporations, predatory politics and corruption.[108] According to David Bilchitz and David Landau, this 'decline' has led to 'a crisis of confidence in

[105] Sam Basil, 'Prime minister in contempt of court again' on *Malum Nalu Blog* (20 February 2011) (online); Frustrated Citizen, 'Watch Papua New Guinea Fall' on *PNG Blog*, 03 March 2011 (online).

[106] *State v Mataio* [2004] PGNC 239 (unnumbered judgment).

[107] *In re Reference to Constitution Section 19(1) by East Sepik Provincial Executive* [2011] PGSC 41, [65].

In re Reference to Constitution Section 19(1) by East Sepik Provincial Executive [2011] PGSC 41, [65], [604]; *Namah v O'Neill* [2015] PGSC 77, [46]; *In re Application by Ila Geno* [2014] PGSC 2, [40]; *Morauta v Pala* [2016] PGSC 46, [22]. Even James Madison noted that it was not uncommon for elected officials to 'forget their obligations to their constituents and prove unfaithful to their important trust': James Madison, 'Notes of Debates in the Federal Convention' (1787), 378 cited in Hickok McDowell, *Justice vs Law* (The Free Press, 1993) 206-7.

[108] 'A Global Report on the Decline of Democracy' on *Foreign Affairs* (17 April 2018) (online); Tom Ginsburg and Aziz Huq, *How to Save a Constitutional Democracy* (University of Chicago Press, 2018) 26, 143.

political institutions across large swaths of both the developing world and the mature democracies'.[109] Hickok McDowell argues that as parliamentary deliberative functions decline, courts are increasingly compelled to 'fill the void' left by Parliament.[110] Of striking relevance to Papua New Guinea, McDowell states:

> The decline in the deliberative character of *Parliament* is best illustrated by the members themselves, who understood their job primarily to be taking care of constituents. The modern *Parliament* thrives on constituent casework; its members survive by "bringing home bacon" to their districts. Both of these activities help to provide members with campaign advantage for re-election.[111]

McDowell further observe that this decline in the deliberative functions of Parliament 'increas[es] the presence and scope of judicial review as the legislature abdicates its responsibilities' and ultimately 'elevates the courts and judges to the level of partners in the policymaking process'.[112]

These views find support in statements by Chief Justice Brennan in Australia, who argued that 'courts have been prompted to widen the boundaries of judicial review in response to a perceived diminution of legislative control over executive power'.[113] Justice McHugh of the Australian High Court lamented that '[g]one are the days when Parliament stood between the people and the excesses of executive power' and noted that 'the power of Parliament to control the Executive is limited'.[114] This 'decline in democracy', according to Justice Sackville of the Australian Federal Court, means 'political constraints on the conduct of the executive were simply too weak to afford adequate protection to the individual'.[115] His Honour argued that widening judicial power becomes critical, as 'the courts have seen themselves as filling a gap created by the failure of political forms of accountability'.[116]

While these observations arise in the context of jurisdictions with limited exercise of judicial review, they point to a common pathology in the democratic system—the decline of the accountability functions of the parliament. This decline is more severe in the case of Papua New Guinea, characterised by rampant corruption, clientelism, and political volatility. If judicial intervention is deemed essential in Australia, it is even more critical in Papua New Guinea. It is therefore imperative that the courts maintain their larger guardianship role as the guardian of the country's

[109] David Bilchitz and David Landau (eds), *The Evolution of the Separation of Powers between the Global North and the Global South* (Edward Elger, 2018) 19.

[110] McDowell, above n 107, 213.

[111] Ibid 212.

[112] Ibid.

[113] Sir Gerard Brennan, 'The Purpose and Scope of Judicial Review' in Michael Taggart (ed), *Judicial Review of Administrative Action in the 1980s: Problems and Prospects* (University of Auckland, 1988) 19.

[114] Michael McHugh, 'Tensions between the Executive and the Judiciary' (2002) 76 *Australian Law Journal* 567, 571.

[115] Ronald Sackville, 'The Limits of Judicial Review of Executive Action—Some Comparisons between Australia and the United States' (2000) 28 *Federal Law Review* 315, 317.

[116] Ibid.

democracy, a role that can only be sustained through continued exercise and maintenance of their liberal powers with clear interest in the wide socio-political affairs of the country.

Another facet of the 'decline in democracy' necessitating judicial intervention is the weaknesses and volatility in the political party system. A robust political party system typically ensures a robust legislature that holds the executive accountable.[117] However, as Landau observed, in many developing countries, 'political parties are extremely weak, rendering the legislature a largely incoherent body'.[118] This weakness is characterised by multiple parties with 'loose or non-existent ideological platforms' and undisciplined behaviour, contributing to political instabilty.[119]

These observations resonate strongly in Papua New Guinea, where the political party system is fragmented and lacks robust ideological foundations. The country has never had an established political party system, with political parties existing more as a tool for political bargaining than as a reliable platform for leadership on critical issues. This has led to frequent party jumping and a long history of instability.

This political context of Papua New Guinea creates a gap in the political accountability system, necessitating the judiciary to be proactive in using its liberal powers to secure the country's democracy and constitutionalism. It also underscores the need for a reconceptualisation of the judicial role, tailored to Papua New Guinea's unique political context. As Landau pertinently argues in the context of developing countries, 'differences in the configuration of political institutions should bear upon the way courts do their jobs'.[120] In clear application to Papua New Guinea, Landau observes that 'any attempt to build a theory of judicial role in [developing] countries must begin with [an] assessment of their political institutions and not with theories borrowed from the United States' or Australia for that matter.[121]

For Papua New Guinea, maintaining the liberal character of the judiciary is not merely a response to recent democratic decline, but a pre-existing mandate. Acting Judge Bernard Narokobi, a key figure in drafting the Constitution, foresaw the judiciary's role in safeguarding against an overbearing executive in a context of declining political accountability:

> I foresaw an over anxious executive, having every command of the legislature, enacting laws, taking away or restricting human liberties, under written laws and leaving the aggrieved with no recourse to a Court of law, and justice and conscience.[122]

---

[117] David Landau, 'Political Institutions and Judicial Role in Comparative Constitutional Law' (2010) 51 *Harvard International Law Journal* 320, 329; Dary Levinson and Richard Pildes, 'Separation of Parties, not Powers' (2006) 119 *Harvard Law Review* 2311.

[118] Landau, ibid 330.

[119] Ibid 329–32.

[120] Ibid 321

[121] Ibid.

[122] *Mase v State* [1980] PGNC 82 (Narokobi AJ) (unnumbered judgment).

While the decline in institutions of democracy may be a recent concern for some constitutions, for Papua New Guinea, it has been part of the socio-political pathologies that the liberal judiciary was intended to remedy from the outset and that can only be realised by maintaining its liberal character.

Legitimate expectation for the judiciary to maintain its liberal character

The second reason why the judiciary should not retreat from maintaining its liberal character amidst the challenges is that there is a legitimate expectation from the people for the judiciary to uphold its liberal character. As demonstrated in Chap. 2, the people of Papua New Guinea, through the extensive consultation process that underpinned the creation of their 'home-grown' Constitution, intended the judiciary to have a broad and liberal character to ensure meaningful engagement with and contribution to the country's socio-legal and political developments.

This expectation is further legitimised in Section 158(2) of the Constitution which declares that the 'judicial authority of the People is vested in the National Justice System'.[123] As Chief Justice Frost held in *Yamba v Geru* (1975), this direct conferral of judicial power meant 'the Royal Prerogative as *parens patriae* has been displaced' and that 'the judicial power of the people is as plenary as the Royal Prerogative which attached to the Queen as the dispenser of justice'.[124] Deputy Chief Justice Salika further clarified in *Vaki v Baki* (2014):

> The judicial power that the courts wield and exercise is the judicial power of the people of Papua New Guinea. This means that when the courts make decisions they are exercising the judicial powers of the people.[125]

The people are therefore 'the exclusive and ultimate source of [judicial] authority' in Papua New Guinea.[126] The constitutional intimacy between the people and the courts has greatly influenced the liberal approaches adopted by judges. In *Somare* (1981), the Supreme Court rejected arguments to limit standing that was based on the policy rationale of 'opening the floodgates' argument and insisted that 'the judicial power belongs to the people [and] [i]t is the people's court [so] let them come by the hundreds if they have the right to come'.[127]

This constitutional intimacy further positions the courts as legitimate intermediators between the people and the State, with the expectation that they act to counter and protect the people from adverse social and political forces. Being 'charged with the judicial power of the people', the National and Supreme Courts have maintained that they 'have a constitutional duty to seriously take into account the peoples

[123] S 158(1).

[124] *Yamba v Geru* [1975] PGNC 22 (Frost CJ) (unnumbered judgment).

[125] *Vaki v Baki* [2014] PGNC 21, [25].

[126] *Aihi v The State* (No 1) [1981] PGSC 9 (Kearney DCJ) (unnumbered judgment).

[127] *Somare, Re* [1981] PGLawRp 589 (Kapi J) (unnumbered judgment); See also *Namah v Pato* [2014] PGSC 1, [38]–[39].

wishes…[128] and that 'the judges have not taken lightly [and should not take lightly] the direct vesting of the people's judicial power in the Courts'.[129]

It is therefore incumbent upon the judges to honour the expectation of the people, legitimised by the Constitution. As the Supreme Court frankly attested in *Public Prosecutor v Don Hale* (1998), '[t]he courts are bound under the philosophy of the constitution to be in touch with the aspirations and attitudes of the people of PNG'.[130] It is clear that the 'aspirations of the people', as entrenched in the Constitution, intend for a judiciary that maintains its liberal character, allowing the courts to impact the many facets of Papua New Guinea society despite the challenges outlined above.

Lack of constitutional culture

The third reason why the judiciary should not retreat from its liberal character and its transformative role as the guardian of Papua New Guinea's democracy amidst the challenges is the general lack of constitutional culture in the country. In his research on constitutions in developing countries, Landau describes societies lacking a 'constitutional culture' as those in which the 'political elites and ordinary people flout or ignore the constitution rather than take it seriously'.[131] Miguel Schor noted in the context of Latin America that political elites tend to readily 'ignore or change' constitutional rules to suit their political interests.[132] Consequently, citizens distrust constitutional institutions, realising that 'rules could be readily changed by those in power' and institutions bend to their will.[133]

These observations resonate with Papua New Guinea's experience since 1975. The country has had over forty constitutional amendments, driven mainly by the executive with very minimal debate and very little constituency deliberations.

There is a growing culture of exploiting and undermining the constitutional system and rule of law, while systemically embedding bad governance. Consequently, widespread popular distrust in the formal state system has emerged, with people, disconnected from the State and suspicious of their political leaders, often resorting to self-help mechanisms for governance and justice. According to some observers, it has created a situation where 'the legitimacy of state institutions of all kinds has been called into question'.[134] Robert Foster noted further that in Papua New Guinea, 'many people not only distrust politicians, whom they vote out of office at an astounding rate, but they also refuse to accept the idea of the state'.[135]

---

[128] *State v Winston* [2003] PGNC 146 (Kandakasi J) (unnumbered judgment) (emphasis added).

[129] *Reference by Allan Marat & Reference by the National Parliament* [2012] PGSC 20, [44]—[5] (emphasis added).

[130] *Public Prosecutor v Hale* [1998] PGSC 26 (unnumbered judgment).

[131] Landau, above n 221, 326.

[132] Miguel Schor, 'Constitutionalism through the Looking Glass of Latin America' (2006) 41 *Texas International Law Journal* 1, 5.

[133] Ibid 25.

[134] Colin Filer and Nikhil Sekhran, *Loggers, Donors and Resources Owners* (PNG National Research Institute, 1998) 68.

[135] Robert J. Foster, 'Bargains with Modernity' in Bruce M. Knauft (ed), *Critically Modern: Alternatives, Alterities, Anthropologies* (Indian University Press, 2002) 69.

Despite this popular distrust, the judiciary remains the least distrusted institution. As Justice Kirriwom poignantly described, it is 'the last bastion of hope for the survival of the country'.[136] The liberal function of the judiciary is crucial in providing guardianship and enforcing the Constitution to counteract the decline in democratic and constitutional culture. Chief Justice Injia made this clear in the *Marat Case*:

> [A] fearless National Judicial System, as the custodian of the *Constitution*, is jealously guarding the *Constitution* to ensure that its provisions are not flouted, subverted or destroyed by powerful elements within the society that control the very democratic processes that the *Constitution* itself has availed to them to operate within prescribed limits.[137]

Injia CJ firmly emphasised an active role of the court in 'guarding the Constitution' and criticised 'powerful elements' actively undermining the constitutional order. Vesting liberal powers in the judiciary thus entails an expectation for the courts to play a larger role in the development of the Papua New Guinea society—not just policing the legal system but also overseeing and fostering social and political reform and strengthening an accountability and constitutional culture.

5 Conclusion

The case for maintaining the liberal character of the judiciary in Papua New Guinea faces significant institutional challenges both internal within the judiciary and from external actors and institutions. However, the analysis in this chapter shows that there is a far greater and more compelling need to maintain and promote the liberal character of the judiciary. It further demonstrates that there are sufficient regulatory and institutional mechanisms to deal with concerns about judges abusing their liberal powers.

Amidst the decline of democratic institutions and a serious lack of accountability and constitutional culture, there is legitimate expectation backed by constitutional mandate, for the judiciary to play a larger role in intervening and shaping Papua New Guinea society. The unique and indispensable role of the judiciary in this context is aptly captured by Deputy Chief Justice Salika (as he then was):

> The general opinion of the community at large is that respect for the legislature and the executive arms of government have waned and that the last bastion of our system of governance that is holding the country together is the judiciary of this country.[138]

The argument in this chapter further resonates with the prescient views of Chief Justice Sir Arnold Amet in a lecture to audiences in Australia in 1996. Acknowledging that Papua New Guinea's judiciary 'is vested with very powerful roles to play in

---

[136] Oseah Philemon, 'Independent judiciary is key for PNG: Judge', *The National* (online) 02 February 2010. Justice Davani also noted that 'the courts are the last bastion in a sea of uncertainty', see *State v Mataio* [2004] PGNC 239 (unnumbered judgment).

[137] *Reference by Allan Marat & Reference by the National Parliament* [2012] PGSC 20, [91].

[138] *Moiga v Devete* [2010] PGNC 240, [16].

the shaping of the country,' Amet CJ noted: ' [T]he judiciary has been willing to accept the challenges involved in its role', [and has] a very challenging yet important position for the overall development of the country into the twenty-first century and beyond'.[139]

Amet CJ observed that some of these challenges may force the 'courts into open conflict with the overall economic and political trends' in the country.[140] However, he elevated the importance of the courts' role above these challenges, describing the Supreme Court as having 'an increasing consciousness of the threat to constitutionalism', and showing 'willingness to be involved in promoting change' and adopting 'a more interventionist approach'.[141]

These views firmly demonstrate that while acknowledging the diverse challenges to the judiciary's role, the courts have a much higher function in Papua New Guinea society. For many, including judges, the judiciary is 'the last beacon of hope'[142]—a responsibility that extends beyond adjudicating legal issues to one that demands judges sacrifice personal and professional comfort and sensibilities to enforce their constitutionally-mandated reformist and liberal functions meaningfully.

Judges are therefore encouraged to guard against any tendency to adopt ready-made principles or subscribe to uncritical legalistic approaches developed elsewhere under the guise of judicial restraint. Further, they should be wary of conservative forces within the judiciary and legal profession that seek to suppress the judiciary's interventionist and liberal mandate.

Chief Justice Kidu reinforced this in his reprimand of his colleague judges in *Aihi v The State* (No 1) (1981), rejecting differing conceptions about the liberal judicial functions:

> *We cannot cut down the powers of this Court if the Constitution has invested it with extra jurisdiction or power*, [instead], we must be bold in stating the fact [and in exercising it]...[w]hatever the nature or extent of this power might be.[143] (emphasis added)

This view was further affirmed by Chief Justice Injia in the *Marat Case,* where his Honour stated that the 'potential for conflict [with the other two arms of government] is no reason for the courts and judges to become recalcitrant and abdicate our constitutional duty'.[144] Injia CJ acknowledged that having liberal powers 'is always fraught with the potential for conflict between the Courts and the legislature and the executive'.[145] However, his Honour held that 'the framers of our *Constitution* was fully conscious of that risk but it deliberately chose to vest the Supreme Court with [its liberal powers],' knowing the greater societal and constitutional importance of

---

[139] Sir Arnold Amet, 'Issues facing the Supreme Court of Papua New Guinea' in Cheryl Saunders (ed), *Courts of Final Jurisdiction: The Mason Court in Australia* (The Federation Press, 1996), 261.

[140] Ibid.

[141] Ibid.

[142] *State v Mataio* [2004] PGNC 239 (unnumbered judgment).

[143] *Aihi v The State* (No 1) [1981] PGSC 9 (unnumbered judgment) (emphasis added).

[144] *Reference by Allan Marat & Reference by the National Parliament* [2012] PGSC 20, [90].

[145] *Reference by Allan Marat & Reference by the National Parliament* [2012] PGSC 20, [89].

such a mandate.[146] The argument of this chapter, advocating for the discovery and maintenance of the liberal character of the judiciary despite the challenges, aligns firmly with these views.

146 Ibid; P. N. Bhagwati, 'The Role of the Judiciary in the Democratic Process: Balancing Activism and Judicial Restraint' (1992) 18 *Commonwealth Law Bulletin* 1262, 1265. Indian Chief Justice Bhagwati adds that 'merely because a question has a political complexion that by itself is no ground why the Court should shrink from performing its [constitutional] duty'.

Chapter 10
Conclusion

Abstract Papua New Guinea embarked on a historic and unparalleled constitution-making process to create a truly 'home-grown' Constitution. A remarkable outcome was the establishment of a liberal judiciary with unique social and political interventionist functions. Judges have a duty not to relinquish their liberal powers or substitute them with conceptions of judicial power derived from sources elsewhere that do not align with the 'home-grown' constitutional intents. While challenges for the liberal powers of the judiciary may persist, they can be overcome through concerted efforts to clarify understandings of the judiciary's role. Strengthening Papua New Guinea's governmental system involves reassessing assumed structures and doctrines of government towards recognising the judiciary's larger societal role as the guardian of Papua New Guinea's democracy. The judiciary's unusual liberal mandate and the establishment of independent constitutional institutions in the Constitution mean Papua New Guinea has a modified separation of powers doctrine, encompassing four governmental branches rather than the traditional three branches. The ingenuity of establishing the liberal judiciary is better understood when considering this modified separation of powers framework as part of the broader innovation characterising the 'home-grown' Constitution.

Keywords Home-grown constitution · Liberal judiciary · Papua New Guinea democracy

Papua New Guinea embarked on a historic and unprecedented process of constitution-making in decolonial history to craft a truly 'home-grown' Constitution. The Independent Constitution, entered into force on September 16, 1975, represents a transformative document as explored in Chap. 4. It aimed to challenge the colonial order and its institutional ideologies, rectify the historical injustice through detailed rights and enforcement mechanisms, and envision a future driven by independent institutions empowered to promote a culture of accountability and constitutionalism.

A defining aspect of this autochthonous constitution-making process, critical to its transformative vision, was the establishment of a judiciary endowed with powers beyond the traditional character of a judiciary. Chapter 5 delved into the twelve

B. Kama, *Rethinking Judicial Power in Papua New Guinea*,
https://doi.org/10.1007/978-981-97-2946-3_10

textual indicators in the Constitution that firmly establish the judiciary's liberal character. Complementing this aspect of the Constitution's transformative intent are the independent constitutional institutions. They exist outside of the three arms of government, constituting the 'fourth arm' of government.

The independence of these institutions from the conventional three arms of government, coupled with the unconventional liberal role of the judiciary, necessitates a reevaluation of the doctrine of separation of powers. Under the 'home-grown' Constitution, this doctrine should be understood not as a tripartite, but rather as quadripartite, as detailed in Chap. 7.

The argument for the enlivening of the judiciary's liberal character and the resulting modification of the separation of powers doctrine is not without challenges. As discussed in Chap. 6, constitutional crises cases such as *Rooney* (1979) and the *East Sepik Province* (2011) demonstrated resistance against the judiciary's expansive review powers from other branches of government, leading to significant constitutional and societal ramifications. Challenges also persist within and outside the judiciary, hindering the full realisation of its liberal character, as discussed in Chap. 9.

However, Chaps. 8 and 9 underscore that the imperatives for maintaining the judiciary's liberal character outweigh these challenges. The broad constitutional mandate of the judiciary has elevated it to a new role as the guardian of the country's democracy. Considered as 'leaders' by the people and through the Constitution, the role of the judges lies not only in the narrow confines of legal matters but also in shaping Papua New Guinea's larger socio-political and developmental landscape. Amidst declining democratic and accountability institutions and rising social frustration with persistent governance issues, there is a legitimate expectation from the people that their liberal judicial power, vested in the judiciary, is faithfully implemented to meaningfully address these conditions.

Judges, therefore, should steadfastly engage their liberal functions to uphold the transformative intent of the Constitution. This requires constitutional stability going forward, necessitating acceptance by the other branches of government—mainly the executive and the legislature—of the judiciary's reconceptualised role and the modified doctrine of separation of powers.

In conclusion, the book presents three implications. First, in the realm of constitutional law in Papua New Guinea, the findings challenge members of all *four* arms of government to reconsider their understanding of the judiciary's role vis-à-vis their own powers, fostering a more constructive relationship and reducing potential for constitutional and political tensions. Second, the findings empower judges to depart from ready reliance on and uncritical adoption of formalistic judicial restraints and to confidently assert their liberal judicial powers. Third, the findings raise awareness about the judiciary's crucial role in Papua New Guinea society, advocating for engagement with the courts to foster a constitutional and legal culture that promotes, rather than stifles, the use of judiciary's liberal powers, and encourages a vibrant constitutional discourse.

While overt or covert animosities between government branches, as evidenced in constitutional crisis cases discussed in this book, may persist under current political conditions and interpretations of the Constitution, this book does not propose definitive solutions. Rather, it proposes a reevaluation of these animosities, starting with a recognition and acceptance that the judiciary in Papua New Guinea has a distinct role beyond traditional expectations.

The findings in this book may unsettle adherents of orthodox conceptions of judicial power and constitutionalism. However, as Professor Peter Mulphern fittingly noted, '[i]n law, as in science, a phenomenon that refuses to conform with orthodox theory should inspire re-examination of the theory'.[1] The founders of the Papua New Guinea Constitution, when deciding to depart from the Australian model of constitutionalism, undertook that 're-examination' against the traditional conceptions. They cautioned doubters of their innovative proposals:

> We welcome constructive criticism of our proposals...But acceptable criticism must not be based on the arrogant assumption that Papua New Guinean political representatives are unable to think for themselves; or on the belief that radical departures from the institutions and procedures inherited from the colonial power cannot possibly work.[2]

The mission of this book is, at minimum, to revitalise the understanding of the judiciary's role as a critical institution of constitutional innovation under the 'home-grown' Constitution, with a unique capacity to impact the country's developmental trajectory. The book thus invites a reimagining of the 'home-grown' Constitution, beginning with a reconsideration of the judiciary's role. It is hoped that this undertaking will stimulate further inquiry into the value of the Papua New Guinea judiciary, the effectiveness of its functions, and the Constitution as a dynamic document fostering socio-political transformation—not merely a relic of colonial continuity.

---

[1] J. Peter Mulhern, 'In Defence of the Political Question Doctrine' (1988) 37 *University of Pennsylvania Law Review* 96.

[2] CPC Report 1974, Chapter 1[10].

Bibliography

Literature

Ackerman, Bruce, 'The New Separation of Powers' (2000) 113 *Harvard Law Review* 634
Ackerman, Bruce, *We the People: Foundations* (Belknap Press, 1993)
Adams, John, *The Political Writings of John Adams: Representative Selections* 1785–1826 (Hackett Publishing, 2003)
Afigbo, Adiele E., *The Warrant Chiefs: Indirect Rule in South-eastern Nigeria*, 1891–1929 (London, 1971)
Aitkin, Don and Edward P. Wolfers, 'Australian Attitudes Towards the Papua New Guinea Since World War II' (1973) 27 *Australian Outlook* 202
Ako, Rhuks, Environmental Justice in Developing Countries: Perspectives from Africa and Asia-Pacific (Routledge, 2013)
Allison, J.W.F. (ed), *The Law of the Constitution:* A.V. Dicey (Oxford University Press, 2013)
Ananian-Welsh, Rebecca and George William, 'Judicial Independence from the Executive: A First-Principles Review of the Australian Cases' (2014) 40 *Monash University Law Review* 593
Appleby, Gabrielle and Adam Webster, 'Parliament's Role in Constitutional Interpretation' (2013) 37(2) *Melbourne University Law Review* 255
Aristotle, *Politics: The Athenian Constitution*, Book IV (compiled by John Warrington, Heron Books, 1723)
Austin, John, *The Province of Jurisprudence Determined:* And, The Uses of the Study of Jurisprudence 1861 (Hackett Publishing, Reprinted 1998)
Barak, Aharon, 'Unconstitutional Constitutional Amendments' (2011) 44 *Israel Law Review* 321
Barak, Aharon, *Purposive Interpretation in Law* (Princetown University Press, 2005)
Barnett, T.E. (ed), *Magistrates' Note* (Australian National University, 1967)
Bastarache, Justice Michel, 'The Role of Academics and Legal Theory in Judicial Decision-Making' (1999) 37 *Alberta Law Review* 739
Bayne, Peter, 'Judicial method and the interpretation of Papua New Guinea's Constitution' (1980) 11 *Federal Law Review* 121
Bayne, Peter, 'Legal Development in Papua New Guinea: The Place of Common Law' (1975) 3 *Melanesian Law Journal* 9
Bell, Jeffery Graham, 'Agents of Parliament: A New Branch of Government?' (2006) *Canadian Parliamentary Review* 13
Berghoff, Hartmut, Frank Biess, Ulrike Strasser (eds), *Explorations and Entanglements: Germans in Pacific Worlds from the Early Modern Period to World War I* (Berghahn Books, 2018)

B. Kama, *Rethinking Judicial Power in Papua New Guinea*,
https://doi.org/10.1007/978-981-97-2946-3

Bergougnous, Georges, *Presiding Officers of National Parliamentary Assemblies:* A World Comparative Study (Inter-Parliamentary Union, 1997)
Bhagwati, P. N., 'The Role of the Judiciary in the Democratic Process: Balancing Activism and Judicial Restraint' (1992) 18 *Commonwealth Law Bulletin* 1262
Bickel, Alexander M., *The Least Dangerous Branch* (Yale University Press, 1986)
Bilchitz, David and David Landau (eds), *The Evolution of the Separation of Powers between the Global South and the Global North* (Edward Elger, 2018)
Blackham, Alysia, 'Judges and Retirement Ages', (2016) 39 *Melbourne University Law Review* 738
Blackshield, Tony, 'Strict Logic and High Technique' (2003) *Australian Book Review* 8
Blackshield, Tony, Michael Coper and George Williams (eds), *The Oxford Companion to the High Court of Australia* (Oxford University Press, 2001)
Bourke, Michael and Tracey Harwood (eds), *Food and Agriculture in Papua New Guinea* (ANU Press, 2009)
Bowen, Rachel E., *The Achilles Heel of Democracy* (Cambridge University Press, 2017)
Brandt, Michele, Jill Cottrell, Yash Ghai and Anthony Regan, *Constitution-making and Reform: Options for the Process* (Interpeace, 2011)
Brennan, Sir Gerard, 'The Parliament, the Executive and the Courts' (1997) 9 *Bond Law Review* 136
Brewbaker III, William S., 'Found Law, Made Law and Creation: Reconsidering Blackstone's Declaratory Theory' (2006–07) 22 (1) *Journal of Law and Religion* 255
Brian Bix, 'H. L. A. Hart and the "Open Texture" of Language' (1991) 10 (1) *Law and Philosophy* 51
Brown, Bernard (ed), *Fashion of Law in New Guinea* (Butterworths Australia, 1969)
Brown, Paula, 'From anarchy to satraphy' (1963) 65 (1) *American Anthropologist* 1
Brubaker, Stanley C., 'Reconsidering Dworkin's Case for Judicial Activism' (1984) 46 *The Journal of Politics* 503
Buss, William G, 'Andrew Inglis Clark's Draft Constitution: Chapter III of the Australian Constitution and the assist from Article III of the Constitution of the United States' (2009) 33 *Melbourne University Law Review* 718
Butterworth, A. R., 'Australian Constitution' (1901) 17 *Law Quarterly Review* 381
Campbell, Enid and H.P. Lee, *The Australian Judiciary* (Cambridge University Press, 2013)
Campbell, Tom, 'Judicial Activism - Justice or Treason?' (2003) 10 *Otago Law Review* 307
Canadian Human Rights Commission, *Evolution of Human Rights in Canada* (2012). http://www.chrc-ccdp.ca/sites/default/files/ehrc_edpc-eng.pdf
Cane, Peter, 'Reconceptualising separation of powers' (2015) 101 *Amicus Curiae* 2
Carrigan, Frank, 'A Blast From The Past: The Resurgence of Legal Formalism," (2003) 27(1) *Melbourne University Law Review* 163
Chalmers, Donald, 'The Village Courts of Papua New Guinea: Their Introduction, History and Operation Until 1976' (1978) 6 *Melanesian Law Journal* 56
Chemerinsky, Erwin, 'In Defense of Judicial Supremacy' (2017) 58 *William & Mary Law Review* 1459
Clayton, Richard, 'Principles for Judicial Deference' (2006) 11 *Judicial Review* 109
Commonwealth, The, 'Australian Political Chronicle May-August 1969' (1969) 15 *Australian Journal of Politics & History* 81
Conyers, D, *The Provincial Government Debate: Central Control Versus Local Participation* (Institute of Applied Social and Economic Research, 1976)
Coper, Michael and George Williams, *Power, Parliament and the People* (The Federation Press, 1997)
Coper, Michael, 'Comment and Critique: Comment about Judicial Method' (2006) 30 *Melbourne Law School* 554
Coper, Michael, 'Legal Knowledge, the Responsibility of Lawyers, and the Task of Law Schools' (2008) 39 *University of Toledo Law Review* 251

Corrin, Jennifer and Don Paterson, *Introduction to South Pacific Law* (Cambridge, 2013)
Corwin, Edward, 'Marbury v Madison and the Doctrine of Judicial Review' (1914) *12 Michigan Law Review* 538
Crocombe, R. et al (eds), *Culture and Democracy in the South Pacific* (Institute of Pacific Studies, 1992)
de Montpensier, Roy Stone, 'The British Doctrine of Parliamentary Sovereignty: A Critical Inquiry' (1966) 26(4) *Louisiana Law Review* 753
De Vere, Ross, Duncan Colquhoun-Kerr and John Kaburise (eds), *Essays on the Constitution of Papua New Guinea* (University of Papua New Guinea, 1985)
Denoon, Donald and Kathleen Dugan, *Public Health in Papua New Guinea: Medical Possibility and Social Constraint, 1884–1984* (Cambridge University Press, 2002)
Denoon, Donald and Malama Meleisea, *The Cambridge History of the Pacific Islanders* (Cambridge University Press, 2004)
Denoon, Donald and Jude Shanahan (eds), *Emerging from Empire?: decolonisation in the Pacific* (ANU Press, 1997)
Denoon, Donald, *A Trial Separation: Australia and the Decolonisation of Papua New Guinea* (ANU Press, 2012)
Derham, David P., *Report on the System for the Administration of Justice in the Territory of Papua and New Guinea* (Department of Territories, 1960)
Dhingra, Alisha, 'Indian Constitutionalism: A Case of Transformative Constitutionalism' (2014) 2 *Asian Journal of Multidisciplinary Studies* 135
Dicey, A. V., *Introduction to the Study of the Law of the Constitution* (First published 1885, Palgrave MacMillian, 10th ed, 1959)
Dinnen, Sinclair, *Law and Order in a Weak State: Crime and Politics in Papua New Guinea* (University of Hawaii Press, 2001)
Dixon, Owen, 'Concerning Judicial Method' (1956) 29 *The Australian Law Journal* 486
Dixon, Owen, 'The Law and the Constitution' (1935) 51 *Law Quarterly Review* 590
Dixon, Rosalind and George Williams (eds), *The High Court, the Constitution and Australian Politics* (Cambridge University Press, 2015)
Downs, Ian, *The Australian Trusteeship: Papua New Guinea 1945 – 1975* (Canberra, 1980)
Duxbury, N, 'The Birth of Legal Realism and the Myth of Justice Holmes' (1999) 20 *Anglo-American Law Review* 81
Dworkin, Ronald, *Law's Empire* (Harvard University Press, 1986)
Dworkin, Ronald, *Taking Rights Seriously* (Harvard University Press, 1977)
Dziedzic, Anna, 'Forge v Australian Securities and Investments Commission: The Kable Principle and the Constitutional Validity of Acting Judges' (2007) 35(1) *Federal Law Review* 129
Feinman, Jay M., 'The failure of legal education and the promise of Critical Legal Studies' (1985) 6 *Cardozo Law Review* 739
Fenbury, David, *Practice without policy: genesis of local government in Papua New Guinea* (Australian National University, 1978)
Filer, Colin and Nikhil Sekhran, *Loggers, Donors and Resources Owners* (PNG National Research Institute, 1998)
Finnis, J. M., 'Separation of Powers in the Australian Constitution' (1968) 3(2) *Adelaide Law Review* 159
Firth, Stewart (ed), *Globalisation and Governance in the Pacific Islands* (ANU Press, 2006)
Firth, Stewart, 'The Transformation of the Labour Trade in German New Guinea, 1899–1914' (Part I) (1976) 11 *Journal of Pacific History* 51
Fitzpatrick, Peter, *Law and State in Papua New Guinea* (Academic Press, 1980)
Fombad, Charles M. (ed), *Constitutional Adjudication in Africa* (Oxford University Press, 2017)
Gageler, Stephen, 'Chapter IV: The Inter-State Commission and the Regulation of Trade and Commerce under the Australian Constitution' (2017) 28 *Public Law Review* 205
Galligan, Brian, *A Federal Republic: Australia's Constitutional System of Government* (Cambridge University Press, 1995)

Gava, John, 'The Rise of the Hero Judge' (2001) 24(3) *University of New South Wales Law Journal* 747

Gawi, John, Yash Ghai and Abdul Paliwala, 'National Goals and Law Reform: A Report on the Goroka Seminar' (1976) 4 *Melanesian Law Journal* 259

Gencer, Bedri, 'Sovereignty and the Separation of Powers in John Locke' (2010) 15(3) *European Legacy* 323

Ghai, Yash and Anthony Regan, *The law, politics, and administration of decentralisation in Papua New Guinea* (National Research Institute, 1992)

Ghai, Yash (ed), *Law, Government, and Politics in the Pacific Island States* (Institute of Pacific Studies, 1988)

Ghai, Yash, 'A Journey around Constitutions: Reflections on Contemporary Constitutions' (2005) 122 *African Law Journal* 804

Ghai, Yash, 'Establishing a Liberal Political Order Through a Constitution: The Papua New Guinea Experience' (2002) 28 *Development and Change* 303

Gibbs, Harry, 'Judgment Writing' (1993) 67 *Australian Law Journal* 494

Gibbs, Harry, 'The Separation of Powers – A Comparison' (1987) 17 *Federal Law Review* 151

Ginsburg, Tom and Aziz Huq, *How to Save a Constitutional Democracy* (University of Chicago Press, 2018)

Ginsburg, Tom, *Judicial Review in New Democracies: Constitutional Courts in Asian Cases* (Cambridge University Press, 2003)

Gleeson, A. Murray, 'Legal Oil and Political Vinegar' (1999) 10 *Public Law Review* 108

Goddard, Michael, *Substantial Justice: An Anthropology of Village Courts in Papua New Guinea* (Berghahn Books, 2009)

Goddard, Michael, *The Unseen City*: Anthropological Perspectives on Port Moresby, Papua New Guinea (Pandanus, 2005)

Goddard, Michael, *Villagers and the City*: Melanesian Experiences of Port Moresby, Papua New Guinea (Sean Kingston, 2010)

Goldberg, Ann, *Honor, Politics, and the Law in Imperial Germany, 1871–1914* (Cambridge University Press, 2010)

Goldring, John, *The Constitution of Papua New Guinea* (Lawbook Co, 1978)

Grossart, Ian 'Members in the Legislative Council of Papua and New Guinea 1951–1963' (1966) 1 *The Journal of Pacific History* 147

Gonol, David, *National Court Registry Manual on Election Petitions* (Marapa Publications, 2017)

Gore, Ralph, *The Punishment for Crime among Natives in Territory of Papua' Annual Report for the Year 1928–1929* (Canberra, 1929)

Gray, Rachel, *The Constitutional Jurisprudence and Judicial Method of the Australian High Court* (Presidian Legal Publications, 2008)

Griffin, James, Hank Nelson and Stewart Firth, *Papua New Guinea: A Political History* (Heinemann Publication, 1979)

Grigg-Spall, Ian and Paddy Ireland (eds), *The Critical Lawyers' Handbook* (Pluto Press, 1992)

Hart, H.L.A., *The Concept of Law* (Oxford University Press, 2nd ed, 1994)

Hasluck, Paul, *A time for Rebuilding: Australian administration in Papua and New Guinea, 1951–1963* (Melbourne University Press, 1976)

Hassall, Graham and Cherly Saunders, *Asia-Pacific Constitutional Systems* (Cambridge University Press, 2001)

Hau'ofa, Epeli, *Mekeo Inequality and Ambivalence in a Village Society* (ANU Press, 1981)

Hayne, Kenneth, 'Deference—an Australian Perspective' (2011) *Public Law* 75

He, Baogang, Brian Galligan and Takashi Inoguchi (eds), *Federalism in Asia* (Edward Elger Publishing, 2009)

Healey, A.M., 'The Foot Report and East New Guinea' (1962) 34(2) *The Australian Quarterly* 11

Healy, A. M., 'Paternalism and Consultation in Papua, 1880–1960' (1967) 4 *ANU Historical Journal* 19

Heydon, Dyson, 'Judicial Activism and the Death of the Rule of Law' (2004) 10 *Otago Law Review* 493

Heydon, J. D., 'Threats to Judicial Independence: the Enemy Within (2013) 129 *Law Quarterly Review* 205

Hickok, Eugene and Gary L. Macdowell, *Justice vs. Law* (Simon and Schuster, 2010)

Hills, Edward and Guy Powles, 'Magistrates Manual of Papua New Guinea' (University of Papua New Guine Press, 2001) (online copy). http://www.paclii.org/pg/Manuals/Magistrates/Magistrates.htm

Hinton, Colin, R.C. Green and C.J. Lynch, 'Shorter Communications' (1961) 70 *The Journal of the Polynesian Society* 233

Hoffman, Daniel H., *Our Elusive Constitution: Silences, Paradoxes, Priorities* (Suny Press, 1997)

Holmes Jnr, Oliver Wendell, 'Primitive Notions in Modern Law' (1877) 11 *American Law Review* 641

Holmes, Oliver, 'The Path of Law' (1897) 10 *Harvard Law Review* 457

Horn, Nico, 'Interpreting the Constitution: Is Transformative Constitutionalism a Bridge Too Far?' (2014) 2 (1) *University of Namibia Law Review* 1

Hornblower, William B., 'A Century of "Judge-Made" Law' (1907) 7(7) *Columbia Law Review*

House of Assembly, Territory of Papua and New Guinea, *Final Report from the Select Committee on Constitutional Development together with Minutes of Proceedings*, Port Moresby, June 1967

Howie-Willis, Ian, *A Thousand Graduates:* Conflict in University Development in Papua New Guinea 1961–1976 (Australian National University Press, 1980)

Hutchison, A. C., 'The Rise and Ruse of Administrative Law and Scholarship' (1985) 48 *Modern Law Review* 293

Inglis, Amirah, *Not a White Woman Safe: Sexual Anxiety and Politics in Port Moresby 1920 – 1934* (ANU Press, 1974)

James, R.W and I. Fraser, *Legal Issues in a Developing Society* (University of Papua New Guinea, 1990)

Jefferson, Thomas, *The Works of Thomas Jefferson* 1787 (Best Books, Vol. 5, 1904)

Jinks, B., P. Biskup and H. Nelson, *Readings in New Guinea history* (Angus and Robertson, 1973)

Jowell, J. L. and J.P.W.B. McAuslan (eds), *Lord Denning: The Judge and the Law* (Sweet & Maxwell, 1984)

Joyce, R. B., *Sir William McGregor* (Oxford University Press, 1971)

Judicial and Legal Services Commission, *Appointment and Discipline Procedures Handbook* (JLSC, 2015)

Kaireys, David (ed), *The Politics of Law: A Progressive Critique* (Basic Books, 2nd ed, 1992)

Kalb, Johanna, 'Judicial Role in New Democracies: A Strategic Account of Comparative Citation' (2013) 2 *Yale Journal of International Law* 423

Kannabiran, Kalpana, *Tools of Justice: Non-Discrimination and the Indian Constitution* (Routledge, 2012)

Kavanamur, David, Charles Yala and Quinton Clements, *Building a Nation in Papua New Guinea:* Views of the Post-independence Generation (Pandanus Books, 2003)

Kellogg, Fredrick Roger, *The Formative essays of Justice Holmes: The Making of an American Legal Philosophy* (Greenwood Press, 1984)

Kelsen, Hans, *Pure Theory of Law* (University of California Press, 1967)

Kennedy, Duncan and Karl Klare, 'A Bibliography of Critical Legal Studies' (1984) 94 *Yale Law Journal* 461

Ketan, Joseph, *The Name Must Not Go Down: Political Competition and State-society Relations in Mount Hagen, Papua New Guinea* (University of South Pacific, 2004)

Kibet, Eric and Charles Fombad, 'Transformative constitutionalism and the adjudication of constitutional rights in Africa' (2017) 17 (2) *Africa Human Rights Law Journal* 340

King, Anthony and Ivor Crewe, *The Blunders of Our Governments* (Oneworld Publications, 2013)

Kirby, Michael, 'Judicial Activism - A Riposte to the Counter-Reformation' (2005) 11 *Otago Law Review* 1

Kirby, Michael, 'Judicial Activism: Power without Responsibility? No, Appropriate Activism Confirming to Duty' (2006) 30 *Melbourne University Law Review* 576
Kirby, Michael, 'Welcome to Law Reviews' (2002) 26 *Melbourne Law Review* 1
Klare, Karl and Dennis M. Davis, 'Transformative constitutionalism and the common and customary law' (2010) 26 *South African Journal of Human Rights* 403
Klare, Karl E., 'Legal Culture and Transformative Constitutionalism,' (1998) 14 *South African Journal of Human Rights* 146
Knauft, Bruce M. (ed), *Critically Modern:* Alternatives, Alterities, Anthropologies (Indian University Press, 2002)
Kwa, Eric, Alphone Gelu and Wilfred Golman, *Judicial Scrutiny of the Electoral Process in a Developing Democratic State* (UPNG School of Law, 2003)
Kwa, Eric, *Constitutional Law of Papua New Guinea* (Lawbook Co, 2001)
Lal, Brij V., *In the Eye of the Storm: Jai Ram Reddy and the Politics of Post-Colonial Fiji* (ANU EPress, 2010)
Landau, David, 'Political Institutions and Judicial Role in Comparative Constitutional Law' (2010) 51 *Harvard International Law Journal* 320
Langa, Pius, 'Transformative Constitutionalism,' (2006) 3 *Stellenbosch Law Review* 351
Lange, Matthew, 'British Colonial Legacies and Political Development' (2004) 32 *World Development* 905
Larmour, Peter (ed), *Solomon Islands Politics* (University of South Pacific, 1983)
Larmour, Peter, 'Westminster constitutions in the South Pacific: A "policy transfer" approach' (2002) 10(1) *Asian Journal of Political Science* 39
Lee, H. P. and George Winterton, *Australian Constitutional Landmarks* (Cambridge University Press, 2004)
Lessig, Lawrence, 'Post Constitutionalism' (1996) 94 *Michigan Law Review* 1422
Levinson, Dary and Richard Pildes, 'Separation of Parties, not Powers' (2006) 119 *Harvard Law Review* 2311
Locke, John, *Two Treatise of Government* 1689 (compiled by P. Laslett, Cambridge University Press, 1970)
Logan, Justice John, 'A year in the life of an Australian member of the PNG judiciary' (FCA) [2013] *Federal Journal Scholarship* 9
Loughlin, Martin, *'The silences of constitutions' (2019)* 17 *International Journal of Constitutional Law* 18
Lynch, C. J., 'Parliamentary and Executive Control of Delegated Legislation under the Legislative Council for Papua and New Guinea 1951–63' (1966) 5 *Melbourne University Law Review* 329
Lynch, C. J., 'The Achievement of Independence in Papua New Guinea' (1980) 15 *The Journal of Pacific History* 175
Lynch, Joe, "The Adoption of an Underlying Law by the Constitution of Papua New Guinea" (1976) 4(1) *Melanesian Law Journal* 37
Macfarlane, Emmett, *Governing from the Bench: The Supreme Court of Canada and the Judicial Role* (UBC Press, 2013)
Mair, Lucy, *Australia in New Guinea* (Christophers, 1948)
Marai, Leo, 'The Psychology of Consensus in Melanesia' (2007) 1(2) *Journal of Pacific Rim Psychology* 54
Martin, Keir, *The Death of the Big Men and the Rise of the Big Shots: Custom and Conflict in East New Britain* (Berghahn Press, 2013)
Mason, Anthony, 'The Judge as Law-maker' (1996) *James Cook University Law Review* 1, 2
May, Ron and Anthony Regan (eds), *Political Decentralisation in a New State: The Experience of Provincial Government in Papua New Guinea* (Crawford House, 1997)
May, Ron, 'Papua New Guinea's Political Coup: The ousting of Sir Michael Somare' (In Brief 1/2011, State, Society and Governance in Melanesia, Australian National University)
May, Ron, *Micronationalist Movements in Papua New Guinea* (Australian National University, 1982)

May, Ron, *State and Society in Papua New Guinea: The First Twenty-Five Years* (ANU Press, 2004)
McDowell, Hickok, *Justice vs Law* (Free Press, 1993)
McHugh, Michael, 'Tensions between the Executive and the Judiciary' (2002) 76 *Australian Law Journal* 567
McMillan, John, 'Re-thinking the Separation of Powers' (2010) 38 *Federal Law Review* 423
Mikhaiel, Mark Mina, 'The Dangers of the Reference Question: SCC v SCOTUS' (2016) 40 *Canada-US Law Journal* 71
Moke, Paul, *Earl Warren and the Struggle for Justice* (Lexington Books, 2015)
Moore, Clive and Mary Kooyman (eds), *A Papua New Guinea Political Chronicle 1967–1991* (Crawford House Publishing, 1998)
Moore, William Harrison, *The Constitution of the Commonwealth of Australia* (Sweet and Maxwell, 2nd ed, 1910)
Morton, Fredrick Lee (eds), *Law, Politics and the Judicial Process in Canada* (University of Calgary Press, 3rd ed, 2002).
Moseneke, Dikgang, 'The Fourth Bram Fischer Memorial Lecture: Transformative Adjudication,' (2002) 18 *South African Journal on Human Rights* 309
Moss, Tristan, *Guarding the Periphery: The Australian Army in Papua New Guinea, 1951–75* (Cambridge University Press, 2017)
Mulhern, Peter, 'In Defence of Political Question Doctrine' (1988) 137 *University of Pennsylvania Law Review* 97
Munday, Roderick, 'Judicial Configurations' (2002) 61 *Cambridge Law Journal* 612
Murphy, Walter F., 'Civil Law, Common Law, and Constitutional democracy' (1991) 52 *Louisiana Law Review* 91
Murray, Andrew, *Thinking about Political Things: An Aristotelian Approach to Pacific Life* (ATF Press, 2016)
Murray, Hubert, *The Scientific Mode as Applied to Native Land Problems in Papua* (Government Printer, 1931)
Narokobi, Bernard, *The Melanesian Way* (Institute of Papua New Guinea Studies, 1980)
Narokobi, Vergil, 'The testing of two prime minister's saga: Parliament testing the supremacy of the constitution' (2013) 24 *Public Law Review* 81
Nelson, Hank, Stewart Firth and James Griffin, *Papua New Guinea: A political history* (Pearson Education, 1979)
Nelson, Hank, *Taim Bilong Masta: The Australia Involvement with Papua New Guinea* (ABC, 1990)
Neufeld, Matthew, *The Civil Wars After 1660: Public Remembering in Late Stuart England* (Boydell Press, 2013)
Nonggorr, John, 'The Maintenance of Judicial Independence and Integrity in Papua New Guinea: Some Recent Developments' (1992) 18 *Commonwealth Law Bulletin* 1181
Olson, James Stuart, *Historical Dictionary of European Imperialism* (Greenwood, 1991)
Omar, Imtiaz, 'Parliament, Executive and the Court in PNG' (1996) 70 *Australian Law Journal* 313
Opeskin, Brian, 'Judicial Exits: The Tenure of Judges in Three Apex Courts' (2016) *University of Technology Sydney Law Research Series* 2
Orr, Graeme, 'Integrity on the Line: Judicial Power Over Elections in Papua New Guinea' (2017) *LAWASIA Journal* 65
Pangle, Thomas L., *Montesquieu's Philosophy of Liberalism: A Commentary on The Spirit of the Laws* (University of Chicago Press, 1989)
Papua New Guinea Commission of Inquiry, *Final Report of the Commission of Inquiry Generally into the Department of Finance* (2009)
Papua New Guinea Department of Information and Extension Services, *Progress and Growth of Papua New Guinea* 1972 (Port Moresby)
Papua New Guinea Electoral Commission, 'Local-Level Government Elections report for Parliament' (Port Moresby, 2013). http://www.pngec.gov.pg/docs/default-source/annual-reports/electoral-llg-report-2013.pdf?sfvrsn=2

Papua New Guinea, *Constitutional Planning Committee Final Report* 1974. http://www.paclii.org/pg/CPCReport/main.htm
Patapan, Haig, *Judging Democracy: The New Politics of the High Court of Australia* (Cambridge University Press, 2000)
Pearce, Dennis, 'Executive Versus Judiciary' (1991) 2 *Public Law Review* 179
Peasah, Joseph A., *Local-level Government in Papua New Guinea: A Study in Change and Continuity in the Development of Liberal-democratic Self-determination at the Local Level* (PNG National Research Institute, 1994)
Pinsler, Jeffrey D., 'The Inherent Powers of the Court' (1997) *Singapore Journal of Legal Studies* 1
Podolefsky, Aaron, 'Mediator Roles in Simbu Conflict Management' (1990) 29 (1) *Ethnology* 67
Posner, R.A., *How Judges Think* (Harvard University Press, 2008)
Pound, Roscoe, 'Theories of Law' (1912) 2 *Yale Law Journal* 114
Quirk, William J. and R. Randell Bridwell, *Judicial Dictatorship* (Transaction Publishers, 1995)
Ratnapala, Suri, 'John Locke's Doctrine of the Separation of Powers: A Re-Evaluation' (1993) 38 *American Journal of Jurisprudence* 189
Ratnapala, Suri, *Jurisprudence* (Cambridge University Press, 2013)
Ray, Samirendra N., *Modern Comparative Politics: Approaches, Methods and Issues* (Prentice-Hall, 1998)
Regan, Anthony and E. P. Wolfers, 'Aids to Interpretation of the *Constitution* - Some Preliminary Thoughts' (1986) 14 *Melanesian Law Journal* 153
Regan, Anthony J, Owen Jessep and Eric L Kwa (eds), *Twenty Years of the Papua New Guinea Constitution* (University of Papua New Guinea Press, 2001)
Reilly, Benjamin, 'Political Engineering and Party Politics in Papua New Guinea' (2002) 8 *Party Politics* 704
Roberts, Clayton, *The Growth of Responsible Government in Stuart England* (Cambridge Univesity Press, 1966)
Robinson, Nick, 'Expanding Judiciaries: India and the rise of the Good Governance Court' (2009) 8 *Washington University Global Studies Law Review* 1
Rosen, Jeffery, *The Supreme Court: The Personalities and Rivalries That Defined America* (St Martin's Griffin, 2007)
Roux, Theunix, 'Transformative Constitutionalism and the Best Interpretation of the South African Constitution: Distinction without a Difference?' (2009) 2 *Stellenbosch Law Review* 258
Roznai, Yaniv, 'Unconstitutional Constitutional Amendments: The Migration and Success of a Constitutional Idea' (2013) 61 *The American Journal of Comparative Law 657*
Russell, Meg, Daniel Gover and Kristina Wollter, 'Does the Executive Dominate the Westminster Legislative Process?' (2016) 69 *Parliamentary Affairs* 286
Rutherford, Bruce K., *Egypt after Mubarak: Liberalism, Islam, and Democracy in the Arab World* (Princeton University Press, 2013)
Sack, Peter (ed), *Pacific Constitutions,* (Australian National University, 1982)
Sack, Peter and Dymphna Clark (eds), *Albert Hahl: Governor in New Guinea* (Australian National University, 1980)
Sackville, Ronald, 'Judicial Law Making' (2011) 5 *University of Western Sydney Law Review* 59
Sackville, Ronald, 'The Limits of Judicial Review of Executive Action - Some Comparisons between Australia and the United States' (2000) 28 *Federal Law Review* 315
Sahlins, Marshall D, 'Poor Man, Rich Man, Big-man, Chief: Political Types in Melanesia and Polynesia' (1963) 5(3) *Comparative Studies in Society and History* 285
Saunders, Cheryl (ed), *Courts of Final Jurisdiction: The Mason Court in Australia* (The Federation Press, 1996)
Scaglion, Richard, 'Legal Adaptation in a Papua New Guinean Village Court' (1990) 20 *Ethnology* 17
Schlegel, John, 'Notes towards an Intimate, Opiniated and Affectionate History of Conference on Critical Legal Studies' (1984) 36 *Stanford Law Review* 391

Schor, Miguel, 'Constitutionalism through the Looking Glass of Latin America' (2006) 41 *Texas International Law Journal* 1
Shapiro, Ian (ed), *The Federalist Papers* (Yale University Press, 2009)
Shapiro, Martin, *Law and Politics of the Supreme Court* (Free Press, 1964)
Sillitoe, Paul, *An Introduction to the Anthropology of Melanesia: Culture and Tradition* (Cambridge University Press, 1998)
Singh, Virendra, *Indian Polity with Indian Constitution & Parliamentary Affairs* (Neelkanth Prakashan, 2015)
Smith, David, 'A Question of Trust: Parliamentary Democracy and Canadian Society' (2004) *Canadian Parliamentary Review* 25
Smyth, Russel, 'Academic Writing and the Courts: A Quantitative Study of the Influence of Legal and Non-legal Periodicals in the High Court' (1998) 17 *University of Tasmania Law Review* 164
Standish, Bill, 'Papua New Guinea in 1999–2000' (2001) 36 *The Journal of Pacific History* 295
Standish, Bill, 'Papua New Guinea's most turbulent election' (2003) 33(2) *Catalyst: Social Pastoral Journal for Melanesia* 130
Standish, William, 'The dynamics of Papua New Guinea's democracy: an essay' (2007) 22 *Pacific Economics Bulletin* 135
Stellios, James (ed), *Encounters with Constitutional Interpretation and Legal Education* (The Federation Press, 2018)
Stellios, James, *The Federal Judicature: Chapter III of the Constitution* (LexisNexus Butterworths, 2010)
Stone, Julius, *Precedent and Law: Dynamics of Common Law Growth* (Butterworths, 1985)
Strathern, Andrew and Pamela J. Stewart, *Arrow Talk: Transaction, Transition, and Contradiction in New Guinea Highlands History* (Kent State University Press, 2000)
Sturgess, G. and P. Chubb, *Judging the World, Law and Politics in the World's Leading Courts* (Butterworths 1988)
Sunstein, Cass, *Why Societies Need Dissent* (Harvard University Press, 2003)
Thomson, Deryck, 'The Separation of Powers Doctrine in the Commonwealth Constitution: The Boilermakers' Case (1958) 5 *Sydney Law Review* 480
Thornton, Margaret, 'Disabling discrimination legislation: The High Court and judicial activism' (2009) 15 *Australian Journal of Human Rights* 1
Thornton, Margaret, *Privatising the Public University: The Case of Law* (Routledge, 2012)
Troper, Michel, 'Constitutional Justice and Democracy' (1995) 17 *Cardozo Law Review* 273
Tushnet, Mark V., *Arguing Marbury V. Madison* (Stanford University Press, 2005)
Uhr, John, 'Parliament and the Executive' (2004) 24 *Adelaide Law Review* 51
Unger, Robert, 'The Critical Legal Studies Movement' (1983) 96 *Harvard Law Review* 563
van der Walt, A.J, 'Dancing with Codes – Protecting, Developing and Deconstructing Property Rights in a Constitutional State,' (2011) 118 *South African Law Journal* 258
van Maarseveen, Henc and Ger van der Tang, *Written Constitutions: A Computerized Comparative Study* (Brill Nijhoff, 1978)
Vibert, Frank, *The Rise of the Unelected: Democracy and the New Separation of Powers* (Cambridge University Press, 2007)
Vile, M. J. C., *Constitutionalism and Separation of Powers* (Clarendon Press, 1967)
Vilhena, Oscar, Upendra Baxi and Frans Viljoen (eds), *Transformative constitutionalism: Comparing the apex courts of Brazil, India and South Africa* (Pretoria University Law Press, 2013)
Waldron, Jeremy, 'Separation of Powers in Thought and Practice?' (2013) 54 *Boston College Law Review* 433
Ward, M., *The Politics of Melanesia* (Australian National University, 1970)
Weisbrot, David, 'Papua New Guinea: Judges and Politicians' (Part 1) (1979) 4 *Legal Service Bulletin* 240
Weisbrot, David, 'Papua New Guinea: Judges and Politicians' (Part 2) (1980) 5 *Legal Service Bulletin* 214

Weisbrot, David, Abdul Paliwala and Akilagpa Sawyerr (eds), *Law and Social Change in Papua New Guinea* (Butterworths, 1982)
Weller, Patrick and Dean Jaensch (eds), *Responsible Government in Australia* (Drummond, 1980)
West, Robin, 'The Aspirational Constitution' (1993–1994) 88 *North Western University Law Review* 241
Wheare, Kenneth Clinton, *The Constitutional Structure of the Commonwealth* (Clarendon Press, 1960)
Williams, John M, *The Australian Constitution: A Documentary History* (Melbourne University Press, 2005)
Winterton, George, 'Reserved Powers in an Australian Republic' (1993) 12 *University of Tasmania Law Review* 249
Woinarski, J. (ed), *Jesting Pilate and Other Papers and Addresses* (Law Book Co, 1965)
Wolfers, Edward P., 'Discretion, Politics and Governors-General: Some Comparisons between Papua New Guinea and Australia' (1977) 49(2) *The Australian Quarterly* 75
Wolfers, Edward P., *Australia's Northern Neighbours: Independent or Dependent?* (Australian Institute of International Affairs, 1976)
Wolfers, Edward, *Race Relations and Colonial Rule in Papua New Guinea* (Australia and New Zealand Book Company, 1975)
Woolford, Don, *Papua New Guinea: Initiation and Independence* (University of Queensland Press, 1976)
Wright, Harley, 'Sovereignty of the People – The New Constitutional Grundnorm?' (1998) 26 *Federal Court Review* 165
Zimmermann, Augusto, *Western Legal Theory: History, Concepts and Perspectives* (LexisNexus Butterworths, 2012)
Zines, Leslie, 'The Australian Constitution 1951–1976', (1976) 7 *Federal Law Review* 89
Zorn, Jean and Peter Bayne (eds), *Lo Bilong Ol Manmeri: Crime, Compensation and Village Courts* (University of Papua New Guinea, 1975)

Other Sources

Academic Thesis

Deklin, Anthony, 'Legal Control of the Executive under the Papua New Guinea Constitution' (PhD Thesis, Australian National University, 1985)
Dziedzic, Anna Maria, 'The use of foreign judges on courts of constitutional jurisdiction in Pacific island states' (PhD Thesis, University of Melbourne, 2018)
Kari, Sam Sirox, 'The Origin and Setting of the National Goals and Directive Principles in the process of writing the Constitution of Papua New Guinea' (PhD Thesis, Queensland University of Technology, 2005). https://eprints.qut.edu.au/16071/
Narokobi, Vergil, 'The implementation of Papua New Guinea's national goals and directive principles and basic social obligations' (PhD Thesis, Victoria University of Wellington, 2016). http://researcharchive.vuw.ac.nz/xmlui/handle/10063/5030
Ritchie, Jonathan, 'Making Their Own Law: Popular Participation in the Development of Papua New Guinea's Constitution' (PhD Thesis, University of Melbourne, 2003)

Speeches, Discussion/Conference Papers and Parliamentary Debates

Cannings, Justice David, 'Compliance with the Enforcement of Decisions of Public Authorities' (Paper presented at the Third Underlying Law Conference on Administrative Law, Port Moresby, Papua New Guinea, 27–28 November 2017)

Chief Justice Willy Mutunga, 'Theory of Interpreting Kenya's Transformative Constitution', (Speech delivered at the Inaugural Distinguished Lecture Series on the 2010 Constitution of Kenya and its Interpretation: Reflections from the Supreme Court Decisions, University of Fort Hare, 16 October 2014)

Chief Justice Willy Mutunga, 'Transforming Judiciaries in Africa: Lessons from the Kenyan Experience' (Speech delivered at the Nigerian Bar Association International Conference, Abuja, Nigeria, 23 August 2015)

Dinnen, Sinclair, 'Building Bridges – Law and Justice Reform in Papua New Guinea' (Working Paper No 01/3, State, Society and Governance in Melanesia Project, Australian National University, November 2015). http://ssgm.bellschool.anu.edu.au/sites/default/files/publications/attachments/2015-12/workingpaperdinnen01_3_0.pdf

French, Chief Justice Robert, 'The Courts and the Parliament' (Speech delivered at the Queensland Supreme Court Seminar, Brisbane, 04 August 2012). http://www.hcourt.gov.au/assets/publications/speeches/currentjustices/frenchcj/frenchcj04aug12.pdf

Geno, Ila, 'Public Interest Litigation – Private Sector Perspective' (Paper presented at the Third Underlying Law Conference on Administrative Law, Port Moresby, Papua New Guinea, 27–28 November 2017)

Ghai, Yash, 'Interpreting Kenya's Transformative Constitution' (Paper presented at The International Conference on Interpretation and Shaping of Transformative Constitutions Conference Paper, Nairobi, 9–10 June 2014)

Ginsburg, Tom, 'Courts and New Democracies: Recent Works' (Public Law & Legal Theory Working Paper No.388, University of Chicago, 2012)

Gleeson, Chief Justice Murray, 'The Role of a Judge in a Representative Democracy' (Speech delivered at the Judiciary of the Commonwealth of the Bahamas, Nassau, 4 January 2008)

Gonol, David, 'Enforcement of the Underlying Law: Customary Law Perspective' (Paper presented at the National Conference on the Judicial Development of the Underlying Law, Port Moresby, November 27–28, 2017)

Hon. Justice Edwin Cameron, 'Judges, Justice and Public Power: The Constitution and the Rule of Law in South Africa' (Speech delivered at High Court of Australia Public Lecture, Canberra, 11 October 2017). http://www.hcourt.gov.au/assets/publications/speeches/lecture-series/Cameron-Judges-Justice-and-Public-Power-Oct17.pdf

International Institute for Democracy and Electoral Assistance (IDEA), 'Fourth Branch Institutions' (Paper presented at the Workshop on the Tuvalu Constitutional Reform, University of New South, 27 February 2018)

John Momis, 'The Making of the Papua New Guinea Constitution' (Speech delivered at the 2nd Pacific Constitutions Conference, Emalus Campus, University of South Pacific, December 5, 2017)

Justice Robert J. Sharp, 'Interpreting and Shaping a Transformative Constitution: The Canadian Experience' (Paper presented at the International Conference on Interpretation and Shaping of Transformative Constitutions Conference Paper, Nairobi, 9–10 June 2014)

Kiefel, Hon. Susan, 'Judicial Methods in the 21st Century' (Speech delivered at the Supreme Court Oration, NSW Supreme Court, 16 March 2017)

Lady Hale, 'The Supreme Court: Guardian of the Constitution?' (Speech delivered at the Sultan Azlan Shah Lecture, Kuala Lumpur Malaysia, 2016)

Ley, John, 'Challenges and Achievements of the Constitutional Planning Committee 1972–1975' (Paper presented at Hindsight: A workshop for participants in the Decolonisation of Papua New Guinea, Australian National University, 3–4 November 2002
Logan, Justice John, 'Executive Intervention in Judicial Functions and Judicial Encroachment into Executive Functions – Defining the Boundaries' (Paper presented at the National Conference on Development of the Underlying Law on Administrative Law, Port Moresby, 27 November 2017)
Lord Neuberger, 'Sausages and the Judicial Process: the Limits of Transparency' (Speech delivered at the Annual Conference of the Supreme Court of New South Wales, Sydney, 1 August 2014)
Masi, Peter, 'Ombudsman Tolerance and Investigations amidst disorderly democracy: Can the PNG Ombudsman survive?' (Speech delivered at the 22nd Australasia and Pacific Ombudsman Region Conference, Wellington New Zealand, 10 February 2005)
Momis, President John, Keynote Address (Speech delivered at the State of the Pacific, Canberra, 08 September 2015).
Papua New Guinea, *House of Assembly Debates*, House of Assembly, 09 March 1967
Papua New Guinea, *House of Assembly Debates*, House of Assembly, 23 June 1972
Papua New Guinea, *House of Assembly Debates*, House of Assembly, 23 May 1975
South Africa, *Debates of the Constitutional Assembly*, Constitutional Assembly, 1994 Issues 1–2
Spigelman, Chief Justice James, 'The Integrity Branch of Government' (Speech delivered at the Australian Institute of Administrative Law National Lecture Series on Administrative Law [No. 2], Sydney, 2004)
Standish, William, 'The "Big-man" model reconsidered: power and stratification in Chimbu' (Research Discussion Paper 22, Institute of Applied Social and Economic, 1978)
Yalo, Nemo, 'Public Interest Litigation – Under Sections 18(1) of the Constitution: When the Sentries Sleep at their Posts' (Paper presented at the Third Underlying Law Conference on Administrative Law, Port Moresby, Papua New Guinea, 27–28 November 2017)

MIX
Papier aus verantwortungsvollen Quellen
Paper from responsible sources
FSC® C105338

If you have any concerns about our products,
you can contact us on
ProductSafety@springernature.com

In case Publisher is established outside the EU,
the EU authorized representative is:
Springer Nature Customer Service Center GmbH
Europaplatz 3, 69115 Heidelberg, Germany

Printed by Libri Plureos GmbH
in Hamburg, Germany